The Commons in Perspective

PHILIP NORTON

Longman
New York

Published in the United States of America, its territories and
dependencies, and the Philippines by Longman Inc., 19 West 44th
Street, New York, New York 10036.

First published in 1981 by Martin Robertson & Company, Ltd.,
108 Cowley Road, Oxford OX4 1JF, England.

Library of Congress Cataloging in Publication Data

Norton, Philip,
    The Commons in perspective.

    Includes bibliographical references and index.
    1. Great Britain. Parliament. House of Commons.
I. Title.
JN675 1981.N67   328.41'072   81—830
ISBN 0-582-28294-2   AACR2

Printed and bound in Great Britain

Contents

List of figures

List of tables

Preface

The purpose of this book is simply stated: it seeks to provide an overview of the contemporary House of Commons, in as concise a form as possible, for the undergraduate and for anyone else with a serious interest in the subject of politics. Although I have drawn upon research of primary sources and interviews with Members of Parliament and others, this is primarily a work of synthesis. It seeks to bring together existing material and to present interpretations (including my own) which have appeared elsewhere, but which collectively are not readily available to the student.

Although there is now a growing literature on the House of Commons, much of it (as with my own previous works) has been of a somewhat specialised nature. There are few existing texts which provide an overview, a general perspective, of the Commons. Of those that do exist, none combines the advantage of being recently published with being concise, inexpensive and fairly comprehensive. For example, Peter Richards's standard work *The Backbenchers* was published in 1972; *The Commons in the Seventies*, now revised as *The Commons Today,* covers many, but not all, of the important features of the House (it contains no sustained consideration of party, for instance); and Dr Eric Taylor's *The House of Commons at Work*, while it appeared in its ninth edition in 1979, remains, as Bernard Crick once observed, a work on procedure. In teaching the subject of Parliament to undergraduates I have been conscious of the need for a short, up-to-date work providing a general overview: this offering seeks to answer that need. Whether or not it achieves that aim will be determined by others: my efforts are a necessary but not sufficient condition for its success. If readers find it useful, I will be well pleased; if they enjoy reading it as much as I enjoyed writing it, I will be delighted — and not a little surprised. As with my other contributions in this field, the writing of it has been a labour of love.

In the course of preparing this work, I have incurred a number of obligations which I am pleased to take the opportunity to acknowledge. My first thanks must go to my publishers, Martin Robertson and Company, and especially to Edward Elgar, formerly of Martin Robertson, for first suggesting the work to me, and to Michael Hay for seeing it through to publication. My grateful thanks are due to those Members of

Parliament who have kindly shared with me over the past few years the benefit of their ideas and experience, and to my colleagues in the Study of Parliament Group for the benefit of their wisdom. Spending time with MPs and friends in the SPG has helped me appreciate the nuances of the House of Commons and has encouraged me to think more deeply about its role and future. Though it is perhaps a little unfair to single out Members by name, I would wish to thank especially Sir Bernard Braine on the Conservative side of the House, and George Cunningham on the Labour side, for providing me with much useful information during the research for this work; and, among Ministers, especially Norman St John-Stevas, Chancellor of the Duchy of Lancaster and Leader of the House of Commons, Leon Brittan, Minister of State at the Home Office, and Mrs Lynda Chalker, Under-Secretary of State for Health and Social Security. My appreciation is owing also to academic colleagues for their support, and especially to Stuart Walkland, Reader in Politics at the University of Sheffield. Although he and I do not always agree in our interpretations of the functions and the behaviour of the House of Commons (as will be apparent in Chapter 9), he has been a constant source of support and encouragement, for which I am most grateful. I am grateful also to the students who take and have taken the course on the influence of Parliament which I teach here at Hull: their questions and comments have helped me give thought to various points that I otherwise might have missed.

The responsibility for everything that appears in this book is mine alone. The reaction of my own students to what I have written will come as a matter of course, but I would be happy to receive also the comments of interested readers.

Philip Norton

Department of Politics
The University of Hull
October 1980

1
Introduction

England (and, by comparison with other countries, Britain) is an old nation. It is noted for having a Constitution (the fundamental rules and principles by which a nation is governed) which is 'unwritten' in that it is not embodied in one binding document, and a history marked by the adaptation of traditional structures of government and law-making to meet changing conditions.[1] * As the basis of authority has, in the terminology of Max Weber, shifted from being 'traditional' to being 'rational–legal',[2] so the new has adapted and been superimposed upon the old. The locus of political decision-making[3] has changed, but the traditional structures of government and law-making remain, and it is *through* them that the effective power of decision-making is exercised. Over the centuries the effective (though not exclusive) centre of power has shifted from monarch and Parliament to the executive (and, some would now argue, from the executive to extra-governmental bodies), yet Ministers remain, and perform functions as Her Majesty's Ministers – with certain powers accruing from that position – and they can effect changes in statute law only through and with the approval of Parliament. The result is that one may distinguish what might appropriately be termed the *formality* from the *reality* of political decision-making, while nevertheless having to appreciate the interrelationship of the two. Each is a necessary but not sufficient condition for explaining the contemporary political decision-making process in Britain today.

The formality – which used to be emphasised by the institutional, descriptive approach to politics and which is still emphasised by a number of constitutional lawyers – is that Parliament is sovereign, and has been since 1688. 'Parliament' in this context means not, as may be popularly assumed, the House of Commons and the House of Lords, but the 'Queen-in-Parliament', that is, the monarch with the two Houses acting together (strictly, though not in practice, the monarch on the throne in the Lords with the Commons assembled at the bar of the House). Parliamentary sovereignty, in the words of the great nineteenth-century constitutional lawyer A. V. Dicey,

> means neither more nor less than this, namely, that Parliament thus
> defined has, under the English constitution, the right to make or un-

---

* Notes are to be found at the end of each chapter.

1

make any law whatever; and, further, that no person or body is recognised by the law of England as having a right to override or set aside
the legislation of Parliament.[4]

In short, Parliament (the Queen-in-Parliament) can pass any law it
desires, and such law is binding and cannot be overridden. If it wished,
it could remodel the British Constitution, pass retrospective legislation,
give dictatorial powers to the Government, legalise illegalities,[5] and
even — despite de Lolme's famous assertion to the contrary — provide
that, in law, a woman is a man and vice versa.[6] As Quintin Hogg observed in *The Purpose of Parliament*, 'legally Parliament is omnipotent.
It can do anything.'[7]

To state the formal position is necessary to an understanding of the
decision-making process in Britain, but in itself is insufficient and not a
little misleading. As Bernard Crick has pointed out, to state what is
legally possible tells us little about what is politically possible. While
Parliament may be unrestrained in its legal powers, it is far from unrestrained in what it finds politically feasible. The monarch and the two
Houses have never been completely free of external influences. In the
nineteenth century, Dicey sought to reconcile the rise of a mass electorate with the doctrine of Parliamentary sovereignty by distinguishing
between legal sovereignty, which continued to reside with Parliament,
and political sovereignty, which he deemed to rest with the electorate.[8]
This distinction, while a clumsy one, as Marshall and Moodie have
noted,[9] has a certain utility, but it does not go far enough to explain
the shift in political power in the nineteenth century. The growth of
the mass electorate was to motivate the development of organised, mass-
membership political parties and, through them, to facilitate a shift of
political power to the executive. The law-making power remained
formally with Parliament, but the decisions as to what measures were to
be introduced and their content were taken increasingly by the Cabinet,
responding in turn to demands made upon it by organised interests,
these demands having grown in more recent years. The passage of such
measures in the House of Commons was made possible by the existence
of a party majority. Recognition of the 'political sovereignty' of the
electorate reduced the political willingness of the unelected House of
Lords to obstruct such measures, a reluctance turned into a legal restraint by the Parliament Acts of 1911 and 1949. The monarch's formal
power to veto measures approved by both Houses had succumbed to
political reality before the nineteenth century and was confirmed in
that century by Queen Victoria's acceptance of advice not to attempt
to veto a measure of which she disapproved. Within the confines of the
triumvirate of the Queen-in-Parliament, the House of Commons emerged
as the dominant element, but the very factor which made it that (the

emergence of a mass electorate) served also to transfer decision-making power to the executive. Measures which emerged from Parliament, having received the assent of the two Houses and the Crown, remained legally binding — hence the continuing importance of the formality of the Queen-in-Parliament — but the initiation and formulation of such measures lay elsewhere, with their passage usually (albeit not always) assured by a majority in the Commons House of Parliament.

The result is that in the twentieth century decisions which are to be binding upon society, and are accepted as such, are usually, though not exclusively, expressed formally by or under the authority of the Queen-in-Parliament, though in reality they are taken by what may appropriately be termed the Prime Minister-in-Cabinet. The latter (comprising a party leader and his or her lieutenants) bases its power on a party majority, usually a one-party majority, in the House of Commons and exercises it through the formal constitutional structures, a number of constitutional conventions (unwritten rules based on precedent, which are accepted as binding) and political procedures (for example, Government control of the House of Commons' timetable) having developed to facilitate this relationship. Strong party government has adapted and been superimposed upon the traditional constitutional structure, which hardly recognises formally the existence of parties, yet in practice could not now operate without them.

Parliament and the decision-making process

If one wished to express the contemporary position of Parliament (hereafter meaning the Houses of Commons and Lords) in the decision-making process in a more structured, and possibly more comprehensible, form, then a simple systems model might suffice.

A systems approach to politics, pioneered by David Easton in the 1950s, seeks to provide an overview of the political 'system', identifying within it the body or bodies responsible for making authoritative decisions about public policy and the relationship of the decision-making bodies to the other elements of the 'system'. The political system is represented diagramatically through a model, as shown in Figure 1.1.

The inputs of a political system are based upon supports (the beliefs, customs and rules upon which a political community is based), resources (the availability of wealth and material), and demands made upon the political system, demands which are articulated and channelled through political parties, pressure groups of one kind or another, elections, opinion polls, individuals in touch with decision-makers, and so on. These inputs are received by the decision-making body and converted into policies (the output), which are then implemented and enforced; reaction to them and their effect constitute feedback. This feedback in

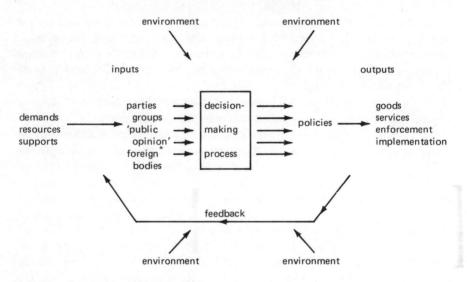

Figure 1.1 A political system model

turn influences the inputs (effect upon values and resources, whether new demands need to be made or old ones modified), so that the process is a continuous and interactive one — in short, it is dynamic. If it is not, the systems approach is designed to help identify where the problem may lie.

In itself, the systems approach has certain drawbacks: it is very general, and by seeking to delineate a 'process' of decision-making may obscure both the exceptions and the complexity of how decisions are reached. A political system is rarely as systematic as the name may imply, and decisions are rarely reached in such a clear, black-and-white manner as a neat systems model may suggest. For that reason, it is important to stress that a systems model serves as a guide to, not a definitive statement about, how public policy is formulated. Its utility, though, lies in the fact that it does serve as a guide. It helps to give some shape to the complexity of facts and relationships with which a student is faced in trying to comprehend the workings of a political community, and provides a simple means by which the general position of one element of a political community may be expressed in relation to other elements. It is for that reason that we employ it here.

We propose to employ a systems model to provide some indication of Parliament's position in the political process in Britain. Before doing so, it may be useful to provide a simple systems model of another nation, not only to demonstrate the utility of the approach but, more important for our purposes, to provide a comparison which may make Parliament's position in the British model more comprehensible.

Let us consider a systems model of the political process in the United States of America. British students are generally more familiar with the politics of the United States than of any other country (excepting, of course, Britain). The legislative branch of American government, Congress, is very different from that of this country. It is thus useful for our purposes to compare the two. A model of the American political process may be represented as in Figure 1.2.

As can be seen, the three traditional branches of government in the United States — executive (the President), legislative (Congress) and judicial (the Supreme Court) and lower courts — all form an important part of the decision-making process. As a consequence of the constitutional structure (the separation of powers, fixed-term elections, and federalism) as well as the supports of the political system (the framework of values and beliefs), both the executive and legislative branches exercise power independently. The President is not dependent upon Congress for his continuance in office. Congress can and does challenge, amend or reject the President's legislative proposals; although the initiative in policy formulation has passed largely to the executive, it has by no means done so exclusively — policies can be and are formulated within Congress itself. The two Chambers of Congress control their own procedures and timetables; and in determining Congressional voting behaviour, President and party are but two, and far from being necessarily the dominant, influences. Even a President with a Congress dominated by members of his own party is not assured of the passage of measures which he proposes, as President Carter discovered when he

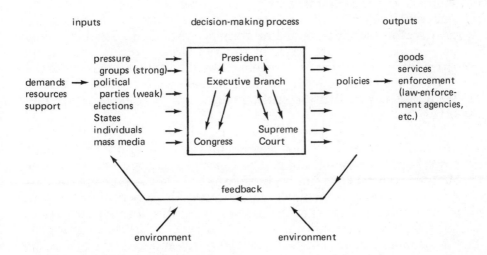

Figure 1.2 The federal political system of the United States

entered the White House. The Supreme Court, at the apex of the federal judiciary, also exercises power independently within the decision-making process. American courts have the power (effectively read into the Constitution by the Supreme Court itself in 1803) to interpret the Constitution and to declare unconstitutional congressional measures and executive actions deemed to conflict with the provisions of the document. It could be argued that since this power is largely negative (it is the power to strike down rather than to initiate and formulate) and has been employed only rarely to strike down federal measures, the Supreme Court (to which cases of constitutional interpretation are normally appealed) does not form a significant part of the decision-making process. However, the Court, which determines its own time-table and chooses which case it will hear, does enjoy the ability to engage in *de facto* policy-making ('judicial law-making', as it is some-times described in this context) because of the vague language of the Constitution. The wording of the Constitution is general and imprecise (what, after all, constitutes 'cruel and unusual punishment', which is proscribed by the Eighth Amendment?), and can be subjected to what might be termed creative interpretation by those vested with the authority to declare what it really means. An obvious and notable example would be the Court's holding in *Brown v. Board of Education of Topeka* in 1954, in which it interpreted the phrase 'the equal protec-tion of the laws' to mean that the segregation of schools was unconsti-tutional, thus giving a lead in the field of civil rights which the executive and legislative branches had been and still were reluctant to give them-selves. This ability to engage in 'judicial law-making' is facilitated by the supports of the political system, notably by what has been called the Lockean ideology.[10] Within this political system, the factors which provide for the three branches' forming part of the decision-making process also encourage weak parties and strong pressure groups, the latter filling something of a vacuum created by the weakness of parties.

How, then, does such a politicial system compare with the British? We would suggest that the British political system could be represented by Figure 1.3.

Unlike the American system, only the executive (the Government and its officials) forms the major decision-making body in Britain. Through powers already granted, and in their capacity as Ministers of the Crown, Ministers can take certain decisions which do not require approval by Parliament (though sometimes requiring the formal assent of the Crown); in other instances, notably the passage of legislation and the levying of taxes, Ministers do require the assent of Parliament. Parliament (primarily the Commons as the dominant House) fulfils an important role as the legitimiser of Government decisions and, prior to giving its legitimisa-tion, as scrutineer of those decisions. As we shall detail later, these are

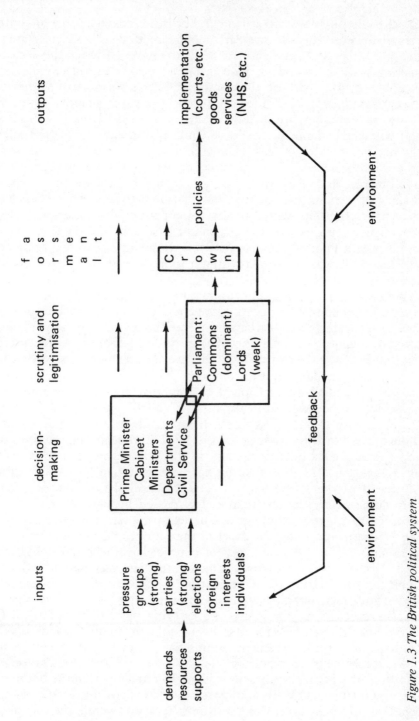

Figure 1.3 The British political system

not the sole functions of Parliament, nor is their exercise free of contro-versy. However, they do give Parliament something of a special status in the political process, as Figure 1.3 seeks to convey. Though the decision-making body is dependent upon it and its legal sovereignty, Parliament is not a central part of that body. Policy is formulated within the executive, and is usually then approved by a party majority within the House of Commons. We shall have cause to consider later why this is so, and whether Parliament should or could play a more significant role in the decision-making process (a liberal view of the Constitution) or not (the Whitehall view). For the moment, we content ourselves with the observation that Parliament is not a major part of the decision-making process in this country, but that nevertheless that process has a special relationship with, and is dependent upon, Parliament: legal sovereignty remains with the Queen-in-Parliament, and the Government is dependent upon the approval of this triumvirate (a formality by con-vention in the case of the Crown; not so in the case of the two Houses) for its exercise.

We may also note, again in contrast to the American system, that the courts do not constitute a central element of the decision-making process. The legal sovereignty of Parliament places them (willingly, as parliamen-tary sovereignty is a legal doctrine) in the outputs role of interpreters and implementers of statute law. The law of Parliament is sovereign and cannot be overridden by the courts. If the courts interpret the law in a way not intended by Parliament (in practice, by the Government), a new law can be passed to overrule the courts' interpretation, as, for example, with the 1972 Northern Ireland Act. It is important to note, though, that with the passage of the 1972 European Communities Act and Britain's consequent accession to the European Communities (EC) on 1 January 1973, this position has been modified somewhat. Under the terms of the Rome Treaty, certain EC legislation has precedence over domestic legislation (that is, law passed by Parliament), and re-sponsibility for resolving conflicts between the two is vested largely in the judiciary, including the Court of the European Communities as well as domestic courts. So far, cases of conflict have been rare, and Parlia-ment has, via the Government, some indirect and very limited influence upon the formulation of EC legislation. The doctrine of Parliamentary sovereignty is maintained, arguably anyway,[11] by the fact that in giving EC law precedence, the courts are carrying out the provisions of the 1972 Act (though nevertheless being able to 'unbind' other laws in consequence), and Parliament retains the power to put an end to this new arrangement by repealing the 1972 Act. (Some would raise the question of whether or not this is likely to remain within the bounds of what is possible politically, as opposed to what is possible legally, though repeal would be a breach of the Rome Treaty.) Overall, the role of the courts in this country remains chiefly, though no longer exclusively, one of the interpretation and implementation of common and statute law. In time, in consequence of EEC membership and a greater assertiveness on the part of the judiciary, this role may change.[12]

To summarise: Parliament is not the body in Britain which makes public policy. That body is primarily the executive, of which part is drawn from Parliament (that is, Government Ministers as opposed to civil servants), and which depends upon Parliament for legitimisation, both of itself and its legislative measures. Through its ever-present formal power to deny legitimacy, Parliament can, and to some extent does, seek to oversee and influence the Government's decision-making. With the acceptance of the political sovereignty of the electorate, the Commons has become the dominant element of the Queen-in-Parliament, and it is through the Lower House that scrutiny and influence is predominantly exercised or at least attempted. It is with the Commons and its attempts at scrutiny and influence that we are concerned in this work.

In Chapter 2, we shall seek to explain how power was transferred from Parliament to, or at least consolidated in, the executive in the nineteenth·century, and how, within Parliament, the Commons became the dominant chamber. The conduit for this change was the growth and operation of political parties (the product of a mass electorate, new demands, and a parliamentary form of Government), and the result was what has sometimes been termed 'party Government'. The relevance of party we shall seek to establish by examining both this shift in executive—legislative relations in the nineteenth century and, in Chapter 3, its relevance within the Commons in the twentieth. Having established this changed relationship — the Commons dominated by party and no longer a regular part of the decision-making process — we shall consider in Chapter 4 what functions the contemporary House of Commons may be deemed to fulfil. In particular, we shall concern ourselves with the general scrutinising function which we have briefly identified above. We shall not only consider it from the perspective of the procedures available for the scrutiny of legislation and executive actions (Chapters 5 and 6), but we shall also examine, specifically in Chapter 7, how such procedures are employed by the Commons in its relations with the different elements of the domestic decision-making process (Ministers, civil servants and executive agencies) — and now also the supra-national decision-making body of the European Communities — and, in Chapter 8, how it employs them in specific policy sectors: for example, is the Commons more effective in the scrutiny of the Government's foreign than it economic policy? If so, why? Penulitmately, in Chapter 9, we shall review the issue of how functional the House actually is through a consideration of various contemporary approaches to parliamentary reform. In so doing, we shall seek to relate developments within the Commons in the 1970s — the most significant decade in terms of post-war (and possibly twentieth-century) political behaviour — to these approaches, and posit our own individual, though not necessarily original, view of the role and effectiveness of the House of Commons. For convenience, the author — pretentiously, if characteristically — has termed this the 'Norton view'. We shall conclude (in Chapter 10) with some observations about the future of the House of Commons — or, as Professor Crick would put it: 'Whither the Commons?'

NOTES

1   See especially Richard Rose, *Politics in England Today* (Faber & Faber, 1974), pp. 43—4.
2   Weber distinguished three types of authority: traditional, based on what has usually or always existed; rational—legal, based on an acceptance by the population that the rules laid down are legitimate; and charismatic, based on the belief that a leader has God-given or extraordinary powers.
3   That is, where decisions are taken resolving disputes on measures of public policy.
4   A. V. Dicey, *Law of the Constitution*, 10th ed. (Macmillan, 1959), pp. 39—40. The first edition was published in 1885.
5   Sir Ivor Jennings, *The Law and the Constitution*, 5th ed. (University of London Press, 1959), p. 147.
6   Quoted in Ivor Jennings, *Parliament*, 2nd ed. (Cambridge University Press, 1957), p. 2. (One could contend that this actually happens given that male references in some Acts — 'he shall be deemed', etc. — encompass women as well as men.)
7   Quintin Hogg, *The Purpose of Parliament* (Blandford Press, n.d.), p. 52.
8   Dicey, *Law of the Constitution*.
9   Geoffrey Marshall and Graeme Moodie, *Some Problems of the Constitution*, 4th revised ed. (Hutchinson, 1967), p. 16.
10   See especially Louis Hartz, *The Liberal Tradition in America* (Harcourt, Brace & World, 1955).
11   Some constitutional lawyers now question whether the doctrine of Parliamentary sovereignty remains valid in consequence of EEC entry. See Gillian Peele, 'The Developing Constitution', in C. Cook and J. Ramsden (eds), *Trends in British Politics since 1945* (Macmillan, 1978), pp. 6—8.
12   See Gillian Peele, 'Change, Decay and the British Constitution', *Hull Papers in Politics No. 1* (Hull University Politics Department, 1978), pp. 2—8. See also Lord Hailsham, *The Dilemma of Democracy* (Collins, 1978), pp. 175—7.

2

The transfer of power: the rise of party government in the nineteenth century

The origins and establishment of Parliament

Parliament may be said to have its origins in the Great Council of the Norman kings, though the tradition of the king seeking the advice of his leading vassals had already been established through the Anglo-Saxon *witena gemot*. Through the Great Council, the king was expected to consult with his tenants-in-chief (the earls, barons and leading churchmen of the kingdom) in order to discover and declare the law, and to have their counsel before any levies of extraordinary taxation were made. This expectation was to find documented recognition in the Magna Carta of 1215, by which the king recognised it as a right of his subjects 'to have the Common Council of the Kingdom' for the assessment of extra-ordinary aids (that is, taxation).

From the Great Council evolved what came to be recognised as a *parlement* or Parliament. The Great Council, as it was composed originally (of the baronage and leading churchmen), was the precursor of the House of Lords. In 1254 two knights from each shire had been summoned to a Council 'to consider . . . what aid they will be willing to grant us in our great need',[1] and in 1264, acting in the king's name, Simon de Montfort issued writs for the return of four knights from each shire to discuss the state of the realm. The following year, he issued writs for the return not only of two knights from each country but also of two burgesses from each borough, and this is often viewed as the beginning of the Commons: 'The Commons had arrived.'[2] In 1275, Edward I held his 'first general Parliament', to which knights, burgesses, and citizens were summoned in addition to the barons, and he held some thirty Parliaments during the first twenty-five years of his reign. However, representatives of the communities, or *communes* (the Commons), played no part in the discussion of high policy, and indeed were not always summoned; there is no evidence of their having been called to more than four of Edward's Parliaments. Their attendence became more regular under Edward II, and they were summoned regularly after 1325. Under Edward III, who had to have constant resort to Parliaments to raise extra taxes for the wars he pursued, the Commons began to make the grant of supply conditional upon the redress of grievances. Hence, Edward's demands 'were to be the foundation of parliamentary influence with the Executive exerted through control of the purse'.[3] At various times in the fourteenth century the Commons deliberated separately from the barons, and there developed the formal separation of Lords and Commons.

· The status of Parliament was enhanced under the Tudors, especially under Henry VIII and Elizabeth I, and for the first time a seat in the Commons became something that was sought after. Henry used the Commons to approve the statutes effecting his break with Rome and determining the succession to the throne. While the king had little difficulty in achieving this through a supportive Commons, it helped to create a precedent for the high matters on which the Commons might deliberate and give consent. Although Elizabeth called few Parliaments, the Commons became more assertive during her reign, prodding her to go further than she wished, and taking the initiative in introducing a number of measures. Parliament 'became only second to the Crown as a power in the State'.[4] Such a position created tension under the Stuarts, especially under Charles I, who sought to maintain the 'divine right' of kings to rule and to deny the privileges acquired by Parliament. The disagreement between Crown and Parliament was to lead eventually to the Civil War and the beheading of the king. With the abolition of the monarchy came a brief period of rule by the Council of State elected by the Rump Parliament, and then military dictatorship. With the Restoration in 1660 came also the restoration of traditional institutions. Although the claim to levy taxes without the consent of Parliament was abandoned, the relations between Crown and Parliament were not well-established and under Charles II 'showed a steadily increasing tension'.[5] Under James II they worsened, with the Catholic king seeking to reassert the 'divine right' to rule and with Parliament combining against him. In 1688 James fled, being replaced under Parliament's will by William of Orange. The new king owed his position to Parliament, and the latter's dominance was established. The constitutional position was asserted in statute by the Bill of Rights. The 'pretended power of suspecting or dispensing with laws, or the execution of laws, without the consent of Parliament' was declared to be illegal, as was 'levying money for or to the use of the Crown, by pretence of prerogative, without grant of Parliament for longer time or in other manner than the same is or shall be granted'. Thirteen years later, the Act of Settlement was to affirm that

> the laws of England are the birthright of the people thereof; and all the Kings and Queens who shall ascend the throne of this realm ought to administer the government of the same according to the said laws; and

all their officers and ministers ought to serve them respectively according
to the same.

Parliament's position in the constitutional structure was established.
The king was expected (through, increasingly, his Ministers) to govern
– those responsible for the Bill of Rights wanted 'a real, working, governing king, a king with a policy'[6] – but to do so with the consent of
Parliament. The king retained prerogative powers, but new laws and taxes
had to have the approval of Parliament. The formal position thus established has remained unchanged.

Reform and the growth of party

During the eighteenth century, Parliament was powerful but rarely
assertive. Little public legislation was passed, and Members generally
accepted that they had a duty (albeit not always fulfilled) to support
the king's Government. The presumed independence of Members of
Parliament[7] was undermined by the dominance of the aristocracy. Many
Members were returned for pocket boroughs through the patronage of
members of the Upper House; a table compiled in about 1815 indicated
that 144 peers, along with 123 commoners, controlled 471 seats in the
House of Commons.[8] Indeed, the monarch and the aristocracy tended
to dominate the political community. In the fifty years prior to the first
Reform Act, the membership of the Cabinet was drawn predominantly
from the House of Lords (for many years Pitt was the only commoner
among its members),[9] and the political decisions of the day were taken
by this limited political community, operating almost solely within
'parliamentary circles and the drawing-rooms connected with them'.[10]
Outside interests and the mass of the population – disenfranchised and
lacking the means of political expression (except perhaps through riot)
– were ignored. The general populace, in fact, paid little heed to politics.
'It was', wrote Ostrogorski, 'the pet hobby of a select group, the sport
of an aristocracy.'[11] The Reform Act of 1832, which enlarged the electorate by 49 per cent, helped to bring this sport to an end.

As Lord Blake has pointed out, the Reform Act could never have been
passed peacefully if a section of the aristocratic class which dominated
Parliament had not supported it.[12] It was, in fact, passed by the descend-
ants of the Foxite Whigs who, for the twenty-five years prior to 1830,
had been the 'outs' in politics. Ironically, the Government which promoted the Bill was one of the most aristocratic the country had ever
seen.[13] The widening of the franchise helped to extend political power
beyond the drawing-rooms of the aristocratic houses, and created an
electorate of such a size that it could not be influenced solely by connection or the power of the nobility. To retain its position of power the

political aristocracy was forced to seek novel channels of communication with the new electors. Some form of *organised* communication was clearly necessary, or at least desirable, and hence the growth of embryonic political organisations in the 1830s: political clubs were set up; registration societies were formed; election funds were created (the Conservative Party, for example, instituted an election fund in 1834); and in some areas, notably Lancashire, constituency associations were established. Yet the Act of 1832 did not create the transfer from an aristocracy to a form of representative democracy sometimes claimed for it. The period between the 1832 and 1867 Reform Acts still bore many similarities to pre-1832 days: the redistribution of seats had been essentially a conservative one; rotten boroughs were by no means fully abolished; the aristocracy still held great political sway;[14] and the franchise remained highly restrictive. However, the Act did help to create conditions which marked out the period between the two Reform Acts as a transitional one between an aristocracy and some (albeit limited) form of representative democracy. This was to be reflected in the choice of Government. Prior to 1832, it had been chosen by the monarch — it was tried for the last time in 1834 — and after 1867 it came to be determined by the voting of the electors. In the interval, as Cecil Emden has noted, ' after the Sovereign ceased to have unfettered ability to choose Ministers, and before the people gained the power to choose between rival Ministries, the change of Government often depended on the voting in the House of Commons.'[15] This was to be the period sometimes described as the 'golden age' of the Commons.

During this period, Parliament and primarily the Commons came to form what was effectively part of the decision-making process. It did not itself govern — it has never done so — but it did exercise an effective negative (checking) and sometimes positive (initiating) power in the decision-making process, especially after 1846. Walter Bagehot attached much importance to what he described as the 'elective function' of the Commons. It was, he wrote, 'a real choosing body: it elects the people it likes. And it dismisses whom it likes too.'[16] Members could and did replace one Government with another without suffering a dissolution (as, for example, in 1852, 1855, 1858 and 1866), and could and did remove individual Ministers who had erred (as, for instance, Lord John Russell in 1855 and Lord Ellenborough in 1858).[17] Members collaborated in the shaping of various Government measures as well as in amending or rejecting legislation on the floor of the House ('the existence of numerous independent and earnest members with a great deal to say and the right to say it meant that no Government could with any certainty plan any legislative programme');[18] ministerial policy on various occasions was overruled; the Ministry was sometimes forced to divulge information (for example, about negotiations with foreign powers); and debate really counted for something. 'There was always a possibility that a speech might turn votes; the result of a division was not a foregone conclusion.'[19] With the exception of the period from 1841 to 1846 party cohesion was almost unknown. Members were able to change parties (or remain members of none) and 'party votes' were rare. According to the researches of Lawrence Lowell, the percentage of divisions in which both sides of the House cast party votes was less than 23 per cent in 1836 and less than 7 per cent in 1860.[20] The position of the Commons during this golden age (sometimes known as the period of 'classical parliamentary government', though government in the sense of government *by* Parliament is a misnomer), has been aptly summarised by Victor Wiseman. 'From 1832 to 1867', he wrote, 'Cabinets were responsible for policy though they worked under the *informed observation and control* of the Commons.'[21] The golden age was to be short-lived. It came to an end essentially in consequence of the effects of the Reform Act of 1867.

The reasons for the introduction and passage of the Act of 1867 are complex, and various schools of thought on the subject exist. The Act itself put into practice the principle recognised by the 1832 Act, that of the extension of the franchise, and increased the electorate by 88 per cent. In the boroughs, the increase was 140 per cent. For the political parties, such an enormous and sudden growth of the electorate meant that 'a system of centralization became inevitable.'[22] Political leaders realised that they would have to make efforts to cater for the political aspirations of middle-class and some working men, and to attract their support, through constituency-based organisations and through legislation in Parliament. This could be achieved only by the development of large-scale party organisations (not warranted by the limited franchise extension of 1832), with Members united in the House of Commons to ensure the passage of promised measures. The Conservative and Liberal parties were both restructured to form mass-membership organisations − the Conservative National Union and the National Liberal Federation being created as a direct response to the new conditions − and Members of Parliament began to adhere more firmly to party labels. The traditional methods of ensuring election gradually disappeared. The size of the electorate helped to discourage bribery; intimidation and corrupt practices were removed largely by the Ballot Act of 1870 and the Corrupt Practices Act of 1882; and the electorate proved too ill-educated to appreciate the discriminating political judgement of independently minded Members in parliamentary cross-voting. Members of Parliament increasingly became reliant upon their newly developed constituency associations − the more so as the franchise was further extended in 1884 − while at the same time having to support the general policy of one of the political parties with which sections of the electorate could identify. As John Mackintosh has noted:

The mid-century House of Commons had been able to distinguish between the total record of a ministry and its individual proposals. A mass electorate wanted its MPs to be consistently Liberal or Conservative. This was in part because the public could not be expected to scrutinise too many specific policies. The loyalty of large blocks of voters, once established, was not easily shaken.[23]

The result of a large electoral roll, the growth of party competition, and the development of large, centralised party organisations all modified the position of Members of Parliament. The parliamentary action of an individual Member was no longer his own concern or that of a limited few — it was now that of his constituents and party; electors no longer identified with Members as individuals but increasingly with party, and it was on the strength of their party labels that Members were elected. The dominant force of British political life became the political parties, a development which was gradual but sure. As mass parties assumed positions of dominance, the effect on Parliament and parliamentary life was profound.

With the passage of the second Reform Act came the end of the brief golden age of the House of Commons. The wishes of the electorate, aggregated and expressed through political parties, began to determine the composition of the Government: its fate was no longer decided (other than exceptionally) on the floor of the House of Commons, but by the opinion of the enfranchised population. Members of Parliament were gradually relegated to being representatives of that opinion, and their freedom of parliamentary action was correspondingly diminished. Members who had previously regarded public interest in their proceedings in Parliament as an intrusion now sought publicity in a new responsiveness to public opinion. It was a situation which had been predicted with uncharacteristic insight by the Earl of Carnarvon, an arch-opponent of reform. Speaking during the Second Reading of the Bill in the Lords in 1867, he declared:

> Suppose that the very same men are returned that now sit in the House of Commons. I still contend that their course of conduct must be different, because, though they may sit for the same seats, they will be returned by constituencies of a very different nature. There will, as I think was once said, be all the difference between these men, now and then, that exists between an actor who speaks to the boxes and an actor who speaks to the gallery.[24]

It was not only individual Members who had to play to the gallery, but party leaders as well. Realising that political power was now determined by the country and not primarily by the House of Commons, leading politicians began to develop the technique of speaking directly to the electors. Increasingly, less attention was paid to influencing debates on the floor of the House. As long as the Government had the support of the country, it had little fear from widespread dissent among its parliamentary adherents — representatives of that support — in the division lobbies. Major speeches in Parliament came to be delivered more for external consumption than for the benefit of assembled Members. This shift of elective power, from Commons to a mass electorate, was given almost instant recognition when Disraeli, after being defeated on the new franchise in 1868, resigned without waiting for a defeat in Parliament. It was, observed Spencer Walpole, 'the first open recognition in history that the House of Commons itself was of less importance than the electors'.[25] Disraeli, who before 1868 had confined his speeches to the Commons and his constituency, followed up this resignation in 1872 by addressing two mass rallies (both of the party faithful) in Manchester and at Crystal Palace; while Gladstone, in response to the demands of the crowds, had to stop to address meetings at the major stations on the way from his country home to Midlothian in 1879, thus becoming the first statesman to 'stump the country'. Lord Selbourne commented that the result of the Midlothian campaign removed 'the political centre from Parliament to the platform'.[26] The short-lived elective function of Parliament was thus transferred to the new electors.

The advent of a mass suffrage and the growth of party deprived the House of Commons not only of its elective function, but also of another function ascribed to it by Bagehot, namely 'the function of legislation, of which of course it would be preposterous to deny the great importance'.[27] As the idea of the mandate developed, so Government-inspired legislation, promised at the polls, began to take priority over the Bills of private Members. Concomitant with this, as party leaders appealed to and rested their power on the decisions of the voters, Ministers became less willing to be overruled on matters of policy, while the increase in legislation itself — which Gladstone attributed not only to the new role of Government (responding to a large and new class of electors) but also to the extension of trade relations and the growth of empire — and its increasing complexity further reduced the influence of individual Members: private Members had neither the facilities nor the knowledge to prepare the complex Bills which were becoming a feature of parliamentary life.[28] The result was the gradual domination of Parliament by the Cabinet. Prior to 1867, the Cabinet had rested its authority on Parliament; Ostrogorski referred to it as 'only a committee of the two Houses'. After 1867, it began in effect to be chosen by the electors through party voting, and derived its authority from such voting. Parliament became subordinate to its wishes. Having voted for a party and a programme, as John Mackintosh has noted, both the electors and those MPs in tune with the times expected that Parliament would enact the

programme. 'The task of the House of Commons became one of supporting the Cabinet chosen at the polls and passing its legislation . . . By
the 1900s, the Cabinet dominated British government.'[29] The effect on
the House of Commons of the rise of political parties, the product of a
mass suffrage, was thus to deprive it of both its elective and its legislative
functions, the former going to the electorate, the latter to the Cabinet.
Classical parliamentary government was at an end. Power now rested
not on the floor of the House but, with the consent of the electors, in
the Cabinet, a party Cabinet, at the head of which was a Prime Minister
who was party leader.

In the Commons, the parliamentary parties became significantly more
cohesive. In 1871, four years after the passage of the second Reform
Act, party votes were cast in just over 35 per cent of divisions. In 1881,
this figure was 76 percent.[30] By 1899, the number of divisions in which
neither side cast a party vote was negligible. Yet the increase in the size
of the electorate does not, by itself, account for the high degree of cohesion. If we may be permitted to state what may be an obvious point
underpinning most of the foregoing analysis, it requires a parliamentary
system to facilitate the emergence of this cohesion. Although the Commons lost its elective function to the electors, the electorate could
exercise this function only *through* the Commons. Lacking a system of
government based upon a separation of powers between executive and
legislative branches and fixed-term elections, a ministry was (and still is)
dependent upon the support of a majority in the House of Commons
not only for the passage of its measures but also for its continuance in
office. Failure by members of the party in government to support the
Government in the division lobbies could lead to defeat and, if defeats
were frequent or on a vote of confidence, to resignation; hence, 'maintaining a government in office became their responsibility.'[31] While
cohesive parties are not absolutely necessary for the proper functioning
of Government under the separation of powers (note the experience of
the United States), the parliamentary system, as Ergun Ozbudun has
succinctly concluded, creates a strong initiative for maintaining party
cohesion by making important votes in the legislative assembly almost
tantamount to votes of confidence in the Government. 'In other words,
effective working of a parliamentary system depends on the existence
of cohesive political parties.'[32]

Changes in procedure

The development of party government further affected the workings of
the House of Commons in that it necessitated a reform of procedure.
The shift of power, and especially of the legislative function, from the
floor of the House to the executive made it more and more necessary

for the parliamentary timetable to be revised in favour of the ministry — it was impossible to pass many Government measures as long as procedure discriminated in favour of the private Member — while, at the same time, the growth of party competition led to the realisation that the very existence of Parliament rested upon its rules of business as a foundation. The result was that 'the need of framing a new and adequate system became too urgent to be evaded. For the first time procedure came to be recognised as an independent problem in the spheres of political life, of parliamentary law and of the constitution itself.'[33]

The need for some measure of procedural change had been recognised in the transitional period between 1832 and 1867, but despite the appointment of Select Committees on Procedure in 1837, 1848, 1854 and 1861, little was achieved.[34] Members were jealous of their rights, and were prepared to defend them. Following the second Reform Act, Select Committees were appointed in 1869 and 1871, but again (despite many important recommendations made to the 1871 Committee by Sir Erskine May) not much was achieved. A further Committee, appointed in 1878, achieved a few concrete results, and by 1880, as a result of various piecemeal reforms, 'a great deal of the dead wood had been cleared away.'[35] However, it was not until the reforms introduced in order to deal with the obstruction by Irish Members (which began in 1877 and was brought to an end by the reforms of 1882) that procedure began to discriminate clearly in favour of the Government. The reforms, introduced by Gladstone, 'represented the watershed between the old and the new Government-managed Parliament'.[36] The closure, which has now become a normal instrument for the curtailment of debate, was introduced, followed by the guillotine (in effect, a timetable motion); the right of Members to raise adjournment debates on matters of urgency was severely restricted; Mr Speaker was empowered to direct a Member to discontinue a speech for irrelevance or tedious repetition, and his powers to 'name' a Member strengthened; the 'rule of progress' was applied to going into Committee of Supply; and a rule made in 1877 against making two dilatory motions on the same question was now extended to all proceedings, whether in committee or in the House, and debate on such motions confined strictly to the matter of the motion.[37] Such changes diminished the power of the individual Member and of minorities, while strengthening the Government, backed by its parliamentary majority. Although introduced to deal with Irish obstruction, it is likely that changes of this nature would have been introduced anyway. As Redlich has observed, the actions of the Irish Members helped accelerate the reforms, but they were not the true cause of them: 'The real motive power came from the alteration in the nature of British Government itself.'[38] Once these procedural changes had taken place, the Government ensured that they remained, and further reforms followed.

In 1882, Gladstone — again aided by the results of Irish obstruction in debating Bills in Committee of the whole House — introduced a scheme providing for two Standing Committees (one for legal, one for trade Bills), which, after lapsing for a period, were provided for by standing orders in 1888 and extended to all public Bills, except money and provisional order Bills, in 1907. In 1888, the procedural reforms were systematised, and Mr Speaker was given the power to bring the sitting to a close at 1.00a.m. without the question being put. In 1896, the number of days for discussing supply was limited to twenty, when the Opposition had the right to determine the debate, and thereafter was normally allocated for general debates. In 1902, the Leader of the House, A.J. Balfour, introduced a comprehensive scheme of procedural reform, including precedence for Government business except during the latter half of Tuesdays and Thursdays and on the whole of each Friday, with further reforms following in the sessions of 1906 and 1907.[39] The result was the domination of the parliamentary timetable by the executive. Josef Redlich, writing shortly after the turn of the century, was thus able to assert that in the previous quarter of a century three tendencies had stood out in bold relief: the strengthening of the disciplinary and administrative powers of the Speaker, the continuous extension of the rights of the Government over the direction of all parliamentary action in the House, and, lastly, the complete suppression of the private Member, both as to his legislative initiative and as to the scope of action allowed him by the rules. 'Not one of the three is the consequence of any intentional effort; they have all arisen out of the hard necessity of political requirements.'[40]

Relationship of the two Houses

In the period prior to 1867, the House of Commons could be said to form a major part of the decision-making process. In consequence of the developments we have identified, it ceased to do so, coming instead to occupy the position in the political process which we have illustrated in Chapter 1 (Figure 1.3, p. 7). However, while the Common's place in the political process was changing, so too was its relationship to the other House, the House of Lords. The cause of the Common's changed role was, within the context of Parliament, to make it the dominant of the two chambers.

In financial matters, the Commons had achieved some priority over the Lords before the nineteenth century. As Kenneth Mackenzie has noted, the Commons owed their place in Parliament to the necessity of securing their assent to aids, and it was perhaps inevitable that the House of Commons, as the ultimate source of revenue, should become eventually the effective controller of taxation.[41] The Commons became the exclusive originator of taxation, a position affirmed by Henry IV in 1407 and reasserted after the Restoration when a number of Lords' Bills to impose taxes were refused First Readings. Also after the Restoration, the Commons began to deny the right of the other House even to amend money Bills. The Lords objected, 'but from this time onwards the Commons' claim, if not yet formally admitted, had in practice to be conceded.'[42] However, the right of the Lords to amend and reject non-money Bills remained (the Upper House was formally co-equal with the Commons in dealing with such legislation), and important members of the Lords remained powerful through their control of seats in the Commons.

The authority of the Lords was undermined in the nineteenth century with the gradual transfer to a rational—legal system of limited representative democracy. The authority of the House of Lords was traditional, and could be accommodated in a rational—legal system only through its acceptance of subordination to the chamber which was elected by 'the people'. However, 'the people' granted the vote by the 1832 Act were not numerous (it was the principle of the Act that was important), and the Lords could still, on occasion, cause problems. Prior to Peel's second ministry the Lords tended, in Greville's words, 'to bowl down [Whig] Bills like ninepins'.[43]

The 1867 Reform Act largely removed the remaining authority, if not formal power, of the Lords to resist the will of the Commons. The effect the measure was to have on the Upper House was noted by the Earl of Shaftesbury during its Second Reading in the Lords. His Lordship observed perceptively:

> When we come to look at the House in which I have now the honour to address your Lordships, I ask how it will be affected by this great democratic change? So long as the other House of Parliament was elected upon a restricted principle, I can understand that it would submit to a check from a House such as this. But in the presence of this great democratic power and the advance of this great democratic wave . . . it passes my comprehension to understand how an hereditary House like this can hold its own. It might be possible for this House, in one instance, to withstand a measure if it were violent, unjust, and coercive; but I do not believe that the repetition of such an offence would be permitted. It would be said, 'The people must govern, and not a set of hereditary peers never chosen by the people.'[44]

Shaftesbury's prophetic insight was to be justified by events, although it was not until the Parliament Act of 1911 that the Lords were forced statutorily to accept their diminished status. They were jealous of their former power and fought to retain it. The theory was developed, especially by Conservative peers (who were in a permanent majority in the House), that the House of Lords could reject any major Government legislation on which it felt the opinion of the country was not adequately known, and force a dissolution in order to ascertain that opinion.

The tactics of the Conservative peers were clear: they hoped to compel any Liberal Government to go to the polls every time a controversial measure was introduced in order that the Conservatives might have the opportunity to return to power. As Sir Charles Dilke put it in 1881, 'the claim of Lord Salisbury to force us [the Liberals] to "consult the country" is a claim for annual Parliaments when we are in office and septennial Parliaments when they are in office.' In 1884, the Conservative peers employed their obstructionist tactics and refused to pass the franchise Bill until a scheme of redistribution was also introduced. 'Their attitude', recorded G. Lowes Dickinson, 'aroused a storm of indignation. Mr Gladstone quoted Shakespeare in the House [and] Mr Morley hit off the famous assonance "mend or end" ';[45] while the radical Member Mr Labouchere introduced a motion calling for 'such alterations in the relations of the two Houses of Parliament as will effect a remedy to this state of things'.[46] The policy of 'mending or ending' became part of the 1891 Newcastle programme, and when the Lords threw out the Home Rule Bill in 1893, the Liberal Conference, meeting in Leeds the following year, passed a resolution in favour of abolishing its veto. Ten years of uninterrupted Conservative rule then intervened, but the problem returned with the Liberal Government of 1906.

From 1906 onwards the Lords adopted an approach of almost consistent obstruction, striking down Bills on education, licensing, plural voting, Scottish smallholdings, and land valuation, culminating in 1909 in their refusal to accept the budget 'until it has been submitted to the judgement of the country'. The tactic backfired, with the Government going to the country not on the issue of the budget but on the reform of the Upper House. The result, after two elections, was the Parliament Act of 1911. The Act provided that a non-money Bill could be delayed by the Lords for only two successive sessions (reduced by a further session by the Parliament Act of 1949),[47] the Bill being enacted into law if passed by the Commons again in the next session, and that a money Bill, as certified by the Speaker, was to become law one month after leaving the Commons, whether approved by the Lords or not. The only power of veto retained by the Upper House was that of Bills to prolong the life of a Parliament, of provisional order Bills, and of delegated legislation. 'The whole experience of this struggle forced the Lords to appreciate and be content with the position to which they had been relegated when Cabinets became dependent first on the House of Commons and then on the electorate.'[48] Despite their struggle, the Lords were forced to submerge, though not quite drown, under Shaftesbury's foreseen 'democratic wave'.

Conclusion

With its origins in the thirteenth century at the latest, Parliament developed (at times erratically) to achieve a formal position of dominance in connection with the raising of taxes and the promulgation of law in this country. In practice, it rarely played a positive role in the decision-making process. Its power was based on the ability to give, and hence to deny, consent to taxes and to legislation. Only in the period between the two Reform Acts can it be said that the House of Commons constituted a regular part of the decision-making process (the House of Lords was already clearly starting to take second place to the elected House), exercising both a negative (checking) and, based on that, a limited positive (initiating) power. This golden age of the Commons was to prove of short duration. Following from the effects of the 1867 Reform Act came a shift of power from the Commons to the executive. It resulted in the virtual suppression of the independence of the private Member in the Commons, and a corresponding increase in, and new emphasis upon, the power of the Cabinet, necessarily reflected in the reform of parliamentary procedure and the growth of party cohesion in the division lobbies. Both the elective and the legislative functions of the Commons as identified by Bagehot were transferred elsewhere, the former in practice to the electors, the latter to the Cabinet; while the House of Lords was forced to acquiesce, albeit with reluctance, in the decisions (though now originating elsewhere) of the newly representative House. The political sovereignty identified by Dicey[49] rested now with the new electors, and was channelled through, and exercised on their behalf by, political parties. The House of Commons was 'transformed into an organ of power put at the disposal of a political group to whom the electorate majority has for a term of years accorded its confidence in the expectations that election promises will be adequately[50] fulfilled. Party government had arrived.

By the beginning of the twentieth century, the position of Parliament in the political process — as identified in Chapter 1 — was established. It was not part of the decision-making 'black box' as such, but it did perform a number of important functions in the political process. The decision-making process was dominated by the executive, and the link between it and Parliament, primarily the Commons, was provided by party. Such remains the position today.

NOTES

1   Kenneth Mackenzie, *The English Parliament* (Penguin, 1968), p. 15.
2   *ibid.*
3   Ronald Butt, *The Power of Parliament* (Constable, 1967), p. 35.
4   Henry Morrison and Wilfrid S. Abbott, *Parliament*, 2nd ed. (Pitman, 1935), p. 3.

5   David Ogg, *England in the Reign of Charles II*, Vol. II, 2nd ed. (Oxford University Press, 1963), p. 455.

6   F.W. Maitland, *Constitutional History of England*, quoted in H.V. Wiseman (ed.), *Parliament and the Executive* (Routledge & Kegan Paul, 1966), p. 5.

7   The term 'Members of Parliament' had applied to Members of the Commons since the time of the Restoration. Previously, it had applied to Members of both Houses.

8   Moisei Ostrogorski, *Democracy and the Organisation of Political Parties*, Vol. I: *England* (Macmillan, 1902), p. 20.

9   W.L. Guttsman, *The British Political Elite* (Macgibbon & Kee, 1968), p. 36.

10   Ostrogorski, p. 15.

11   *ibid*.

12   Robert Blake, *The Conservative Party from Peel to Churchill* (Eyre & Spottiswoode, 1970), pp. 100—1.

13   Guttsman, ch. 2.

14   It has been calculated that the House of Commons in 1841 contained 343 sons of peers, baronets, or near relations of peers. See D.G. Wright, *Democracy and Reform 1815—1885* (Longman, 1970), p. 51.

15   Cecil Emden, *The People and the Constitution*, 2nd ed. (Oxford University Press, 1956), pp. 159—60.

16   Walter Bagehot, *The English Constitution* (Fontana ed., 1963), p. 150.

17   John Mackintosh, 'Parliament Now and a Hundred Years Ago', in D. Leonard and V. Herman (eds), *The Backbencher and Parliament* (Macmillan, 1972), pp. 246—7, and, by the same author, *The Government and Politics of Britain*, 3rd revised ed. (Hutchinson, 1974), p. 130.

18   Kenneth Swinhoe, 'A Study of Opinion about the Reform of the House of Commons Procedure 1945—68', unpublished PhD thesis, University of Leeds, 1971, p. 27.

19   Lord Campion, 'Parliament and Democracy', in Lord Campion (ed.), *Parliament: A Survey* (Allen & Unwin, 1952), p. 15.

20   A. Lawrence Lowell, *The Government of England*, Vol. II (Macmillan, 1924), pp. 76—8. A 'party vote' was one in which 90 per cent or more of members of one party voting in a division voted in the same lobby.

21   Wiseman, p. 10 (my emphasis).

22   Charles Seymour, *Electoral Reform in England and Wales* (David & Charles, 1970), p. 313.

23   John Mackintosh, *The British Cabinet*, 2nd ed. (Methuen, 1968), p. 189.

24   *Parliamentary Debates*, Vol. 188, col. 1837.

25   Quoted in Emden, p. 163.

26   Quoted in Mackintosh, *The British Cabinet*, p. 178n, and Emden, p. 289.

27   Bagehot, p. 153.

28   See Sir Courtenay Ilbert's introduction to Josef Redlich, *Procedure of the House of Commons*, Vol. I (Archibald Constable, 1908), p. xix.

29   Mackintosh, *The British Cabinet*, p. 174.

30   Lowell, pp. 76—8.

31   Leon D. Epstein, *Political Parties in Western Democracies* (Praeger, 1967), p. 320.

32   Ergun Ozbudun, *Party Cohesion in Western Democracies: A Causal Analysis* (Sage, 1970), p. 380.

33   Author's introduction to Redlich, p. xxxii.

34   Though in 1846 two days a week were allocated to Government business, increased to three days in 1851.
35   Lord Campion, *An Introduction to the Procedure of the House of Commons*, 3rd ed. (Macmillan, 1958), p. 38.
36   Butt, p. 88.
37   See Redlich, Vol. I; Butt, pp. 83—9; Mackenzie, pp. 137—43.
38   Redlich, p. 210.
39   See generally Swinhoe for details.
40   Redlich. p. 206.
41   Mackenzie, p. 69.
42   Mackenzie, p. 70. For details of the Commons' privilege in finance, see Sir David Lidderdale (ed.), *Erskine May's Treatise on the Law, Privileges, Proceedings and Usage of Parliament*, 19th ed. (Butterworth, 1976), ch. 31, pp. 795—810.
43   Quoted in A.J. Anthony Morris, *Parliamentary Democracy in the Nineteenth Century* (Pergamon, 1967), p. 99.
44   *Parliamentary Debates*, Vol. 188, col. 1925—6.
45   G. Lowes Dickinson, *The Development of Parliament during the Nineteenth Century* (published 1895), p. 102.
46   *Parliamentary Debates*, Vol. 294, col. 141—2.
47   One year has to elapse between the Second Reading of the Bill in the Commons in the first session and its passing in the Commons in the second.
48   Mackintosh, *The British Cabinet*, p. 223.
49   A.V. Dicey, *Law of the Constitution*, 10th ed. (Macmillan, 1959), pp. 39—40.
50   Sir David Lindsay Keir, *The Constitutional History of Modern Britain since 1485*, 8th ed. (Black, 1966), p. 463.

3

Party in Parliament: the role of party in the twentieth century[1]

Central to an understanding of the House of Commons in the twentieth century — its composition, procedure, and output, as well as the voting behaviour of MPs and their activity on and off the floor of the House — is *party*. Strictly speaking, political parties are unofficial bodies, and as such are not recognised as part of the formality of the constitutional structure; they are, though, at the heart of the reality of British politics.

With the development of a mass electorate in the nineteenth century (further and more comprehensively extended in the twentieth), political parties became highly organised and centralised to serve as channels through which the elective function of the Commons was transferred primarily to the electorate, and the legislative function to the Cabinet. 'Party within Parliament', as Quintin Hogg noted, 'is the instrument whereby Government retains control of its time and gives coherence and meaning to its policy. In the country at large, Party is the means whereby the public exercises its control over Government.'[2] This development we have outlined in Chapter 2. The importance of party established in the nineteenth century remains, even more pronounced, in the twentieth. Now as then, party serves to provide alternatives and to aggregate opinions. It helps to give meaning and shape to the votes of over forty million electors. It is on the basis of party that most electors vote; it is on the basis of party that most candidates are nominated. Members are returned formally as Members of Parliament, but in reality usually as Conservative Members of Parliament or Labour Members of Parliament (Labour replacing the Liberal party in the 1920s as one of the two largest parties). As one MP has observed, 'first and last, a Member of Parliament is a member of a political Party';[3] and it is interesting to note that a number of practising politicians writing on Parliament, from Quintin Hogg in the 1940s to Fred Willey in the 1970s, have referred to party with a capital P.

Party determines the composition of the House of Commons, and the composition determines which party, or coalition of parties, will form the Government. As Viscount Samuel once aptly commented, party provides a continuity of responsibility (a party in Government can be held accountable at the next election); without it, the Commons would comprise merely a 'fortuitous collection of atoms'.[4] The May 1979 general election saw the return not of an array of atoms, but of 339 Conservative, 268 Labour, 11 Liberal, 10 Ulster Unionist (of one hue or another), 2 Scottish National, 2 Plaid Cymru, and 3 other Members (interest on election night being focused not so much on who was returned but on the parties that they represented), and the leader of the party with an overall majority in the Commons, Mrs Thatcher, formed a Conservative Government. The measures of that Government are passed by the House of Commons through the Conservative majority in the House.

Party cohesion in the division lobbies has been a feature of the Commons in the twentieth century, especially in the period from 1945 to 1970 (less in the 1970s, though it is still the norm);[5] there were actually two sessions in the 1950s in which not one Conservative Member cast a dissenting vote. Even in divisions in which a free vote is allowed, with the party whips off and no official advice offered by party spokesmen, Members often vote on party lines. In the 1974—9 Parliament, for example, it was common for Members to divide along party lines in free votes on ten-minute rule Bills. The procedure of the House, as we detailed in the preceding chapter, is based upon the existence of party government, and assumes the existence of a party (or parties) forming the Government and another forming the official Opposition. In short, the reality of party has adapted and been super-imposed upon the formal decision-making structure.

The importance of party in Parliament is further reflected and rein-forced by the growth of structured party organisations within the Commons. The development of organised mass parties, which was, as we have seen, a feature of the nineteenth century, had a profound effect on parliamentary behaviour and procedure. However, the formal struc-ture of parties within the Commons changed little. When Lawrence Lowell wrote in 1908 that 'the whips may be said to constitute the only regular party organisation in the House of Commons unless we include under that description the two front benches',[6] he was describing a position that had remained essentially unchanged for over a century. Today, that description would be unrecognisable. For if the growth of a formal party organisation outside Parliament was a feature of the nineteenth century, the development of a more structured party organis-ation *within* Parliament has been a feature of the twentieth.

Party organisation

Throughout this century, there has been a steady growth of parliamentary party organisation, a change which has taken place away from (and has attracted Members from) the floor of the House. As William Deedes, a former Member with twenty-four years' service in the Commons, wrote in 1978:

> The volume of political business done *outside* the chamber has increased, is increasing and is unlikely to be diminished. It is a bi-partisan failing. The Tory 1922 Committee share every bit as much blame for this development as the Parliamentary Labour Party. Private laundries have become the vogue.[7]

Each parliamentary party this century has developed some form of infrastructure, the most extensive being within the Parliamentary Labour Party (the PLP) and the Conservative parliamentary party. Although this development has not been uniform between the parties but is related both to their nature and the size of their parliamentary ranks, there are sufficient similarities to allow us to identify four main elements of parliamentary parties today: (1) party whips, (2) an organised parliamentary party with regular meetings and elected officers, (3) party committees, and (4) the election of the party leader. All four constitute essential features of the two largest parliamentary parties in 1980, with party whips and in some instances regular meetings and elected officers also constituting features of the smaller ones. As we shall have cause to argue, the development of organised parliamentary parties has served to give Members, through their positions as party Members, a useful means of influencing their party leadership and hence, when in Government, the decision-making process.

Party whips

Party whips are probably the best-known and most misunderstood elements of parliamentary parties. They have existed since the latter half of the eighteenth century; they increased in number and effectiveness during the nineteenth and, by the turn of the century, constituted still the only regular form of party organisation in the Commons. Although other forms of party organisation have been established during this century, the whips have continued to form a central element of parliamentary parties, every parliamentary party that has existed in this century having appointed one or more. Even one of the two Scottish National MPs in the current Parliament acts as a whip.

The duties of the whips have been much misunderstood and maligned. A popular view is that they perform a positive service on behalf of their leaders, but a negative one for backbenchers. References to the 'tyranny of the whips' appear popular. In practice, they fulfil functions of value to both front and back benches. These functions may be identified as those of management, communication, and persuasion, all three of which are closely related.

The management function derives from a party's need to maximise its strength in the division lobbies. If supporters are to be present in the lobbies as occasion demands, then it is obviously advantageous for a party to keep its own Members informed of current business as well as monitoring their whereabouts during sittings. Keeping Members informed and soliciting their attendance is achieved principally through the issuance of a written whip; the degree of underlining indicates the strength of party commitment on each item of business. An item may be underlined once, twice or three times, the latter (known as a three-line whip) indicating a major item on which the party is strongly committed. The written whip serves an important communicative function and is a document to which Members respond as much because they want to as because they feel they have to. With the increasing inter-party conflict and the greater complexity of legislation during the century (as well as small or non-existent Government majorities in some Parliaments and increased intra-party dissent in the lobbies in the 1970s) the managerial role of the whips has become the more important, both in the marshalling of forces in the lobbies (and, since 1945, in Standing Committees) and in the organisation of the business of the House. In conjunction with the Leader of the House, and through what are known as the 'usual channels' (contact between the whips' offices),[8] the Government Chief Whip is responsible for arranging the timetable of Government business in the House.

The communicative function of the whips may be seen as following closely the managerial. If the whips are to ensure a full turnout of supporters in the lobbies, it is to their advantage to know in advance what Members' views are on the issue in question and that the Members are conversant with their leaders' views. The whips thus constitute a channel of communication between front and back benches. It was and is their business, as Lowell noted, 'to know the disposition of every member of the party on every measure of importance to the ministry, reporting it constantly to their chief'.[9] Frontbenchers, especially when in Government, do not have the time personally to consult the majority of their supporters in the House. They rely upon the whips, who, having between them consulted all their backbenchers, convey the view of the parliamentary party to the Minister concerned or, through the Chief Whip, to the Cabinet. For the backbencher, this contact provides a valuable, and private, means of making his views known to his leaders, and one which is often effective. An adverse reaction to a measure conveyed through the whips can influence a change in front-bench intentions. As one Conservative whip has claimed, if the Chief Whip comes to the conclusion, on the basis of sounding out the parliamentary party, that something cannot be done, then, as a general rule, that is that: it cannot be done.[10]

With the growth of Government legislation (and parliamentary party activity), the written whip, as we have noted, has become an important instrument of communication. The greater the volume of business transacted, and the greater the complexity, the greater the need for guidance. As Hugh Berrington has observed in his analysis of the nineteenth-century House (and as we noted in the preceding chapter), 'increasing technicality meant Members could no longer advert to their own judgement or experience; the resulting vacuum was filled by party.'[11] The written whip communicates the parliamentary business for the forth-coming week (as well as details of meetings of Standing, Select, party and other committees) and guidance, through the underlining of items, as to the party line on specific items of business and the importance attached to them. Without the document, a Member would have little idea of what was happening in the House, nor, having insufficient grasp of every issue, would he know how to vote in most divisions. Vernon Bartlett, an independent Member in the 1940s, found himself in such a position and often abstained from voting, sometimes hiding during divisions to avoid well-meaning reminders that a vote was taking place;[12] the Scottish National Member who sat in the period from 1967 to 1970 (Mrs Ewing) apparently encountered similar difficulties.

The negative view which some commentators entertain of the whips derives not from their managerial—communicative role but from their resulting task of persuasion. It is the job of the whips 'to know the disposition' of Members on issues coming before the House. If Members are disposed to oppose the party line, it is the whips' task to dissuade them from such opposition. It is often believed that they achieve this through employing strong disciplinary measures. In practice, they do no such thing, if for no other reason than that they have no strong disciplinary powers. What power they did once have (other than those of persuasion) have generally disappeared. The 'secret service' fund of £10,000 a year, reputedly used by the Government Chief Whip to help candidates with election expenses, was abolished in 1886, while the threat of a dissolution has lost much of its potency since the majority of candidates ceased to pay their own election expenses. Nor do the whips have the power, as many assume they do, to withdraw the party whip (receipt of which signifies membership of the parliamentary party): on the Conservative side it has fallen into disuse (it was last employed in 1942, and apparently last contemplated in the 1959—64 Parliament), while on the Labour side the whips have never had it (the Labour whip can be withdrawn only by the parliamentary party itself, a power acquired in 1913, and since retained and employed). Other formal powers associated with the whips (the selection of Members to serve on parliamentary delegations and certain committees, the influencing of appointments, and the dispensing of some patronage) are of limited importance. Considerations other than a Member's voting record come into play, especially in the case of projected promotion to the front bench; and as Uwe Kitzinger has observed, preferential treatment for delegations and committees constitute 'the small change of political life, with which habits of conformity can be cemented, but with which no one would expect to buy great votes of principle'.[13] The whips can attempt to cajole, threaten or rebuke recalcitrant backbenchers — the Conservative Chief Whips in the inter-war period were particularly prone, as one MP of the period recalled, to treat dissenters 'as if they were defaulters on parade', while even today the Labour Chief Whip has the power to issue formal reprimands — but such attempts are often unproductive. Members are inclined to resent them, and rebukes *after* a dissenting vote has been cast are somewhat pointless. The trend since 1945 has been to try to persuade Members not to dissent, especially on the Conservative benches and increasingly (since the late 1960s) on the Labour benches. Potential dissenters have been reasoned with and the party's case put to them; if they are unpersuaded, the whips have usually arranged for them to see the frontbenchers concerned for further discussion. If they are still unpersuaded, there is little the whips can do. As the Conservative Deputy Chief Whip once put it: 'We have no powers of sanction. I mean, if a Member of Parliament says he's not going to do anything, well, he jolly well doesn't do it, and there's nothing I can do about it. I can't bribe him.'[14] If Members do engage in serious dissent, then — as the experience of some Members on both sides of the House demonstrated during the European Communities debate in the 1970-4 Parliament — the important pressure to conform comes from sources other than the whips.[15]

Despite a notable increase in intra-party dissent in the division lobbies in the 1970s, it is important to record that in most divisions the whips are merely working to facilitate cohesion among those who wish to be cohesive. Members generally respond to the written whip and vote with their party because they want to. As one leading MP, Sir Ian Gilmour, has noted, 'MPs have a predisposition to vote for their party, otherwise they would not be there.'[16] Just as a consensus of opinion is a prerequisite for effective party discipline, rather than vice versa, so a parliamentary party whose Members wish to vote in the same lobby is a prerequisite for the effective functioning of the whips.

Organised parliamentary parties

Party meetings were sometimes called by party leaders in the eighteenth and nineteenth centuries, but such meetings were called on an *ad hoc* basis for the purpose of one-way communication: leaders to followers (in order to 'exhort, not to consult', as Lowell put it). Not until the formation of the Parliamentary Labour Party in 1906 did a parliamentary party start to meet on a regular basis. Motivated by a belief in internal party democracy, and aided by the fact that it was starting from scratch, the PLP was able to create a more organised (and, in principle, internally more communicative) parliamentary party than was the case with the Conservatives and Liberals. At its first meeting on 12 February 1906, it elected officers (both the existence of officers *and* their election distinguished the PLP from the other two parties) and decided to meet weekly (the officers met daily) to 'discuss the business before the House; allocate speakers for the debates; and to receive reports from the various party committees set up to deal with parliamentary activity in its different phases'.[17]

Although it was to face a number of problems during its first sixteen years of existence, the PLP was able to maintain itself as a formally organised, if not altogether autonomous, parliamentary party. Its growth to form the official Opposition in 1922, and later the Government, created new problems: the principle of intra-party democracy upon which the PLP was founded was not altogether compatible with certain conventions of the Constitution, but these problems were generally resolved under Ramsay MacDonald's guidance in favour of the Constitution. MacDonald began to be styled 'leader' of the parliamentary party and, upon becoming Prime Minister, employed his prerogative to choose his own Cabinet. While in Government, the practice of annually electing the leader, PLP executive (first formed in 1923) and whips was also abandoned. Nevertheless, certain concessions were made to the principle of intra-party democracy: party meetings were continued (on a fortnightly basis in 1924, monthly in 1929), and a different form of executive committee — 'composed of twelve Members not in Government, plus three Ministers, to act as a liaison committee between the Party and the Government'[18] — was elected. An identical committee was formed in 1929 (and proved equally ineffective), while more effective liaison committees, with different compositions, were elected in the 1945–51, 1964–70 and 1974–9 periods of Labour Government. In 1929, the PLP also adopted standing orders on discipline which, although occasionally suspended or modified, have remained with the party since.[19] The basic component of these rules (despite the various changes) has been a prohibition on voting against PLP decisions in the division lobbies, but with some latitude for abstention on the grounds of conscience.

In the 1945 Parliament, the PLP established 'subject' committees (that is, committees formed to consider specific subjects on a regular basis) on a more systematic basis than before; in the 1964–6 and

1966–70 Parliaments it met more regularly than had previously been the case when the party was in Government (eventually meeting weekly, as it does currently in Opposition); and in 1970 the posts of leader and chairman of the PLP, combined when in Opposition, were separated. Currently, the PLP, meeting weekly, with its own elected officers and leaders, liaison committee when in Government and parliamentary committee when in Opposition (the name was changed from the executive committee in 1951), subject committees and written disciplinary code, constitutes the most highly organised of the parliamentary parties.

On the Conservative benches, backbenchers began the process of forming a regular organisation in the 1920s, not in response to the structure of the PLP but rather because of the Carlton Club meeting in October 1922, when Conservative Members voted in favour of leaving the Lloyd George coalition. That event helped to demonstrate the failings of communication between front and back benches and motivated a number of Members, newly returned at the subsequent election, to form the Conservative Private Members (1922) Committee 'for the purpose of mutual co-operation and assistance in dealing with political and parliamentary questions, and in order to enable new Members to take a more active interest and part in Parliamentary life'.[20]

At its first meeting on 23 April 1923 the Committee elected officers and an executive committee, and proceeded to meet weekly throughout the session. It received some co-operation from the Chief Whip, Leslie Wilson, and gradually expanded its membership. In 1925 it was decided to invite all Conservative private Members to join. By the end of 1925, the 1922 Committee, as it became known, had produced a structure which has remained essentially unchanged since. Meetings were held weekly (though at some time fortnightly and, during the 1926 General Strike, daily), preceded by a meeting of the executive to draw up the agenda. Committee meetings would normally comprise the chairman's opening of the proceedings, a whip's announcement of the business for the forthcoming week and his answers to questions about it, reports (if any) from committees, a discussion on any matters raised by the executive or other Members, and/or an address by an invited guest (either a frontbencher or an outside speaker). Over fifty years later, the format remains the same. The influence of the Committee depends largely on the personality of the chairman as well as on that of the party leader, to whom the former has right of access. As we shall see, the 1922 Committee acquired the power to elect the party leader in 1965 (and the power of re-election in 1975), but it still remains less highly organised than the PLP, its counterpart on the other side of the House.

Following its decline to third-party status in the 1920s, the Liberal parliamentary party started to meet regularly, and (despite its reduced members) has done so ever since, usually on a weekly basis. It currently meets on Wednesdays when the House is sitting (at 6.00 p.m.), with meetings lasting up to ninety minutes. Most of the other parliamentary parties since 1945 have also met regularly. The National Liberal Members convened regularly in the 1945—50 Parliament, and, despite their effective merger with the Conservative Party in 1947, continued to meet as the Liberal Unionist group in the 1950s; not until 1966 did the group (only four strong) relinquish a room assigned to it and become an integral part of the Conservative parliamentary party.

The Scottish National Party (SNP) emerged as a parliamentary party in 1974 (seven SNP Members were returned in the February election, and eleven in the October one), and started to meet on a weekly basis; in addition to electing its office holders, it adopted standing orders. Reduced to only two MPs in the current Parliament, the need for regularly scheduled meetings has disappeared (the two Members occupy adjoining offices), but one of them nevertheless continues to act as a whip. The United Ulster Unionist Coalition also emerged as a parliamentary party in 1974 (following the rift in the 1970—4 Parliament between the Conservatives and their Ulster Unionist allies), and met regularly, electing annually a leader and two deputy leaders. The Coalition came to an end on 4 May 1977, following an abortive loyalist strike in Northern Ireland, the six official Ulster Unionists then forming the Ulster Unionist parliamentary party. Five official Ulster Unionist Members were returned in the 1979 election, and they currently meet weekly on Wednesday mornings under the leadership of James Molyneaux. The leader is elected annually (Mr Molyneaux has been leader since the parliamentary party was formed), and he appoints the party spokesmen.[21] One Member serves as whip; a written whip is issued on Thursday evenings. The three Plaid Cymru Members to sit in the 1974—9 Parliament also found it convenient to meet weekly, and to keep formal minutes of their proceedings with one of their number acting as a whip. Reduced (like their Scottish counterparts) to two in number in the current Parliament, one of them is designated convenor and is responsible for the administrative side of their parliamentary work. (Both MPs share the same office, so regular meetings are not necessary.) They enjoy the facility of a full-time parliamentary research officer.[22] Joining the ranks of the parliamentary parties is one which appeared for the first time in 1979, the Democratic Unionist Party of Northern Ireland. Comprising three MPs, it is led by Ian Paisley, who was the party's only Member in the three preceding Parliaments. Though it appears the least well-organised of the parliamentary parties (its leader also combining membership of the Westminster Parliament with that of the European Parliament), one of the three does act as a liaison for the purpose of communicating with the whips.

Overall, the experience of these smaller parties shows the extent to which some form of basic organisation is deemed necessary for the effective functioning of a parliamentary party, however small.

Party committees

For committees of parliamentary parties of whatever type to be established, a prerequisite is the existence not so much of a highly organised party (various Conservative committees preceded the formation of the 1922 Committee, for example) but rather of a party with a sizeable membership. It is difficult for a small parliamentary party to sustain a number of active committees. Thus it is not surprising that various committees evolved within the Conservative parliamentary party, which has been one of the two largest parties throughout the century, prior to a similar development within the PLP, with a membership which has exceeded 200 only in the 1929—31 Parliament and since 1945. The Liberal parliamentary party entered its political decline at the time that Conservative committees were beginning to get under way and was thus unable to follow suit.

A number of 'attitude' groups (that is, unofficial groupings formed, usually on a temporary basis, to promote a particular cause) existed within the Conservative parliamentary party during the first two decades of the century, set up by backbenchers in response to apparent failings of the party leadership and the absence of an effective Opposition in wartime. There was only one subject committee, namely the Agriculture Committee, which met before and after the First World War. In 1923 a number of other committees were formed with official blessing, though they were more akin to the policy committees of the 1964—70 period (party committees extending beyond a parliamentary membership) than purely parliamentary party committees. They were reorganised after the 1924 election as *parliamentary* party committees, and these committees — covering such subjects as foreign affairs, agriculture and finance — soon started operating in a manner that was to become the norm; they met regularly (sometimes weekly) to discuss matters affecting their area of interest and to listen to guest speakers. The committees flourished in the 1930s (the Agricultural, Foreign Affairs, and India Committees often holding crowded and sometimes stormy meetings), and were reorganised again and expanded in the 1945—50 Parliament.

The officers of the committees were brought together with frontbenchers to form a Business Committee, which was re-established in the 1964—70 and 1974—9 periods of Opposition (meeting weekly on Wednesdays in the 1974—9 Parliament), while Winston Churchill established the practice of frontbenchers chairing committees when in Opposition. When the party is in Government, the committees elect their own chairmen as well as the other officers (each committee has a minimum of one vice-chairman and one secretary); Ministers are excluded from membership. In 1980, the committees numbered twenty-four subject committees[23] and seven 'area' committees (each comprising Conservative Members returned from a particular region). Most subject committees meet weekly (parliamentary business permitting) at a regular time within the period 4.00 to 7.00 p.m., Monday to Thursday. Meetings are open to any Conservative private Member who wishes to attend, and attendance at meetings (which usually last about an hour) is generally between five and twenty-five Members; an important guest speaker can push the figure up to well over a hundred. These committees are supplemented by the various attitude groups, such as the Monday Club, the Selsdon Group, the Tory Reform Group, and the somewhat less ideologically based Bow Group (as well as more temporary groupings such as the pro- and anti-Common Market groups in the 1970–4 Parliament),[24] but such bodies usually lack official blessing and do not confine their membership to MPs; indeed, with the exception of the Bow Group, their parliamentary membership is very limited.

Even less official, though confined to a parliamentary membership, are the occasional dining clubs formed by small, often exclusive, groups of Members. In the early part of the 1970–4 Parliament, for example, Nicholas Scott organised a small dining group (known by some as 'Nick's Diner') of liberal Members, and in the current Parliament two separate dining groups of new MPs exist – the 'Blue Chip' group, comprising twelve backbenchers who meet every second Tuesday at the home of one of their number, and the 'Guy Fawkes' group, comprising eleven Members who dine together each week. Of these two, the latter has been described as 'perhaps more obviously left-wing in its attitudes'.[25] Such groups do not form part of the parliamentary party structure (though they traditionally inform the whips of their existence) and tend not to acquire a permanent existence, though a number have existed for several years. They provide a congenial environment in which like-minded Members can meet together.

Had the PLP a large membership at the time of its creation, it might have succeeded in establishing an active system of subject committees before the Conservatives. Its report to the Labour Party Conference in 1908 revealed that it had set up five subject committees and five special committees to deal with specific Bills in the 1907 session, and its report the following year referred to much 'unseen work . . . accomplished by the respective Committees appointed by the Party',[26] but no more is subsequently heard of them. Although a number of sectional groups did exist within the PLP – notably the Trade Union and separate miners' group, as well as the Independent Labour Party[27] – and occasional emergency committees were established in the 1920s and some advisory

committees in the 1930s, it was not until the 1945—50 Parliament that
the PLP was able to create subject committees on any systematic basis,
with twenty subject groups being set up. They have, though, come in
for criticism on the Labour benches for not being as effective as they
might be (a criticism heard from the start) and also for not being well-
organised. The number of committees, or subject groups as they are
called, suffered from inflation, and by 1976 there were no less than
thirty-five subject groups and nine regional groups. Following a report
from a special committee set up in 1976, the PLP reduced the number
of subject groups to nineteen, attempted to create a more ordered timetable for meetings, and introduced various reforms designed to increase
communication between front and back benches. The reforms did not
appear to remove the problems previously complained about: Members
continued to criticise the groups for failing to provide adequate two-
way communication; meetings were still often poorly attended; and the
timetable for meetings was not always adhered to. Nevertheless, PLP
subject groups have not been totally ineffective, and a number of group
chairmen in 1977 contended that their groups had had some influence
on Government policy.[28]

Such groups have been supplemented by the better-known and unofficial attitude groups such as the Tribune Group (the successor to the
'Keep Left' group of the 1950s and arguably, of the Independent
Labour Party of the 1920s) and the Manifesto Group, representing the
left and right of the party respectively. In the current Parliament, the
Tribune Group has a membership of seventy Members (as at June 1980),
and meets every Monday during sittings at 4.15 p.m. Attendance averages
about thirty members, depending on parliamentary business and the
topic to be discussed.[29] It meets, according to one of its members, 'to
discuss — or, even more frequently, debate — the issues before the movement, including the current business of the House of Commons, particularly campaigns demanding attention and action, and wider questions of
party policy'.[30] Officers are elected sessionally, and it is usual practice
for the vice-chairman to become chairman. The Manifesto Group has a
membership of about seventy-five (it declines to publish a membership
list), and meets each week on Wednesday evening. Attendance varies
between fifteen and fifty Members, again depending on parliamentary
business and the topics to be discussed; votes are rarely taken.[31] Officers
are elected sessionally. Among other things, the Group has published a
number of discussion documents and reports, and exists for the purpose
of working

> for the implementation of the policies set out in the Labour manifesto
> and to support a Labour Government in overcoming the country's acute
> economic difficulties; to act as a forum for constructive discussion

designed to relate democratic socialist philosophy to the needs of the
present age; [and] to endeavour to achieve a truly democratic socialist
society through our democratic and representative parliamentary
system.[32]

In its factional behaviour, it tends to be less cohesive than the Tribune
Group,[33] and in 1980 its treasurer, Neville Sandelson, resigned on the
grounds that the Group had failed to stand up for what it believed in.[34]
In March 1980, a group of about thirty Labour MPs, including many
former junior Ministers, formed a body known as Labour First, with
the object of representing the mainstream of Labour opinion in Parliament and in the country.[35] Many Labour Members are also members of
the Fabian Society, though this — rather like the Bow Group on the
Conservative side of the House — is not confined to a parliamentary
membership and constitutes more of a quasi-independent research
organisation than an attitude group.

Election of the party leader

The election of the party leader is a relatively recent innovation in all
three main parties. The PLP, at its first meeting in 1906, did elect
officers (chairman, vice-chairman and whip) but not a leader. Not until
1922, when it became the official Opposition, was MacDonald's title
expanded to 'chairman and leader' of the parliamentary party. As
Leader of the Opposition, and subsequently Prime Minister, it was not
difficult for MacDonald to extend the mantle of leadership to encompass
the whole party. Thereafter, whenever it elected its leader, the PLP was
electing, *de facto,* the leader of the party. In Opposition, the leader
remained subject to re-election, but this practice was not continued in
Government; as we have seen, the annual election of leader, deputy
leader, executive committee (styled the parliamentary committee since
1951), and whips, was suspended in 1924 (though a separate chairman
and vice-chairman were elected), and this has been the practice in subsequent periods of Labour Government. The method of election established in the inter-war years has not changed greatly since, and today,
when in Opposition, the PLP elects sessionally a leader, deputy leader,
chairman (since 1970) and Chief Whip (the election of the leader, deputy
leader, and Chief Whip usually, though not always, being a formality if
the incumbent wishes to continue in office), as well as twelve Members
from the Commons to serve on the parliamentary committee along with
the officers, and the leader, Chief Whip and one elected representative
from the Labour peers in the Lords. In Government, the PLP elects
sessionally a chairman and (under a procedure adopted in 1974) six
backbenchers to serve on the liaison committee; and, upon retirement
of the incumbent from office, a leader and deputy leader. Although it

can be argued that in order to comply with Constitutional conventions the PLP has deviated somewhat from the principle of annual election when in office, elective powers are nevertheless retained which are not matched by those of either of the other two main parties.

It was only after its rapid decline following the First World War that the Liberal parliamentary party introduced election as a standard practice, and even then it was only to elect a chairman, a post that existed for some time concurrently with that of leader. It was not until 1935 that the practice of electing a leader upon the retirement of the incumbent appears to have been established, and that only after a certain amount of confusion.[36] This power was to remain with the parliamentary party until 1976, when a new method of election was approved (one which had been seriously contemplated in the 1930s) under which the electorate comprised the party's paid-up members. Each constituency party was allocated a number of votes determined by a set formula, with every party member having the right to participate, though Liberal MPs alone could nominate and be nominated for election. This new system was employed shortly afterwards, following Jeremy Thorpe's resignation; David Steel was elected. As party spokesmen in Parliament are appointed by the leader (and always have been), and the parliamentary party has no officers other than the leader, Liberal Members as a body now enjoy no power of election.

For the Conservative Party, the election of the party leader has been an even more recent innovation. Until as late as 1965 it maintained its tradition of a leader 'emerging' and, in case of doubt, relying upon the choice of the sovereign; on the one occasion when it looked as if the parliamentary party would be called upon to choose a leader by ballot (in 1911), a suitable compromise candidate 'emerged'. For the first half of the century the practice served the party reasonably well, but following the controversies surrounding the Queen's choice of Harold Macmillan in 1957 and the disputed 'emergence' of Lord Home (subsequently Sir Alec Douglas-Home) in 1963, it came in for much often bitter criticism. Sir Alec Douglas-Home responded to the criticism by agreeing to a new procedure, with formal rules for the election of the party leader upon the retirement of the incumbent. This new procedure (entailing, as does the Labour procedure, more than one ballot if necessary)[37] was adopted officially in February 1965 and employed in July of the same year, following Sir Alec's resignation as leader. It resulted in the election of Edward Heath.

The rules for election applied only when an incumbent retired from the leadership; there was no provision for the leader to be subject to re-election. Following the two successive general election defeats of 1974, pressure began to build up within the parliamentary party for Mr Heath either to resign or to offer himself for re-election. After initially resisting this pressure, Mr Heath agreed to submit himself for re-election and appointed a committee to review the election rules. The committee recommended a slightly modified version of the 1965 rules, with the inclusion of a new rule that a leadership ballot should be held between three and six months after a new Parliament has assembled, with annual ballots thereafter within twenty-eight days of the start of each session, a provision (though not made explicit at the time) with applicability when the party was in Government as well as in Opposition. The recommendations were agreed to in January 1975 and put into operation the following month. Mrs Margaret Thatcher defeated Mr Heath in the first ballot and was elected leader on the second one. In keeping with tradition, a new Conservative leader is still presented to a meeting of MPs, peers, candidates, and members of the National Union Executive Committee for formal accalamation, though the new procedure adopted in 1975 makes provision for some consultation with peers and the National Union Executive Committee prior to the election itself,[38] formalising to some extent what had been past practice.

The consequence of this latter development and the procedure adopted by the Liberal Party has been that formally the PLP, as H.M. Drucker has noted, now has the least 'open' procedure for electing a party leader.[39] An attempt to have the leader elected by a wider constituency was narrowly defeated at the 1979 Labour Party Conference, and in 1980 the PLP rejected a proposal by a party commission of inquiry that the leader be elected by a special electoral college.*

Effect upon the House of Commons

Having briefly sketched the development of the formal organisation of the parliamentary parties in this century, it is appropriate now to consider the effect that this organisation has had upon the House and the Members within each parliamentary party.

The effect, as well as the development, of party organisation has not been uniform between the parties. On the Conservative side, the 1922 Committee and party committees appear to have been more effective forums for communicating backbench opinion, especially dissenting or critical opinion, than the PLP and subject groups on the other side of the House. In part, this may be attributable to what Malcolm Punnett has described as 'two-way deference' between leaders and led on the Conservative side,[40] a deference which is essentially alien to the PLP, especially given its factional nature. The factionalism of the Labour

---

* The 1980 Labour Party Conference voted for the leader to be elected by a wider party body but was unable to agree on the composition of the new electoral body. A special party meeting was called for January 1981 to decide its composition.

Party lends itself to a left-right division across the party as a whole, and left-wingers in the House may thus ignore the PLP, where they are normally in a minority, in favour of taking their case to extra-parliamentary forums such as the Party Conference.

This difference is encouraged by structural factors. No votes are taken at meetings of the 1922 Committee, whereas they can be (and sometimes are) at PLP meetings; in Government, Conservative Ministers are not eligible to attend the 1922 Committee (except by invitation), whereas Labour Ministers can and do attend PLP meetings. Labour backbenchers may thus face the possibility of their case being voted down, the likelihood of the leadership winning any vote being enhanced by the presence of Ministers.[41] Similar variables operate in party committees. No votes are taken in Conservative committees, and meetings are open to any Conservative private Member who wishes to attend; attendances can serve as a guide to party feeling (large attendances and vocal criticism providing an early-warning system for the whips, one of whom will be in attendance), and Members may express their views knowing that they will not be voted upon, hence avoiding the possible appearance of a conclusive rejection. Contact between the committees and frontbenchers is close in Opposition (Opposition spokesmen usually chair the appropriate committees), with all officers having the opportunity to influence the leadership through the Business Committee. In Government, Conservative Ministers often, though not always, heed the views expressed by the relevant committees. In PLP subject groups, by contrast, votes are taken; front benchers do not always serve as chairmen when in Opposition; and in Government Labour Ministers have had a reputation (more perhaps in pre-1964 Labour Governments than since) for often ignoring the PLP and its constituent parts. Unlike their Conservative counterparts, subject groups have suffered from irregular meeting arrangements, and this, coupled with the view of various Members that such meetings achieve little, has led often to poor attendances.[42] The PLP, as we have noted, tried to deal with this by reforming subject groups; though the reforms have not apparently solved the problems, they may have helped to ameliorate some of them. Despite the discrepancy in effectiveness between the two sides, PLP subject groups have sometimes been able to influence front-bench policy, and it would be misleading to regard them as altogether ineffective.

Although there are differences between the actual operation of each party in the election of the party leader, there is at the moment little apparent difference in effect between the two main parties, each producing a leader acceptable to a majority of the party's Members in the House of Commons. Conversely, in so far as there is a difference between the whips, it is rather one of effect than operation. Because of the factional nature of the Labour Party, the Labour whips tend to have less harmonious relations with some backbenchers than do the Conservative whips, though the latter have had to contend with a notable increase in dissent since Mr Heath's premiership.

The above differences are not so great that we cannot generalise about the effect of the foregoing developments on the House, which overall has been a positive one for the Commons. The effect of the whips we have outlined already. Although there have been periods when the operation of the whips has not been without its problems (most notably in the inter-war period), the whips have generally fulfilled functions of value to both front and back benches. As managers, communicators, and persuaders, they fulfil roles central to the smooth working of any parliamentary party. As A.P. Herbert, who sat as an independent Member, once observed: 'It is quite a mistake to think of the whips as cruel ogres whose only purpose is to lash the terrified legislators into the wrong lobbies. The whips — at least, the good whips — are the guides, philosophers and friends of the Members.'[43] No parliamentary party this century has been able to exist without them.

The most notable effect on the Commons of organised parliamentary parties and party committees has been the transfer of Members' activity from the floor of the House to private party meetings. As early as 1931 Sir Austen Chamberlain commented: 'When I have said, "But why are there so few fellows on our benches?", I have been told, "Our Committee on India is meeting," or something of that kind.'[44] With the further expansion of committees, this change has been most marked in post-war Parliaments. However, it should not be misunderstood. It is easy to assume that it represented and represents a further decline in the influence of the House of Commons in relation to the executive. In fact, it may be said to represent the reverse. As we have seen, the main transfer of power from the Commons took place in the nineteenth century, when the parties acted as a conduit for its delivery to the executive. The residual power left to Members was the power occasionally to embarrass or threaten the Government's majority in the lobbies, a power which could only be used sparingly; it was not necessarily allied to the need for Members to be present on the floor of the House during most of the parliamentary day. By attending party meetings, Members were not reducing the power of the House; power was no longer exercised collectively by Members on the floor of the House (except negatively on occasion), but was exercised instead through party. By establishing party forums within Parliament, MPs were, to some limited degree, regaining a slight measure of influence which they had clearly lost in the nineteenth century.

Through these new, regular forums, Members could express views to their party leaders (officially private views, though they have tended to become semi-public through reports and leaks to journalists) which the leaders could sometimes only ignore at their peril. As both Anthony King and the late Richard Crossman (an MP for twenty-five years and Cabinet Minister for six) noted, Government backbenchers are the most important Members in the House as far as the Government is concerned.[45] The Government has to carry its own parliamentary party with it. Failure to respond to backbench criticism from its own side of the House can lead to public, and hence embarrassing, dissent for the Government, or even, in extreme cases, defeat in the division lobbies, as both Mr Heath and Messrs Wilson and Callaghan discovered in the 1970–4 and 1974–9 Parliaments respectively. Mr Heath's case, though, is perhaps exceptional. For reasons already outlined, Conservatives tend to be more effective in influencing the party leadership than Labour, though on both sides of the House parliamentary party and committee meetings provide forums for the exertion of influence by backbench Members which otherwise would not occur. Their effect has been a positive one for Members, not a negative one.

It is possible to argue also that the creation of organised parliamentary parties has helped to strengthen the position of Members in relation not only to their own front benches, but also to their extra-parliamentary parties. This is of more importance, perhaps, on the Labour side of the House, as the PLP does not have the autonomy that is enjoyed by the 1922 Committee. By forming organised bodies, MPs of the same party can express themselves as collective entities within their national parties; without such organisation, Members could operate only either as individuals or collectively on an *ad hoc* or (as with the attitude groups) unofficial basis.

The position of the two largest parties is strengthened by the fact that they form the Government and Opposition, hence justifying their claim to elect their respective leaders who, as Prime Minister and Leader of the Opposition, rely upon their continued confidence. This power of election is clearly important, both in itself and because of the implications which flow from the fact that it is the parliamentary parties in which this power is vested. If the power of election were transferred to other parts of either party, then leaders other than those enjoying majority support in the parliamentary ranks might be elected. If the Conservative Party had retained its traditional faith in the 'emergence' of leaders (a process not confined to MPs), it is quite likely, for example, that Reginald Maudling would have become leader in 1965 instead of Mr Heath; if the power had rested with constituency parties, it seems clear that Mr Heath would have remained leader in 1975. On the Labour side, if the power had been transferred to the party's National Executive Committee, it seems highly possible that Mr Foot (or perhaps Mr Benn) would have become leader in 1976 instead of Mr Callaghan. Although the Conservatives have now introduced procedures to allow for more consultation with peers and the extra-parliamentary party in the election of a leader, and the Labour Party is experiencing intense pressure for the leader to be elected by a wider or completely different constituency, both parliamentary parties still jealously guard their rights.[46] If they were to lose them, the implications for British politics could be profound.

Conclusion

The twentieth century has witnessed the growth of highly organised parties within the House of Commons. The earlier element of party organisation, the whips, has remained as an essential component, their managerial and communicative functions becoming more extensive and more time-consuming, their previously perceived function of 'discipline' becoming ever-increasingly one of persuasion. They have been reinforced by organised parliamentary parties with regular meetings (and elected officers as well in the two largest and some of the smaller parties) and, in the two main parties, by subject and area committees and the power to elect the party leader.

The effect of these developments upon the House of Commons has been a beneficial one. Both whips and regular party meetings can make a claim to be essential to the smooth running of parliamentary parties, most parties employing them in one form or another. The whips perform services of value to both front and back benches and are the oil in the machinery of parliamentary business. Parliamentary party meetings and party committees have served (with other variables) to take Members away from the floor of the House, but in so doing have given MPs valuable forums in which they can seek to influence their leaders. Acquiring the power to elect their respective leaders may not have restored to the two largest parties the elective function lost by the House in the nineteenth century, but it has given them the opportunity to make a significant impact upon British politics. The question of which party will form the Government is determined by the results of a general election, but that of who shall be the Prime Minister or his opposite number is determined (in advance) by the membership of the parliamentary parties.

The development of party organisation within the House has been, and is, essentially dynamic, so some of this power — especially that of electing the leader on the Labour side — may be lost. Alternatively, events may strengthen the role of Members within the parliamentary parties. Much may depend upon other parliamentary developments and, as we shall have the cause to consider later, MPs themselves. For the moment, we conclude with the observation that party served as the channel for the transfer of power from the Commons to the executive in the nineteenth century, and that the creation of party organisation *within* the Commons in the twentieth has helped to provide Members, primarily of the two largest parties, with a means by which to influence their party leaders, leaders who have to exercise their power when in Government through a party majority in the House of Commons.

NOTES

1 This chapter is based largely, though by no means exclusively, on the author's article 'Party Organisation in the House of Commons', published in *Parliamentary Affairs,* 31 (4), Autumn 1978, pp. 406—23. For a more detailed treatment, see Philip Norton, 'The Organisation of Parliamentary Parties', in S.A. Walkland (ed.), *The House of Commons in the Twentieth Century* (Oxford University Press, 1979), pp. 7—68.

2 Quintin Hogg, *The Purpose of Parliament* (Blandford Press, n.d.), p. 83.

3 Fred Willey, *The Honourable Member* (Sheldon Press, 1974), p. 158.

4 Viscount Samuel, 'The Party System and the National Interest', in *Papers on Parliament: A Symposium* (Hansard Society, 1949), p. 78.

5 See Philip Norton, *Dissension in the House of Commons 1945—74* (Macmillan, 1975), and, more for the changes of the 1970s, by the same author, *Dissension in the House of Commons 1974—1979* (Oxford University Press, 1980).

6 A. Lawrence Lowell, *The Government of England,* Vol. I (Macmillan, 1908), pp. 455—6.

7 W.F. Deedes, 'The Lobby', in John Mackintosh (ed.), *People and Parliament* (Saxon House, 1978), p. 156.

8 It is because of this contact between the whips' offices, so important in the determination of parliamentary business, that even the smallest parties find it very useful to have one of their number designated a whip.

9 Lowell, p. 452.

10 Ian M. Fraser to author. An exception to this general rule, though, was the period of Mr Heath's premiership. See especially Philip Norton, *Conservative Dissidents* (Temple Smith, 1978), chs. 6 and 9.

11 Hugh Berrington, 'Partisanship and Dissidence in the Nineteenth-Century House of Commons', *Parliamentary Affairs,* 21, 1967—8, p. 370.

12 See Roy Jenkins, 'Party Discipline in the House of Commons', *Listener,* 26 January 1956, p. 128.

13 Uwe Kitzinger, *Diplomacy and Persuasion* (Thames & Hudson, 1973), p. 173.

14 Bernard Weatherill, MP, in a BBC Radio 3 programme, 'The Parliamentary Process: Parties and Parliament', broadcast 12 February 1976.

15 See Norton, *Conservative Dissidents,* chs 6 and 7.

16 Ian Gilmour, *The Body Politic* (Hutchinson, 1971), p. 261.

17 Herbert Tracey (ed.), *The Book of the Labour Party,* Vol. I (Caxton, n.d.), p. 141.

18 *Labour Party Conference Report 1924,* p. 98.

19 They were suspended by the parliamentary party in 1946, reimposed in 1952, rescinded after the 1959 election and replaced by a code of conduct, reintroduced in 1961 and replaced in 1966 by another code of conduct, itself replaced by another code in 1968.

20   Philip Goodhart, *The 1922* (Macmillan, 1973), p. 15. See also Gervais Rentoul, *Sometimes I Think* (Hodder & Stoughton, 1940), pp. 231–9.

21   No deputy leader is elected, though it is understood that in Mr Molyneaux's absence Enoch Powell will act for him.

22   The research officer has been financed since 1978 by the Rowntree Foundation.

23   The latest addition in 1980, bringing the number to twenty-four, was that of a Special Committee on civil defence.

24   See Norton, *Conservative Dissidents,* ch. 3, especially pp. 65–7 and 79–80.

25   Robin Oakley, 'Blue Chips and Guy Fawkes: Mrs Thatcher's Loyal Rebels', *Now!,* 4 January 1980, pp. 44–5.

26   *Labour Party Conference Report 1908*, p. 43, and *Labour Party Conference Report 1909*, p. 29.

27   Hugh Dalton, *Call Back Yesterday* (Muller, 1953), pp. 194–5. Dalton also recorded the existence of an attitude group (the temperance group, 'to which I did not belong'), as well as 'other' groups.

28   See Norton, 'The Organisation of Parliamentary Parties', p. 45.

29   Ms Jo Richardson, MP, Tribune Group secretary, to author.

30   Neil Kinnock, MP, in *Tribune,* 29 November 1974, reprinted in Douglas Hill (ed.), *Tribune 40* (Quartet, 1977), pp. 194–5.

31   George Robertson, MP, Manifesto Group secretary, to author.

32   Outlined in the Group's submission to the party's General Secretary in 1980. *The Times,* 28 March 1980.

33   Norton, *Dissension in the House of Commons 1974–1979,* especially pp. 442–3.

34   *The Times,* 28 March 1980.

35   *ibid.*

36   See Jorgen Rasmussen, *The Liberal Party* (Constable, 1965), especially p. 40.

37   See Norton, 'The Organisation of Parliamentary Parties', pp. 52–3 and 56–7.

38   A copy of the election rules is reproduced in Sir Nigel Fisher, MP, *The Tory Leaders* (Weidenfeld & Nicholson, 1977), appendix 2.

39   H.M. Drucker, 'Leadership Selection in the Labour Party', *Parliamentary Affairs,* 29 (4), Autumn 1976, p. 388.

40   Malcolm Punnett, *Front-Bench Opposition* (Heinemann, 1973), p. 307.

41   See James J. Lynskey, 'Backbench Tactics and Parliamentary Party Structure', *Parliamentary Affairs,* 27 (1), Winter 1973, pp. 35–7. Also note the comments in Anthony King (ed.), *British Members of Parliament: A Self-Portrait* (Macmillan, 1974), pp. 52–3.

42   PLP subject groups (and the PLP generally) also lack the professional research facilities available to Conservative committees, the latter being serviced by the Conservative Research Department.

43   A.P. Herbert, *The Point of Parliament,* 2nd ed. (Methuen, 1947), p. 31.

44   Quoted in Ivor Jennings, *Parliament,* 2nd ed. (Cambridge University Press, 1957), p. 380.

45   Anthony King, 'Modes of Executive–Legislative Relations', *Legislative Studies Quarterly,* 1 (1), 1976, p. 16; R.H.S. Crossman, *The Myths of Cabinet Government* (Harvard University Press, 1972), p. 32.

46   See Drucker, pp. 393–5, and Fisher, appendix 1.

4

The functions of the House of Commons in the twentieth century

England, as we have observed, is an old country, noted for having a Constitution which is not embodied in one binding document, and for a history of traditional structures being adapted to meet changing conditions. The House of Commons and its functions have been so adapted. As we have seen, political developments in the nineteenth century resulted in two of the functions identified by Bagehot in 1867 — those of legislating and choosing the Government — being transferred in practice elsewhere, producing a House with a role and functions different from those that existed in the period between the two Reform Acts and before. What, then, are the functions of the modern House of Commons? The answer is not a simple one, in part because of the factors we have just identified.

Just as the nation itself does not have a Constitution which is embodied in one binding document, so the House of Commons lacks a formal, authoritative document stipulating its functions. As the Commons has evolved, so new functions have been added to or superimposed upon existing functions; others have been dispensed with. Because of the transfer of power facilitated by political parties, a number of functions (such as choosing the Government) have become essentially formal, as opposed to real or regularly exercised, functions. Identifying the latter is complicated by the fact that some politicians and students of the Constitution still emphasise the formal functions of the Commons as if they were the real ones. For example, adherents to the liberal view of the Constitution still stress the sovereignty of Parliament and its function of control of the executive.[1] Others still stress the function of legislating — 'our first task' as one MP has described it.[2] The position is complicated further not only by the fact that there is no clear agreement over the importance of functions as between the formal and the real, but also by the absence of any agreement over what the functions themselves are. The functions of the Commons, both formal and real, are identified and described differently by those who seek to delineate them. Some writers identify two or three main functions of the House, others as many as eight or nine. Some stress functions which others do not. Also, to add to the complexity, even when there is agreement about some of the functions exercised by the House, there is not always agreement that the House should exercise them.

In identifying the functions of the Commons, it is necessary also to distinguish the functions performed individually by Members from those performed collectively by the House. Delineating the functions of the House as a whole is made more intricate by the fact that it has become increasingly difficult to describe the House of Commons as a collective entity at all. 'Parliament', as Keith Ovenden has observed, 'is composed of such a wide variety of political elements that it hardly amounts to a single political institution at all.'[3] The political changes of the nineteenth century have meant that the parts of the House are as important as or more important than the whole.

The House of Commons comprises 635 Members returned by territorially defined constituencies to serve for the life of a Parliament; it meets in plenary session in the 'House' of Commons, and has its own officers, rules of procedure, supporting facilities, and various official sub-units such as Standing and Select Committees. Superimposed upon this structure is the reality of party government. Within the House of Commons one finds 'a cluster of political institutions all of which are related to each other, but most of which can be seen to be quite different'.[4] Thus one has the Government, a party forming the Government party, a party forming the official Opposition party with its leaders forming the Opposition front bench — these parties having developed infrastructures (the parliamentary parties and their various elements as outlined in Chapter 3) which are distinct from their positions as the Government and Opposition parties — and various smaller parties. These elements may be identified simply in diagrammatic form (Figure 4.1). They are linked to and serviced by different bodies outside the House (the Government by the Civil Service, for example; the Conservative parliamentary party by the Conservative Research Department), and they fulfil functions of their own, which are separate from, and which influence and complicate the task of identifying, the functions of the House as a collective entity. The primary task of Government, of course, is to govern; the function of the party in Government, among other things, is to sustain the Government in office; the function of the Opposition is to scrutinise and to provide an alternative, in both views and personnel, to the Government.[5] We have already considered the role of the parliamentary parties. The development of these elements within the Commons has served both to limit the corporate entity of the House, specially given the adversary role of the parties, and to help to shape and modify those functions which can be seen as being now fulfilled by the House as a whole.

The House of Commons

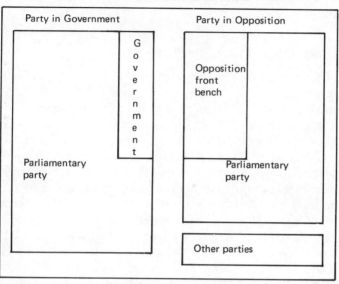

Based on a similar, though not identical, diagram in Anthony King, 'Modes of Executive—Legislative Relations: Great Britain, France and West Germany', *Legislative Studies Quarterly*, 1 (1), 1976, p. 13.

Figure 4.1 Elements in the House of Commons

Having identified some of the problems, we return to our original question: what *are* the functions of the House of Commons? What we seek to do in this chapter is to define those functions which are performed by the House — upon which there is some measure of agreement, albeit variously expressed by those who have written on the subject — and in a way which incorporates not only the relevance of the party political elements within the House but also the traditional or formal functions of the House (upon which some of the existing real functions are based), as well as distinguishing the collective functions of the House from those carried out by Members individually. Adopting this approach, we would suggest that the main functions of the contemporary House are: (1) providing the personnel of Government; (2) representation; (3) sustaining and providing a forum of debate for the Government and Opposition parties; (4) legitimising the Government and its measures; (5) scrutinising and influencing the measures and the actions of the Government; and (6) fulfilling a number of minor though not necessarily unimportant functions, including, as we shall see, a quasi-judicial one. These functions are not mutually exclusive. There are large areas of overlap, and our concern in this work is largely with the functions of legitimisation and scrutiny, under which the other functions we identify may largely be subsumed.

Providing the personnel of Government

The House of Commons no longer performs the elective function identi-fied by Bagehot. As we have seen, the election of the Government is now undertaken not *by* but *through* the House, with a general election serving to determine which party will form the Government. The House chooses neither the Government (though exceptionally, in conditions of minority Government, it may remove it) nor individual Ministers. What it does is provide the means by which the Government is determined and the pool from which the members of Government are drawn.

There is no legal impediment to the appointment of a Minister who is not a member of either House of Parliament, and on rare occasions such an appointment is made. The Law Officers for Scotland in Mr Wilson's Government of 1964–70, for example, were members of neither House; the current Lord Advocate, Lord Mackay, was at the time of his appoint-ment neither an MP nor a peer. (During a brief period in 1963, after renouncing his title and before being elected to the Commons, Sir Alec Douglas-Home was Prime Minister while a member of neither House.) However, convention and political necessity dictate that Ministers should almost always be members of either House. The workings of both Government and Parliament are based upon this convention (among others), a convention well-established by practice and modified only by the post-1867 emergence of the Commons as the dominant House. Given the pre-eminence of the Commons, the Prime Minister must now serve in the Lower House; the last Prime Minister to serve in the Lords was the Marquess of Salisbury (1895–1902), and the convention was confirmed in 1923 when Stanley Baldwin was summoned to Buckingham Palace in preference to Lord Curzon. (Lord Home was appointed to the premier-ship in 1963 but renounced his peerage, as was then possible under the 1963 Peerages Act, and was returned to the Commons at a by-election.) Similarly, most members of the Government must now be drawn from the Commons. Only between two and four peers normally serve in modern Cabinets: the Lord Chancellor, the Leader of the Lords, and one or two others. In May 1979, Mrs Thatcher appointed three peers to her Cabinet, the remaining eighteen members being in the Commons. Of Ministers appointed, most have usually served a parliamentary apprenticeship of ten or more years. Junior Ministers are drawn normally from the backbenches, senior Ministers from the pool of junior Ministers, and the party leader, the Prime Minister, from the ranks of the Cabinet, a similar process pertaining in Opposition. On occasion a Prime Minister may appoint a Minister who has had no parliamentary experience (elevating him to the peerage comcomitant with his appointment, or appointing him upon, or just prior to, his election to the Commons) but such occasions are few, and rarely prove successful; the normal route to office is through a parliamentary career.

The House can play a role in influencing, though not in determining, some of the ministerial appointments made. Given party government, the Commons no longer exercises the power of dismissing individual Ministers, but in some instances it can influence the promotion or demotion of some of them. The power of appointment rests formally with the monarch, in practice with her chief Minister, the Prime Minister, and in choosing his or her administration the Prime Minister will often take into account a Member's parliamentary reputation and his ability to deal with the House. 'It is the House which makes and unmakes ministerial reputations,' declared Harold Laski,[6] perhaps overstating the case; '[The House's] collective reactions to a Minister can make some difference to his career,' noted John Mackintosh a little more realistically.[7]

The collective reaction of the House is but one of the various factors that may influence a Minister's advancement or failure to advance, but it is one that can be important. A Minister's ability at the despatch box, his capacity to answer questions from Members on both sides of the House, his reputation for dealing efficiently and effectively with Member's correspondence and representations — all these contribute to his standing and can help to influence whether he goes on to higher things, stays where he is, or returns to the back-benches. Promotion to ministerial office from the back-benches may be influenced by a Member's performance in the House (it is often all that the Prime Minister and Government Chief Whip have to go on in assessing a Member),[8] and speeches that are effective, be it in style or content, can impress a Prime Minister about to engage in a ministerial reshuffle. As one former premier noted: 'Any politician from the Prime Minister downwards has to make his mark in Parliament and speeches are on the whole the best way to do it.'[9] On occasion, it would appear that a backbencher has actually achieved promotion on the basis of a single though highly effective speech in the House; Iain Macleod in 1952 and Richard Marsh in 1964 are two good examples.[10] The influence of a Member's parliamentary performance in determining promotion (including, once on the ministerial ladder, the ability to answer questions and absorb ministerial briefs) has been attested to by various Prime Ministers,[11] and, in the opinion of one former Conservative Chief Whip, it is this which gains junior Ministers the opportunity for promotion nine times out of ten.[12]

Other influences in determining promotion are provided not only by but through the House. As we have seen, elements within the House — the parliamentary parties — determine the leadership of the two main parties, and the same elements can influence ministerial (or front-bench) promotions. A Minister may be appointed or promoted on the basis of his standing within his parliamentary party; conversely, poor relations with his own backbenchers or party committees may have an adverse effect upon his subsequent career. On one occasion the PLP Transport Group is believed to have been responsible for having a Minister of Transport removed.[13] The House of Commons collectively and its component parts are thus important to a politician seeking ministerial office. Other factors that can contribute to advancement include closeness to the Prime Minister, administrative competence, and standing within the party outside the House.

To summarise: although the House of Commons has lost the elective function which it performed briefly in the last century, it remains important as the channel through which the Government is determined and for providing the pool from which Ministers are drawn; ministerial appointments are made by the Prime Minister, but the House collectively, and some of its component parts, can influence the premier's selection. As we shall have occasion to note later, the House retains also the power, in very exceptional circumstances, to remove the Government itself.

Representation

Collectively and individually, the Commons is deemed to fulfil the function of *representation*. The concept of representation, like that of democracy, has been variously defined and much overworked. The term itself has come into the English language through French derivatives of the Latin *repraesentare*, and did not assume a political meaning until the sixteenth century.[14] It may be said to entail acting on behalf of or in the interests of someone. Rousseau believed that a citizen could alone represent himself (the citizen's sovereignty being indivisible and inalienable), and hence 'representative' government — citizens meeting together to govern through an expression of the 'general will'[15] — was possible only in small city states. Rousseau's interpretation has found little support in British political theory and practice.[16] As it developed in Britain and elsewhere, the concept was interpreted to allow for one person acting on behalf of or in the interests of another. Hence one could have a small assembly of citizens gathered together to 'represent' the interests of society as a whole or the bodies from which they were drawn. It was in this sense that the word entered common usage in Britain from at least the beginning of the seventeenth century.[17]

However, there has been disagreement about how such a 'representative' assembly should be constituted. Hegel believed that representatives should be chosen to represent the classes or trades to which they belonged,[18] a concept now referred to as 'functional representation'. A form of functional representation may be said to have existed in the first Parliaments summoned by English monarchs. Those called to assent to the king's demands were summoned to give assent on behalf of the estates of the realm. This view of representation underwent various modifications, and, though finding some residual support in later concepts of representation, has been largely displaced by the liberal view of representation. Though having its roots earlier in history, the so-called liberal view became the dominant one, and was largely applied in practice, in the nineteenth century.[19] It remains the dominant, though far from unanimous, view today. The essential elements of the liberal interpretation are that an assembly of representatives must be freely elected, and that the representatives must be elected on the basis of 'one man, one vote' (Bentham added 'one value' as well). The emphasis was and is on free election, the electors exercising their judgement as individuals and not as members of a trade or class; functional representation was and is discarded in favour of geographical representation, representatives being returned by those individuals living within defined territorial units. For the House of Commons to be a representative assembly, it has to be freely elected; the election has to be on the basis of 'one man, one vote'; and — this is the basis of representation — those elected are expected to protect and advance the interests of those on whose behalf they were returned. How these interests are to be determined, though, has been a point of contention (especially within the twentieth century Labour Party); also complicating the picture is the fact that not everyone has discarded a belief in functional representation (far from it), and that to a limited extent such a form of representation may be said still to exist. On a related though not identical point, a number of writers have argued that to be representative, those elected should be typical of the social composition of the population from which they are drawn; in other words, if half the population is female, then 50 per cent of MPs should be women.

The House of Commons may be said to constitute a representative assembly in that it is a freely elected body returned to represent the adult population of the United Kingdom. It is impossible for over forty million people to conform to Rousseau's concept of representation by gathering together to deliberate (Rousseau himself realised it was possible only in small communities), so an assembly is elected to perform the task instead. The House is elected at a general election, the election being called formally by the monarch and in practice by the Prime Minister. Under the provisions of the 1911 Parliament Act, the maximum life of a Parliament is five years (previously it was seven); within the five-year period, the Prime Minister can decide when to request a dissolution.

The United Kingdom is divided into geographical units of 635 constituencies,[20] each of which returns one Member of Parliament. Every person aged eighteen years and over has a vote (with a few exceptions: peers, aliens other than Irish citizens, and inmates of prisons and mental institutions) and the candidate receiving a plurality of votes cast in a constituency is deemed elected. Candidates, as we have seen, now seek election on a party label, and the party composition of the House following a general election determines which party (or sometimes coalition of parties) will form the Government.

There appears to be some agreement that the Commons is a representative assembly in so far as it is freely elected. The head of each household is required by law to complete the annual registration of voters form, but there is no formal compulsion to vote in an election, nor to cast one's vote for a certain candidate. (Some would argue, though, that one's ability to exercise freely the right to vote is affected by the disparity of wealth and resources between political parties, some being in a stronger position than others to employ large-scale publicity campaigns and to disseminate propaganda.) The principle of one man (or rather now one person), one vote, has also been conceded, though not until the election of 1950, when university seats ceased to exist, can it be said to have been fully implemented.[21]

However, the Benthamite principle of one man, one vote, one value, has yet to be fully realised. The disparity in the size of constituency electorates (the product of population shifts and the difficulties associated with quickly redrawing electoral boundaries) results in a vote in a small constituency carrying more weight than one cast in a constituency with a large electorate. It was this that Bentham had in mind when he sought equal value for votes, advocating constituencies of exactly equal size. A further disparity arises from the differences between safe and marginal seats. A vote in a closely contested election carries more value than one in an election in which the result is for all intents and purposes a foregone conclusion. The concentration of one party's supporters in certain areas and a more even spread of the supporters of another — resulting in the former party having a large number of safe seats and the latter winning more closely contested constituencies — can result in one party obtaining more votes nationally than its opponent party while nevertheless winning fewer seats; this happened in both the 1951 and the February 1974 elections.[22] Indeed, the 'first-past-the-post', constituency-based system of election produces only a rough correlation between the proportion of votes cast nationally for a party and the proportion of seats obtained by that party in the Commons. The plurality method of voting favours the two largest parties in Britain. A third party, whose candidates obtain several thousand votes in each of the constituencies that the party contests without coming top of the poll in any, can amass a national vote numbering in the millions without winning any seats at all. This is virtually the position in which the Liberal Party finds itself. In May 1979, the Conservative Party received 43.9 per cent of the votes cast in the United Kingdom, and over 53 per cent of the seats in the House of Commons; the Liberal Party gathered 13.8 per cent of the votes cast, and less than 2 per cent of the seats. The Liberals, among others, argue for a reform of the electoral system, with a form of proportional representation being proposed to replace the existing method of election. Such a system, it is contended (See Chapter 9), would make effective the principle of each vote having an equal value.

The House is even less representative in reflecting proportionally the social composition of the electorate than it is the voting support of political parties. The membership of the House is disproportionate to the rest of the population in terms of sex, age, education and occupational background; MPs are generally male, middle-aged and middle-class. This fact is well-known and now well-documented, and it appears that the trend is for the House to become even more middle-class than before.[23] However, in both British political thought and practice, the argument for a socially typical House has never taken root.[24] Certain problems can be identified should the principle ever be conceded. Being a Member of Parliament is essentially a white-collar, middle-class occupation. While Members who are barristers, businessmen and stockbrokers may be able to pursue, to a greater or lesser extent, their pre-election occupations, Members from manual and certain white-collar occupations cannot. Though an ex-miner may know more about the problems of miners than someone who has never been one, he nevertheless knows less about their problems than a man who remains a miner. If one sought a socially representative House based on Members' pre-election jobs, it is difficult to see how this aim could be achieved in practice. The selection of candidates is carried out locally rather than nationally, and while one finds candidates being selected from the same background as a plurality of electors in some constituencies (miners in predominantly mining areas, for example), it would be impossible to achieve the return of 635 Members who reflected proportionally the socio-economic composition of the population as a whole. Professor Birch has suggested that to achieve this a computer would be necessary.[25] In fact, it would appear to require a computer, a list system of election, and the nomination of certain people to stand as candidates, the current supply of potential candidates (those seeking candidature) being socially unrepresentative. The alternative method of achieving this aim, as Hegel realised, would be not to have elections at all. Though there is a growing feeling among certain minorities (and, in the case of women, a majority) that some or more of their number should be returned to represent their interests in the House of Commons, a socially typical House is unlikely to come about. It would introduce what adherents to the liberal view of representation would consider to be the alien concept of functional representation.

The House of Commons thus constitutes a representative assembly in that it is freely elected, election being based on the principle of one man, one vote, though the extent to which it reflects proportionally the party support and social composition of the country as a whole is a point of some contention. Members of Parliament individually also fulfil the function of representation. An MP is elected to 'represent' a constituency, 'to protect and, if possible advance [its] interests' in Professor Birch's terminology, though this aim too has given rise to certain problems of interpretation. Is a Member expected to rely upon his own judgement in deciding what is in the interests of his constituency, or should he exist as a delegate, acting on the instructions of local notables or groups or the body of electors? A Member is returned on a party label. To what extent is he a delegate of his local party? And to what extent is he a delegate of his party nationally? The problem is acute, especially within the Labour Party; its concept of intra-party democracy and of the mandate does not rest easily alongside that of the liberal view of representation.[26] The picture is complicated further by the fact that in practice an element of 'virtual representation' may be said to exist.

In order to clarify the function fulfilled by the individual Member, it is perhaps useful to distinguish two types of representation, each of which may be further subdivided. Each Member may be seen as fulfilling a function of both *specific* and *general* representation. The specific representation, defending and advancing the interests of a constituency and the individuals within it, may be described as the official function, the one adhered to by the liberal view and the basis on which each Member is elected. The general representation may be described as the defence of the causes of wider non-constituency, more functional interests in the country, and, outwith party, takes place on a rather disparate and generally unofficial basis.

Specific representation

A Member is returned to defend and advance the interests of his constituents. This function now largely takes the form of what is referred to as the Member's 'social welfare' role. It is through the Member that constituents can seek to achieve the redress of grievances against the state as represented by the executive. An individual seeking help or correction of some perceived mistake by a Government Department or official will normally approach his or her MP and enlist his aid.[27] As a rule, a Member will make himself available to meet constituents with problems, usually through regularly scheduled local meetings popularly referred to as 'surgeries',[28] as well as by handling such cases through correspondence; and, as we shall see later, there are various means by which Members can fulfil this function of specific representation in the

Commons. In practice, this remains one of the most important functions of the Member of Parliament. A recent survey revealed that respondents placed much emphasis on it, with twice as many people wanting MPs to 'look after local constituency problems' as wanting them to 'help . . . shape national policy'.[29] It is one which Members themselves regard as important — 'evident from the amount of time spent on surgery'[30] — and one which is fulfilled free of party influence. A local party would be concerned if the Member appeared to be neglecting his constituency duties, but otherwise does not impinge upon those duties. Most Members concede that such work has little effect upon their political support in terms of votes, but do it out of a sense of duty as Members of Parliament. 'I do the constituency work, not for a political bonus, because there isn't a political bonus in it,' commented one Member, Roy Hattersley. 'I do it because its part of the job.'[31] It is part of the job which nowadays most Members carry out with a degree of dedication. In a case of real injustice, as one MP noted, 'Members of Parliament can be very relentless indeed and keep forcing [the] case on the Government's attention.'[32] Also, as John Grant has observed, such work has the advantage of keeping an MP in touch with his electors and permitting him to know at first hand their opinions and problems.[33]

A Member's task of representation extends also to his constituents as a body, though in practice constituents may have little in common other than geographical proximity and the fact that they are consumers. Both factors may be relevant at times. Representation of the consuming public may be said to be a 'general' representation performed by Members collectively. Samuel Beer has argued that though Government seeks to mediate between competing demands made by functional groups, it nevertheless cannot ignore the views of consumers who, as electors[34] can turn out at an election.[35] And, in between elections, the representatives of the consumers are MPs. Each Member, though, will seek to perform the function individually, given differences between constituencies; there are variations in consumption, and forms of consumption may differ between areas, as, for example, between urban and rural areas. Geography can also be significant. The population living in a defined area may be threatened by a particular Government policy, and hence seek the help of the local Member. An obvious example would be a Government decision on the siting of a third London airport; an MP in or near whose constituency it was decided to site the airport would be expected by his constituents to oppose the decision. Similarly, an MP whose constituency is directly under the flight path of aircraft approaching Heathrow airport would be expected to favour the building of a third London airport. In practice, this is precisely what has generally happened, with constituency interests being sufficient to overcome party loyalty.[36]

In addition to representing his constituents as individuals and as a collective entity, each Member is expected to represent the many and varied bodies and interests that go to form the constituency. 'He is the Member for a constituency with a primary duty to represent its trades and interests, its corporations and councils,' as one Labour MP once put it.[37] A Member is expected to defend local interests as he defends those of individual constituents; if a local body or organisation is threatened by or suffers from some Government action, the Member will seek to obtain redress for its grievance. Members representing ports such as Hull or Grimsby will maintain a watching brief on matters that affect the fishing industry; a Member returned for a predominantly rural area will normally maintain an interest in agricultural matters; and so on. In other words, a Member will try to look after the interests of his constituents in their capacities as producers and workers as well as consumers, the duality of the role creating the potential for occasional cross-pressures.

A further interest represented is one which is common to each Member (excepting only the rare independent Member) — his local party. A Member is dependent upon his constituency party for his selection, for the organisation of his election campaign, for his renomination, and for support in between elections. A special relationship thus exists between the two. Given this special relationship, it is sometimes believed that Members, or some of them at least, act primarily as delegates of their local parties, acting as mouthpieces for the party activists who control the constituency party organisations rather than exercising their own judgement as to what is in the interests of their respective constituencies. This view was reinforced in the 1970s by a number of cases in which Labour Members were threatened with being, or were, denied renomination following disputes with their local parties; examples include Dick Taverne in Lincoln, Reg Prentice in Newham North-East, Eddie Griffiths in Sheffield Brightside, and Eddie Milne in Blyth. Fears of further such cases were fueled by the vote of the Labour Party Conference in 1979 (following an earlier debate in 1977) that Labour MPs should be subject to compulsory reselection procedures. Against this view must be set the following considerations. Instances of Members being refused renomination are still relatively rare;[38] of those denied renomination in the 1970s, three (S.O. Davies, Dick Taverne and Eddie Milne) were re-elected under independent labels, albeit for short periods in practice but sufficient to undermine the presumed supremacy of local parties,[39] and a fourth, Reg Prentice, successfully crossed the floor of the House and now sits for a safe Conservative seat. Members who have voted in the Commons in a manner at variance with the wishes of their local parties have usually been renominated, a fact most notably demonstrated in the 1970s on the issue of entry into the European Communities (and, later, devolution). No dissenting Conservative Member was denied renomination, despite a number voting against their own Government on a vote of confidence;[40] and out of over seventy dissenting Labour Members only Mr Taverne was disowned by his local party (and that not solely on the basis of his stand on the European Communities issue). Also, local parties comprise voluntary part-time activists who, if they allow 'their political enthusiasms to outweigh other, and perhaps more practical considerations'[41] do so usually only on the major political issues — as a rule they have neither the time nor the expertise to consider the many and often complex issues that command the time and attention of the Commons.

While no Member is likely to ignore his local party, or would wish normally to antagonise it, each does have some latitude in his parliamentary behaviour that goes beyond that of a delegate of his constituency party organisation. Perhaps the most useful generalisation to be made would be that the local party provides the parameters within which a Member may act (and these parameters may vary from local party to local party), but within these parameters the local party does not dictate the Member's action. It should also be remembered that in most instances the Member and his local party operate on the basis of shared beliefs rather than mutual disagreement, with the local party playing a supporting rather than a directing role. A Member will usually have latitude in representing specific and general interests free of the dictates, and more often than not with the support, of his local constituency party.

General representation

A Member is returned for a particular constituency, but he serves in Parliament as a member of a national party. This might be described as a form of general representation, and it continues the most important and the most highly structured form of this type of representation. Members sit and are organised on the basis of parliamentary parties. As we saw in Chapter 2, the wishes of a mass electorate can be realised only through candidates standing on a common platform and supporting that platform through their votes if returned to the Commons. Members are returned for individual constituencies, but general elections are fought on a national basis, between the parties; national party manifestos are issued, and attention is focused on the party leaders. Membership of party helps to shape, albeit not exclusively, parliamentary behaviour. Members sit in the House on a party basis, participate in developed party organisations in the House (as delineated in Chapter 3), and usually, but not always, vote along party lines, more because they want to than because they feel they have to. Though party is the most important, and the common, variable influencing Members' parliamentary activity, opportunities do exist for them not only to pursue the specific representation of constituents' interests but also to represent other interests through or outside the context of party. It is here that Edmund Burke's concept of virtual representation has some relevance.

'Virtual representation', wrote Burke, 'is that in which there is a communion of interests, and a sympathy in feelings and desires, between those who act in the name of any description of people, and the people in whose name they act, though the trustees are not actually chosen by them.'[42] Burke developed the concept to justify a limited franchise, sufficient to prevent absolute monarchy while avoiding the evils of absolute democracy. It was a concept which the liberal view rejects. It conflicted with the liberal view of election (virtual representation lends itself logically to the elimination of election, though that was not what Burke intended), and it could be seen as being akin to some form of neo-feudal functional representation, Members being able to speak on behalf of the classes or trades with which they had some 'communion of interest'. Though the concept has found little favour in British philosophical thought, and the formal constitutional structure and method of election is based on the liberal concept of representation, some form of virtual representation may be said to exist, albeit in a rather limited and disparate form.

As a member of Parliament *qua* Member of Parliament, an MP might, and not infrequently does, seek to represent, to speak on behalf of and further the interests of, a particular body or organisation in the country (not confined to his constituency, indeed not necessarily related to his constituency at all), as well as that most general of interests, the 'national interest', to which we shall turn shortly. The representation of a general interest may derive from a Member's own occupational background: a barrister, for example, may taken an interest in legal matters and in those affecting the legal profession, and may be said to represent its interests; and ex-miner may act as a representative or watchdog for the interests of miners; a former naval officer may act as a guardian of the interests of sailors; and so on. In other instances, a Member may seek to represent a cause or interest because of some personal experience — a physically disabled Member looking out for the interests of the disabled, a Member with a mentally retarded child taking an interest in the care and treatment of such children, for example — or because he is persuaded of the importance or moral validity of a cause (many Members, for instance, take a serious interest in animal welfare, and in the care of the disabled). Some Members also support or may be said to represent interests as a result of their religious and moral convictions and affiliations: Roman Catholic Members supporting anti-abortion organisations, for example, or Anglicans taking a special interest in Church of England measures coming before the House. In such cases (all the foregoing being based on factual examples), the representation may be described as unofficial, the Members concerned having no formal links with the organisations or groups concerned. In other instances, a formal link may exist. A Member may hold a honorary post in an organisation, or, in the case of a number of pressure groups, may be paid a fee or retainer. A number of bodies (including, for example, Police Federation) retain an MP as a parliamentary adviser, while several Labour Members are sponsored formally by trade unions. In May 1979, 148 union-sponsored Labour Members were returned, twenty-one of them sponsored by one union, the Transport and General Workers' Union.[43] Though financial sponsorship may provide the sponsoring body with some means of holding a Member accountable for his actions (albeit limited in practice by parliamentary privilege), such representation is not based on election.[44] Rather, a Member assumes the function because of 'a communion of interests, and a sympathy in feelings and desires' with the organisation or body concerned.

Burke also believed (echoing the traditional Whig view of representation), and again this is pertinent to the contemporary House of Commons, that Members acted not only as representatives of local or general interests, but also of the national community. A Member once returned, was and is often viewed, in Burke's classic formulation, as 'not the Member of Bristol, but the Member of Parliament'. Parliament, in Burke's words, 'is a deliberate assembly of one nation with one interest, that of the whole, where not local purposes or prejudices ought to guide but the general good resulting from the general reason of the whole'. As a Member of Parliament, a Member is able to give his opinion on what he considers to be in the national interest. 'Speak for England, Arthur,' shouted Leo Amery when Arthur Greenwood rose to speak during the crucial debate of 1939 preceding the declaration of war with Germany.[45] It is a concept of representation which remains current. On most occasions, of course, what a Member considers to be in the national interest will coincide with what his party believes to be in the nation's interest: that, after all, is one of the reasons why the Member supports the party that he does. On occasion, though, the two may diverge. An excellent example would be the case of Labour MP Eric Heffer in the 1976–7 session. He found himself in a dilemma over how to vote on the Government's Scotland and Wales Bill. On the one hand, he felt he should support a measure which had been promised in his party's manifesto and supported by the party's National Executive Committee; on the other hand, he had reached the conclusion that the Bill was not in the best interests of the nation. He resolved the cross-pressures by abstaining from voting both on the Second Reading of the Bill and on the fateful guillotine motion which the Government lost in February 1977, effectively killing the Bill in its original form. On most occasions, though, Members are not subject to such conflicts.

A Member of Parliament thus finds himself fulfilling the function of representation, but one which involves representing several interests.[46] More often than not, such interests will converge rather than diverge; local parties (with some exceptions, notably on the Labour side) are supportive of the national party, as are party voters – most seats are safe seats for one or other party. A Member usually shares the views of his national party, and his general interests are normally compatible with his party views; Labour Members with trade-union interests (indeed, the link between the trade union movement and the Labour Party as such is an institutionalised one, though the link with the PLP as such is more tenuous) and Conservative Members with business interests are well-known examples. Representing such interests, which in practice is what Members do, nevertheless provides the potential for occasional conflict between one and another, and on such occasions the Member has to resolve the cross-pressures to which he is subject and determine what course of action to pursue. Burke recognised this. In the last resort, he believed it must depend on the character and the conscience of the individual Member. It was a view most succinctly expressed in 1969 by a Labour Member: 'Last – and perhaps most important – the Member has a responsibility to his own conscience – a need to fit his own actions as comfortably as possible into the view he holds of the world in which he lives and for which he takes some responsibility.'[47] Although party may provide the parameters within which a Member may normally act, his actions may still, on occasions (be they comparatively rare or otherwise), be based on the judgement which adherents of Burke believe he owes his constituents.

Sustaining and providing a forum of debate for the Government and Opposition parties

The developments of the nineteenth century resulted in political life being dominated by political parties, with the two largest tending to attract the most attention. The parties, as we have seen, became organised and centralised, and the Commons became the centre of the well-organised competition between them. The Government and the Opposition, based now on well-marshalled and fairly cohesive parties, became more structured; the procedure and timetable of the House was reformed to accommodate this change. The Government, sustained usually by a parliamentary majority, dominates the timetable, but the smooth working of that timetable and of parliamentary procedure generally depends in large measure upon the co-operation of the parties in the House. That co-operation is founded upon acceptance of the principle that the Government should govern, but that Opposition parties should have the opportunity to debate what the Government puts forward, the result in practice being an adversary relationship between the two sides. As one former Member opined, the whole structure of the parliamentary day is based upon a confrontation between Government and Oppostion. 'Thus, for instance, the whole structure of debates is for and against . . . The whole business of Question Time is patently a confrontation . . . All of this is in terms of the Opposition challenging the Government.'[48] The House sustains competing parties, allowing the Government and Opposition parties to fulfil the functions commented upon in the preceding section, the Government party supporting the Government and its measures, the Opposition party supporting its leaders in providing an alternative to the Government and its measures.

Given the Government's control of the timetable and its command on most occasions of a parliamentary majority, it is argued by some that this debating function is of little relevance. At the end of the day, the Government gets its way; the Commons is no more, so the argument goes, than an ineffective talking shop. That it is a talking shop cannot be doubted. It is supposed to be, and the very name Parliament (Parlement) is founded upon that fact. When critics used to complain to Quintin Hogg that MPs seemed to do no more than talk, he would reply, 'That is why they are called a Parliament.'[49] As a talking shop, though, it can be argued that the Commons serves a useful purpose. The use of debate requires the Government to explain and justify its measures; if it fails to do so convincingly, it knows that the Opposition will exploit that fact and use it to its own ends. Poor performance in debate will be picked up both by the Government's own parliamentary supporters (which is not conducive to good morale) and by the mass media; even if it wins the battle in the division lobbies (which, as we shall see later, is not always guaranteed), the Government may not win the war of argument, and it is believed that this may have some effect, marginal or otherwise, upon the next election campaign. (Whether it does or not is debatable, though the fact that the parties believe it may have is important.)

Some have contended that the proceedings of the House 'constitute a continuous election campaign',[50] and this continuous campaign may be seen as contributing, through the parties, to the fulfilment of the 'expressive', 'teaching' and 'informative' functions identified by Bagehot and echoed more recently by other writers. In the stands which the parties take in the Commons they may be influenced by or seek to reflect public opinion (the expressive function), and they in turn, through their actions and views, may seek to influence public attitudes (the teaching function); also, the putting forward of their various views in the House can mean that 'to some extent it makes us hear what otherwise we should not' (the informing function).[51] On occasion, these functions also may be exercised by the House in a more collective capacity when the Government and Opposition parties leave Members free to determine a contentious non-party issue for themselves.

Less central, but in many respects as important as or more important than the debate between parties, is the occasional public debate within parties. Public confrontation between parties to discourage Members from opposing or criticising publicly their own side (the function of intra-party debate having largely been hived off to the parliamentary parties), but the opportunities do exist for Members to express their dissent in the House if they fail to achieve a response to views expressed in private party forums. The public expression of intra-party dissent within the House is an embarrassment for the party concerned and, if combined with dissent in the division lobbies, can have serious consequences, as we shall see later.

The House's debating function does not force the Government to be as open and forthcoming as many would wish, though it may be said to prevent the Government from being totally closed and arbitrary. Expressed in somewhat Utopian terms, the House is a place for public, rational debate between the parties, representative of different opinions in the country, a place where the dominant party is forced not only to justify its own views (sometimes to its own supporters as well as to Opposition parties) but to listen to those of its opponents as well. This rather idealised, though not totally unjustified, view found reflection in the comments of Michael Foot in 1976, when he was Leader of the House:

> I believe that the process of compelling hon. Members who are in the Chamber, or outside it in Committee rooms, to listen to what other people have to say means that this is a place where we can hear how intelligent, formidable and considerable are the arguments of one's critics or opponents in other parties or in one's own party. That is what the House of Commons is for, and it discharges that function better than many people in the country sometimes acknowledge.[52]

While it may perform the function well, it nevertheless has come in for some criticism. Some would contend that it is one which is not of great significance compared with other functions that the Commons should be performing. On a related point, some argue that the debate between the parties emphasises the Government/Opposition relationship to the detriment of that between private Members and the Government *qua* Government, especially important in connection with the Commons' function of scrutiny. As we shall see in Chapter 9, there are those who believe that this relationship can be and is being modified through increased dissent within the parties, while others believe that, in so far as the debate between parties constitutes an adversary one with certain detrimental consequences, the confrontational relationship between Government and Opposition parties should be ended through the implementation of electoral reform.

Legitimising the Government and its measures

Given the nature and history of Parliament, the functions it performs are not necessarily the same as those of other Parliaments, National Assemblies, legislatures, or Congresses, around the world; as Sir Kenneth Wheare has noted, the variety of functions performed by such bodies are illustrated by the variety of names they bear.[53] However, one function that Parliament (primarily now the Commons) appears to have in common with most, if not all, other national assemblies is the function of legitimisation.[54] It is common for countries to have assemblies (freely elected or otherwise) for the purpose of giving assent to political decisions. In England, it is the most long-standing function of the House of Commons. Originally, as we have seen, the monarch summoned his tenants-in-chief to the Great Council to give counsel and consent prior to the levying of extraordinary taxation; the Great Council, as it was composed originally, was the precursor of the House of Lords. When two knights, representative of each shire, and subsequently two burgesses, representative of each borough, were summoned, it was in order to assent to additional aid. These representatives of the *communes* or Commons were not regularly summoned, and on the occasions that they were in the reign of Edward I it was in order only 'to consent to whatever should be decided'.[55] As we have seen, the later struggle between monarch and Parliament, culminating in the Bill of Rights of 1688, was based on the claim by Parliament that taxes could only be levied and laws changed with the 'consent of Parliament'. With the acceptance of some form of representative democracy in the nineteenth century, the assent of the elected House became much more important, making it the dominant of the two Houses. The importance of the consent of Parliament, expressed for all intents and purposes by the Commons, is that it constitutes the assent of the representatives of the nation's electors to measures that will affect the nation. (Members of the House of Lords, whose writs of summons are personal, represent now no interests other than essentially their own - though an element of quasi-functional representation appears to have crept in with the appointment especially of a number of life peers - hence their weak position in a system based on rational—legal authority.) By assenting to a measure, the representatives are legitimising it on behalf of those whom they represent. 'It represents MPs, the people's elected representatives, giving, if you like, "the seal of approval" to measures drawn up and decided upon by the Government.[56] One observer has also suggested that the Commons is particularly appropriate for this function, 'in that its ancient traditions and esoteric procedures lend it a special mystique'.[57]

The function performed by the Commons today may be divided into two: the legitimisation of the Government, and the legitimisation of the measures proposed by Government. It is an important function in that legitimisation as such is important, and because the Commons retains the power to deny legitimisation, a power that would be considered by many now to be a formal one, but one that can be exercised on rare occasions (and sometimes not so rare occasions).

Following the advent of a form of representative democracy (however imperfect) in the nineteenth century, the legitimacy of the Government rested upon the fact that a majority of its supporters were returned at a general election and that, during a Parliament, it could retain the confidence of that majority. Such remains the position today. During a Parliament, the extent to which the Government retains the support of a Commons majority may be tested by a vote of confidence. Votes of confidence take three forms: explicit votes of confidence (motions expressing confidence in the Government or the lack of it), votes made such by the declaration of the Government (for example, on major measures on which the Government is prepared to stake its continuance in office), and implicit votes of confidence (on items considered so important that they are assumed to be tantamount to votes of confidence without having been declared such), though this latter category appears to have fallen into desuetude. If the Government fails to carry a vote of confidence, constitutional convention requires that it either resign or request a dissolution. In practice, a Government returned with a clear overall majority has few problems in ensuring the support of that majority in votes of confidence. In the twentieth century no Government with an overall party majority has been defeated in such a vote. (In the exceptional wartime circumstances of 1940 a loss of support within his own ranks demonstrated to Neville Chamberlain that he no longer had the confidence of the House, but that was through a reduction in, and not a loss of, the Government's majority.) The nearest a Government with an overall majority has come to losing a vote of confidence in recent years was in 1972, when the Prime Minister, Mr Heath, made the Second Reading of the European Communities Bill a vote of confidence: it was carried by a majority of only eight votes, fifteen Conservatives voting against it and five more abstaining from voting. The real threat to a Government is posed when it does not have an overall majority in the House, and is dependent upon the support or at least acquiescence of another party or parties. If it loses that support, it can be brought down by Opposition parties combining against it in a vote of confidence. Hence, the only three Government defeats on confidence votes in this century (in January 1924, October 1924, and March 1979) have been brought about by Opposition parties uniting against a minority Government. To be assured of continuing in office, of retaining its legitimacy, a Government has to maintain the support of the majority in the House, be it of its own supporters or, if in a minority, of another party (or parties) as well.[58]

The government needs to retain the support of a majority in the House not only to maintain its legitimacy as the Government but also to legitimise the measures it wishes passed. Formally, the House retains the functions of legislating and granting supply. In practice, it does not perform these functions in any significant manner: legislative and financial measures are initiated and formulated elsewhere. If the Government party is in a majority in the House, such measures are normally passed, often with little difficulty. As Hanson and Walles have succinctly expressed the position, the House of Commons 'legitimises but does not legislate'.[59] Nevertheless, the Government does need a majority in the House to pass its measures, whether assent is a formality or otherwise; without the assent of the House a measure cannot become 'law'. It is thus an important symbolic function, though its importance extends beyond this. The Commons can, if it wishes deny legitimisation to a measure — that is, refuse to pass it. The initiation, introduction, and content of most measures are now the responsibility of the Government, but the House retains the power to reject a measure or parts of it. In practice, it is a negative power, rarely exercised. Government supporters, as we have mentioned, are usually prepared to support the Government's measures; it is, after all, one of the essential reasons why they were returned to the House. However, if the Government party is in a minority, it cannot guarantee the passage of Government Bills. On occasion, the Government may be subject also to dissent by some of its own back-benchers. A number of backbenchers on the Government side of the House may decide that a particular measure runs counter to their inter-pretation of party policy, or that it is not in line with what was promised by the party at the last election, or that it conflicts with the interests of their constituents or other interests that they represent. If they resolve the cross-pressures of party loyalty versus opposition to the measure in favour of the latter, they may vote against and help to defeat the measure, or at least threaten to. Given the pull of party loyalty, and the affinity of purpose between the Government and its supporters, such occasions are few, but not as rare as many might believe. Through a combination of Opposition Members and Government backbenchers in the division lobbies, a majority of the House may negate, deny legitimisation, to a Government measure or parts thereof. It may be a power not often used, but it is important to record that it does constitute a power of the House of Commons, one on which the ability of the House to scrutinise and influence the Government is largely founded.

The distinction between legitimisation of the Government and of its measures has often been blurred. A Government, for whatever reason, may choose to resign or request a dissolution. Many MPs believe or used to believe that a Government incurs a constitutional *obligation* to resign or go to the country whenever defeated on an important measure, or indeed on any matter. As early as 1905 Arthur Balfour was observing that it appeared to be assumed in various parts of the House 'that the accepted constitutional principle is that, when a government suffers defeat, either in Supply or on any other subject, the proper course for His Majesty's responsible advisers is either to ask His Majesty to relieve them of their office or to ask His Majesty to dissolve Parliament.'[60] This belief has been current for most of this century, and appears to have been held strongly in the post-war years from 1945 to the early 1970s, having as a result a significant influence on parliamentary behaviour. However, though the efficient functioning of a parliamentary system is based on the premise that the Government will usually be able to achieve passage of its measures (see Chapter 2), the belief that it requires con-stitutionally a majority in every division in order to remain in office has been shown to be a constitutional 'myth'. Though a Government may choose to resign or request a dissolution in the event of any or multiple defeats (few Governments would choose to do so, calculations of electoral behaviour having a much greater influence), it incurs a constitutional obligation to do so only in the event of losing a vote of confidence. By denying legitimisation to a Government measure, the House does not (unless it has been made an explicit vote of confidence) deny legitimisation to the Government.[61] This is a point of some importance, and as we shall see (Chapter 9) one of especial significance in recent years.

The Commons exercises the legitimising function during the course of a Parliament on behalf of the electorate; the electors' representatives assent to measures that will affect those that they represent. It is a function which nevertheless may be described as not being exclusive to the Commons. An element of *de facto* legitimisation is exercised by various powerful groups — sectional interest groups on behalf of their members, for example, and the International Monetary Fund on behalf of the international financial community — upon whom the Government is dependent for advice and co-operation. Many observers take the view that this legitimisation on behalf of functional groups is immeasurably more significant now than that afforded on behalf of the collectivity of electors by the House of Commons.[62] Furthermore, it can be argued that even the legitimisation undertaken on behalf of electors is being and has been modified by the use of referendums. Before deciding whether to retain membership of the European Communities on renegotiated terms in 1975, the House sought the 'advice' of the elect-orate through the use of a referendum;[63] in 1979, the 'advice' of the Scottish and Welsh electorates was sought on whether or not they approved the setting up of Assemblies with devolved powers in their respective countries. Although advisory, such referendums were seen as an abdication by the Commons of its legitimising function: it was per-ceived as seeking legitimisation for measures from the electorate instead of relying solely upon its own power.[64] If the use of referendums was to become common, and especially if they were to be binding rather than advisory, the legitimising function of the Commons would be very seriously undermined: legitimisation by the Commons of important measures might cease to be accepted as the final granting of the 'seal of approval'.

Scrutinising and influencing the measures and the actions of Government

By common consent, probably the most important function of the contemporary House of Commons, interrelated with the foregoing functions, is that of scrutiny and influence of Government. This role has its origins in the fact that the Commons gradually acquired the opportunity, when summoned, to discuss the state of the realm, and in the reign of Edward III began to make the grant of supply conditional upon the redress of grievances. Briefly stated, the role has evolved so that, before assenting to grants of supply or the passage of legislation, the House discusses the proposals of the Government, Members (those not in the ministry) casting a critical eye over such proposals on behalf of their constituents and the other interests they represent. If dissatisfied or worried by such proposals, Members may seek to influence the Government to amend, modify or abandon them; if the Government fails to respond, the House retains the power to deny the Government a majority in the division lobbies, that is, to refuse legitimisation. Such is the formal position; in practice, it is not so simple.

Collectively and individually, Members are deemed to fulfil this role of scrutiny and influence. It is a role modified and given added complexity by the role of party. The collective function has been largely hived off to the party elements within the House. The most consistent, structured scrutiny of Government in the House is provided by the Opposition. 'If Parliament's main function is to criticise, the Opposition is its most important part.'[65] As outline above, one of the functions of the House is to provide the forum in which the Opposition can debate and scrutinise Government measures, with the Government party having the opportunity to support and sustain those measures. On the one hand, the adversary relationship between Government and Opposition means that the Government is placed in a position of having to defend and support its measures in a public forum, knowing that any weakness in its proposals will be picked up and exploited by the party or parties opposite. On the other hand, the adversary relationship tends to ensure that, at the end of the day, the two sides divide along strict party lines, the Government carrying its measure in the division lobbies through its party majority. Hence, as we have observed earlier, the criticism of the Commons as no more than a talking shop.

While there is much to support this criticism, it does not quite convey the whole picture. The function of scrutiny and influence has not been abandoned on the Government side of the House, but is rather performed now within the private or semi-private confines of the parliamentary party. If Government backbenchers have discussed and expressed doubts about a Government proposal in a private forum, and have achieved no satisfactory response to their opinions, the opportunity exists for them then to attempt to influence the Government on the floor of the House. By expressing public disquiet in debate or by threatening to vote against the Government in the division, Government backbenchers are in a position to embarrass their leaders publicly; if they feel strongly on a particular issue, they may be prepared to vote in the Opposition lobby, threatening, by so doing, the Government's majority. While preferring usually the less public confines of the parliamentary party, the fact that Government backbenchers may have recourse to the floor of the House does act as a restraint upon the Government. The Government has to withstand both the public scrutiny of the Opposition *and* the private scrutiny of its own supporters. This reiterates a point already made. To appreciate fully the role of Members of Parliament one has to recognise the importance of what goes on *within* parties in the House as well as what goes on *between* parties. A combination of the two can serve as a perhaps uncommon, but not unimportant, check upon the Government; how uncommon or otherwise we shall have cause to consider later.

An additional point of importance is that the Government may respond in a positive manner to scrutiny and attempted influence, not because it fears that failure to do so may lead to the Opposition's exploiting the point or to its own backbenchers' taking action on the floor of the House, but simply because it has been persuaded of the strength of the case put forward. The Government is not so irrational or so rigid that it cannot sometimes respond to constructive scrutiny and criticism within the House.[66] A prudent Government will also be conscious of the need occasionally to make concessions in order to avoid bad feeling among those upon whom it is dependent for co-operation in ensuring the smooth running of parliamentary business. The result is that the Government does not necessarily bring measures before the House with a closed mind. As one former Minister explained, a Government will not normally be prepared to give way on the Second Reading of a measure, but 'it will watch the Second Reading debate and consider again now at what points would it be wise to make concessions. And so on, throughout the whole process of the Bill.'[67] The scrutiny and influence exerted by the House (in so far as it can be considered to be exerted collectively) may be 'excessively piecemeal, random, and unsystematic', as Bernard Crick has claimed,[68] but at least, contrary to the belief of some critics, it does take place; the extent to which it does we shall investigate in the following chapters.

Individually, Members fulfil the role of scrutiny and influence. They do so not only in their capacities as members of the Government or Opposition party, as actors within the adversary debate between the two sides, but also as Members representing their individual constituencies and other interests. As the Member for a particular constituency, an MP will keep an eye on measures or Government actions that may have some effect upon his constituency; as we have noted, this function of specific representation is often performed outside the context of party politics. If a constituent is denied some benefit as a result of a decision by a civil servant, the Member concerned will seek to achieve redress of the grievance regardless of which party is in power: the letter he sends to the relevant junior Minister or the Question he tables may be the same as that he would submit if the other party were in office. Government Ministers will deal usually with such cases in a non-party manner: they respond as Ministers in charge of a particular Department rather than as Labour or Conservative Ministers in a party Government. Ministers who deal badly or inefficiently with such cases and acquire poor reputations among Members on both sides of the House may find their career prospects harmed; they cannot hide behind party loyalty in such cases. Similar considerations will often apply when a Member seeks to influence Government on behalf of the other interests he represents. Members on both sides of the House may seek to promote causes which are inherently non-partisan, and on which Government Ministers may have to be guided by departmental norms, administrative experience, or basic principles of fairness, rather than by party political doctrine. And in certain instances where the Government may seek to shelter behind party loyalty, its own backbenchers may not be prepared to go along with it. It is in this individual capacity that a Member may have most scope to exert influence. He may seek to promote a cause or interest, his stand on which is not determined by his political philosophy, and through a judicious combination of the means available to him may influence Government policy, either alone or in conjunction with like-minded Members. Through such action some important measures have been subject to considerable amendment.

In brief, Members of Parliament, collectively and individually, perform the function of scrutinising and influencing the measures and actions of Government. It is a complex function. A Member will perform it within the context of the debate between Government and Opposition, publicly on the Opposition side, privately (and sometimes not so privately) on the Government side. He will perform it as the Member for a particular constituency, and as a representative sometimes of other interests as well. Sometimes the two roles may be distinct (one day a Member may attack the other party in debate and later have an adjournment debate on a specific constituency problem); they may overlap (an Opposition Member may criticise the Government for neglecting interests within his constituency); or they may conflict (a Government backbencher may discover that a Government policy will affect adversely his constituency): hence the complexity, a complexity enhanced by the variety of means available to Members to perform this function. It is a complexity for which we seek to provide some structure, incorporating the specific/general representation of the Member with the dimension of the Government/Opposition and House/executive relationships, in Figure 4.2. The lines between the categories are not as distinct as the matrix suggests (some Members may regard a general issue as a non-partisan one to be pursued in the context of the House/executive relationship; others may view the same issue as essentially a party political one), but the figure does serve as a guide, one which helps to give some shape to the complexity of facts and relationships which we have touched upon.

Representation	Relationship involved in fulfilling function of scrutiny	
	Government/Opposition	House/executive
Specific	Attack/support Government for neglecting/helping constituency interests	Asking Minister to take action on behalf of individual constituent
	Use of correspondence, intra-party forums, Questions, debates	Use notably of correspondence, Questions, adjournment debates
	(intra-party disagreement not frequent, but generally viewed without rancour given the motivation)	(rarely seen in party terms; few divisions; opportunity to be persistent free of party ties)
General	Attack/support Government for pursuing policy in/not in national interest, in/not in line with election promises, etc.	Asking Government to introduce or acquiesce in introduction of measures or take action to, e.g., prevent child abuse, promote animal welfare, etc.
	Use notably of intra-party forums and, later, debates for dissent; debates for party competition (concept of 'continuous election campaign' important here)	Use notably of Private Members' Bills and motions, Questions, all-party committees, occasional adjournment debates
	(intra-party dissent restrained by party loyalty; when it occurs, serious and sometimes fundamental)	(rarely seen in party terms; if whips put on, may be overridden by strength of MP's moral convictions)

Figure 4.2 The context of an MP's role in the House

Other functions

In addition to the functions identified above, which we would suggest are the most important ones fulfilled by the House and which incorporate those usually put forward in one form or another by other writers, the House fulfils a number of minor but important functions. These may be summarised briefly as follows.

The House exercises a minor *shared legislative* function. As we have seen, the main function of legislation now resides effectively with the Government. The most important legislation that goes through the House is that of the Government. The Government controls the parliamentary timetable and has the sole right to introduce financial legislation. Because of the Government's party majority in the House, such legislation is usually passed. However, the Government rarely seeks to use parliamentary time exclusively for its own measures. Under the standing orders of the House, some time is available for the consideration of Private Members' and, quite separately, Private legislation, and it is in the consideration of such legislation that the House exercises a small legislative function, one that may be described as shared. It is a function shared between the House (that is, the collectivity of Members who are not Ministers), and the Government, whose acquiescence is usually necessary for the passage of such measures. As a rule, such legislation is considered and voted upon free of party ties, but with the Government offering advice to the House and, where it considers it desirable, making extra time available to facilitate the passage of certain Private Members' Bills. Unlike Government legislation, Private Members' and Private Bills are rarely assured of passage: their sponsors have to persuade both the Government and a majority of private Members who intend voting to support or at least to acquiesce in their passage. Private Members thus enjoy greater freedom of action in this sphere than they do in their consideration of Government measures. Although Private Members' legislation rarely impinges upon Government policy, it may on occasion seek to deal with topics which the Government has neglected or prefers not to touch, and we shall include it, for convenience (along with Private legislation), in our consideration of the scrutiny of legislation in the next chapter.

The House also exercises a number of powers, both formal and real, which may be subsumed under the description of a judicial or *quasi-judicial* function. Of the two Houses, the House of Lords is the one usually associated with a judicial function. However, the Commons has a limited judicial function, though one hardly comparable with the Lords'. Briefly, this function encompasses the following. Committees on Private Bills sit in a quasi-judicial capacity, with promoters and objectors being represented by counsel and witnesses heard under oath.

The House exercises a judicial function in the sphere of its privileges, and has power to punish anyone for breaches of privilege. Certain officers, such as judges, are removable by an address to the Crown by both Houses, and proceedings in relation to the address are of a judicial character. The 1921 Tribunals of Inquiry (Evidence) Act provides that on matters of urgent public importance, by resolution of both Houses, a Tribunal of Inquiry may be appointed by the Crown or a Secretary of State with the powers of a High Court as regards the examination of witnesses and the production of documents.[69] In addition, Parliament (both Houses) retains the formal powers of impeachment and of passing Acts of Attainder, though such powers are now considered to be obsolete.[70] As can be seen, it is an essentially limited function.

Another minor function may be identified within the area of the Commons' privilege, one that can be described as an *internal disciplinary* one. The Commons claims the right to punish breaches of its privilege and also contempt (an offence or libel against its dignity or authority); and if the offender is an MP, the House retains the power not only of reprimand but also of expulsion. It is a power rarely used, in large part because of a fear of setting unfortunate precedents. On occasion, though, it has been employed. In October 1947 the House voted to expel the Labour Member for Gravesend, Garry Allighan, for dishonourable conduct (after he had alleged publicly that certain MPs accepted payment for revealing what went on in private party meetings, it was discovered that he himself was one of the Members in question), and also to reprimand the Member for Doncaster, Evelyn Walkden, for dishonourable conduct (he had given accounts of PLP meetings to the press, for which he had received a weekly retainer of £5).[71] In 1954, Captain Peter Baker, the Conservative Member for Norfolk South, was expelled following his conviction and imprisonment for fraud. More recently, in July 1977, John Cordle, the Conservative Member for Bournemouth East and Christchurch, was found to have engaged in conduct amounting to a contempt of the House (he had used a speech to pursue his own commercial interests, which he had not revealed); he resigned his seat.[72] Such matters, along with other items of privilege, are deemed normally to be 'House of Commons matters', for which the Government has no responsibility, and are determined by free votes of the House. The House and Mr Speaker also retain certain powers to suspend Members for disorderly conduct.

Such minor functions can rarely be said to dominate the time and the interest of the House, and, except for the shared legislative function to which we shall return, are mentioned for the record only: they do not constitute central features of the Commons' main role of scrutiny and influence of Government.

Conclusion

The main functions of the House of Commons may be said to be those of providing the personnel of Government, of representation, of sustaining and providing a forum of debate for the Government and Opposition parties, of legitimising the Government and its measures, of scrutinising and influencing the measures and actions of Government, and of performing a number of minor though not always unimportant functions. These functions may be seen to be largely interrelated. The Government is drawn mainly from, and is accountable to, the House of Commons, and the House fulfils the task of scrutinising and legitimising the Government and its actions in its capacity (collectively and individually) as a representative assembly, such a task carried out largely, though by no means exclusively, within the context of party politics. In short, the central function of the House, collectively and individually, is that of scrutiny. It is a task complicated for the House as a collective body by the elements within it, and for the individual Member by his role as the representative of constituency and other interests and as a party member. It is an intricate relationship to which we have attempted to provide some structure in Figure 4.2.

If one were to seek to provide a simple, one-word description of the central role of the House of Commons, derived from the functions identified above, then the most apt word would probably be 'watchdog'. Collectively and individually, the House watches the actions of Government: collectively through the parties within the House (publicly scrutinised by the Opposition parties, privately and sometimes publicy by the Government party), and individually by Members as representatives of constituency interests, of local and national parties, of their conception of the national interest, and to some extent of their own consciences. In practice, the extent to which the House operates as an efficient watchdog, and the degree to which it is or would be prepared to bare its fangs and actually bite, is a matter of some contention. Some argue that its teeth have for all intents and purposes been pulled; it may bark, but it cannot stop a resolute Government. Others by contrast contend that as long as the House remains the ultimate power to say 'no' to the Government, to deny legitimisation to it and its measures, Government will respond to its influence. It is a power viewed by some as akin to that of the nuclear deterrent: it is not designed for regular use, but the holder of it is listened to with a certain respect by those who may be on the receiving end. And, like the nuclear deterrent, it is an issue on which proponents and opponents are strongly divided.

The House of Commons itself does not and cannot govern. It does not and cannot control the Government in the sense of directing its policies and determining its composition, as it did in the period between the two Reform Acts in the nineteenth century. How, and the extent to which, it can and does continue to scrutinise and influence both the legislative measures and the executive actions of Government are issues which we shall explore in the following chapters. Or, reverting to our canine analogy, we shall seek to discover whether the watchdog is alive and active, slumbering, suffering from a terminal illness, or in need of dental surgery.

NOTES

1   A.H. Birch, *Representative and Responsible Government* (Allen & Unwin, 1964), pp. 77 and 166.
2   Philip Goodhart, MP, 'What's really wrong with the Commons', *Crossbow*, (4) 10, Spring 1960.
3   Keith Ovenden, 'Policy and Self-Perception: Some Aspects of Parliamentary Behaviour', in D. Leondard and V. Herman (eds), *The Backbencher and Parliament* (Macmillan, 1972), p. 173.
4   Ovenden, p. 173.
5   See J. Harvey and L. Bather, *The British Constitution* (Macmillan, 1963), pp. 151—4.
6   Harold J. Laski, *Reflections on the Constitution* (Manchester University Press, 1951), p. 36.
7   John P. Mackintosh, 'The Influence of Backbenchers', in Richard Tames (ed.), *People and Politics* (Knight, 1975), p. 114.
8   The Chief Whip is one of the Prime Minister's principal advisers in this respect; the Chief Whip listens to speeches in the House, especially those of new Members, and conveys his comments on the ability of Members in debate to the Prime Minister, either in conversation or in writing. Robert Mellish, MP, to author.
9   Lord Home to author.
10   Sir Nigel Fisher, MP, *Iain Macleod* (Deutsch, 1973), pp. 80—2; Sir Harold Wilson, MP, to author.
11   As Sir Harold Wilson observed: 'Clearly a Prime Minister would give a lot of weight to parliamentary performance whether considering the appointment of a backbencher to junior office, or planning promotion from the most junior ranks to, say, the position of Minister of State . . . In considering junior Ministers for promotion, ability to handle Questions is probably even more important than ability to make a set speech and no less important is a junior Minister's ability to absorb briefs and handle the kind of matters which are raised in Standing Committee. Probably with the recent development of Select Committees on specific issues, a Minister's performance there could also advance or retard his promotion.' Sir Harold Wilson to author, August 1978.
12   Bruce Headey, *British Cabinet Ministers* (Allen & Unwin, 1974), p. 90.
13   Confidential source to author.
14   Charles A. Beard and John D. Lewis, 'Representative Government in Evolution', in John C. Wahlke and Heinz Eulau (eds), *Legislative Behaviour: A Reader in Theory and Research* (The Free Press of Glencoe, 1959), pp. 22—3.

15   J.-J. Rousseau, *The Social Contract* (first published 1762).
16   The nearest in practice to Rousseau's concept would appear to be parish meetings.
17   Beard and Lewis, p. 23.
18   He believed that electoral participation, unless accompanied by a real sense of belonging to a commonwealth and by actually having an impact on social life, was an empty gesture, leading to alienation and indifference. Shlomo Avineri, *Hegel's Theory of the Modern State* (Cambridge University Press, 1972), p. 213.
19   See Birch, *Representative and Responsible Government*, and, by the same author, *Representation* (Macmillan, 1972).
20   The number was increased from 630 to 635 at the February 1974 election. Constituency boundaries are currently (1980) under revision by the Boundary Commissioners.
21   Women aged thirty and above were given the vote in 1918; the voting age for women was brought into line with that for men — twenty-one years — in 1928. (The voting age was lowered to eighteen years by the 1969 Representation of the People Act.)
22   In 1951, the Conservative Party obtained 13,718,199 votes (48 per cent of the votes cast) and 321 seats; the Labour Party obtained 13,948,883 votes (48.8 per cent) and 295 seats. In February 1974, Labour obtained 11,654,726 votes (37.2 per cent of votes cast) and 301 seats; the Conservatives obtained 11,963,207 votes (38.2 per cent) and 296 seats.
23   See Colin Mellors, *The British MP* (Saxon House, 1978), and also Michael Rush, 'The Members of Parliament', in S.A. Walkland (ed.), *The House of Commons in the Twentieth Century* (Oxford University Press, 1979), pp. 69—123.
24   See the comments of Robert Dowse, 'Representation, General Elections and Democracy', *Parliamentary Affairs*, 15, 1961—2, pp. 331—46.
25   A.H. Birch, 'The Theory of Representation and Practice', in S.E. Finer (ed.), *Adversary Politics and Electoral Reform* (Wigram, 1975), p. 57.
26   On Labour's concept of intra-party democracy, see Birch, *Representative and Responsible Government*, pp. 122—30.
27   One problem, of course, is that the local MP may be a Minister. This is arguably a disadvantage if the problem involves Government policy, and an advantage if it involves a point of detail (because the absence of conflict with Government policy is coupled with Minister's influence). Constituency considerations also may influence a Minister's policy decisions. See Roy Gregory, 'Executive Power and Constituency Representation in United Kingdom Politics', *Political Studies*, 28 (1), March 1980, pp. 63—83.
28   See, for example, Robert E. Dowse, 'The MP and his Surgery', in D. Leonard and V. Herman, *The Backbencher and Parliament*, pp. 46—60; and John Grant, MP, *Member of Parliament* (Michael Joseph, 1974), *passim*. See also Ronald Munroe, 'The Member of Parliament as Representative: The View from the Constituency', *Political Studies*, 25 (4), December 1977, pp. 577—87.
29   Cited in Jenny Jeger, 'The Image of the MP', in John Mackintosh (ed.), *People and Parliament* (Saxon House, 1978), p. 12.
30   Dowse, p. 57.
31   Quoted in 'The case of Flora Ginetio', A. King and A. Sloman (eds), *Westminster and Beyond* (Macmillan, 1973), pp. 26—7.

32 Brian Walden, MP, interviewed in 'The Parliamentary Process', BBC Radio 3, broadcast 25 January 1976.
33 Grant, p. 127.
34 The correlation between electors and consumers is not an exact one, of course, as not all consumers are electors, though all electors are consumers.
35 Samuel H. Beer, *Modern British Politics* (Faber & Faber, 1965).
36 See, for example, Philip Norton, *Conservative Dissidents* (Temple Smith, 1978), p. 134, and J.J. Richardson and A.G. Jordan, *Governing Under Pressure* (Martin Robertson, 1979), pp. 124–6.
37 Leslie Hale, MP, 'The Backbencher', *The Parliamentarian*, 47, 1966, p. 192.
38 See David Butler and A. Sloman, *British Political Facts 1900–79* (Macmillan, 1980), p. 221; and D. Butler and D. Kavanagh, *The British General Election of 1979* (Macmillan, 1980), pp. 280–3.
39 See Anthony King, 'The MPs' New Freedom', *New Society*, 14 March 1974, pp. 639–40.
40 See Philip Norton, *Conservative Dissidents*, ch. 7.
41 Bryan Gould, MP, 'The MP and Constituency Cases', in Mackintosh, *People and Parliament*, p. 92.
42 Letter to Sir Hector Langrishe, *The Works of Edmund Burke*, Vol. III, Bohn's ed., p. 334, quoted in James Hogan, *Elections and Representation* (Cork University Press, 1945), p. 159n.
43 *The Times Guide to the House of Commons May 1979* (Times Books, 1979), p. 275 and errata slip.
44 Nor is it based in any sense on proportion to the strength of the interests in the country as a whole. As Hegel realised, the return of Members with such interests is the product more of chance than design in a system of free elections. See Hegel, *The Philosophy of Right* (Oxford University Press, 1967), p. 202.
45 A.J.P. Taylor, *English History 1914–45* (Penguin ed., 1970), p. 552.
46 See also John P. Mackintosh, MP, 'The Member of Parliament as Representative or as Delegate', *The Parliamentarian*, 52 (1), January 1971, pp. 14–21.
47 Dr David Kerr, MP, 'The Changing Role of the Backbencher', *The Parliamentarian*, 50, 1969, p. 9.
48 Professor Esmond Wright, talking in 'The Parliamentary Process: Government and Opposition', BBC Radio 3, broadcast 8 February 1976.
49 Quintin Hogg, *The Purpose of Parliament* (Blandford Press, n.d.), p. 3.
50 Brian Smith, *Policy Making in British Government* (Martin Robertson, 1976), p. 82; Bernard Crick makes the same point.
51 Walter Bagehot, *The English Constitution* (Fontana ed., 1963), pp. 150–3.
52 *House of Commons Debates*, 909, c. 915.
53 K.C. Wheare, *Legislatures*, 2nd ed. (Oxford University Press, 1968), p. 1.
54 On this, see also Michael L. Mezey, *Comparative Legislatures* (Duke University Press, 1979), pp. 270–4.
55 Kenneth Mackenzie, *The English Parliament* (Penguin, 1968 ed.), p. 22.
56 Philip Norton, 'The House of Commons in the 1970s: Three Views on Reform', *Hull Papers in Politics No. 3* (Hull University Politics Department, 1978), p. 4.
57 Bill Jones, 'The House of Commons', in Bill Jones and D. Kavanagh (eds), *British Politics Today* (Manchester University Press, 1979), p. 71.

58   This paragraph is based largely on Philip Norton, 'Government Defeats in the House of Commons: Myth and Reality, *Public Law*, Winter 1978, pp; 360—78.

59   A.H. Hanson and M. Walles, *Governing Britain* (Fontana, 1975), p. 69.

60   *House of Commons Debates*, CL, c. 49.

61   See Norton, 'Government Defeats in the House of Commons: Myth and Reality'.

62   See the comments in ch. 5 below. (Note also the view expressed by Bob Jessop, as cited in ch. 9 below.)

63   See David Butler and Uwe Kitzinger, *The 1975 Referendum* (Macmillan, 1976), and Anthony King, *Britain Says Yes* (American Enterprise Institute, 1977).

64   See the comments of Mackintosh, *People and Parliament*, pp. 2—3.

65   Sir Ivor Jennings, *The British Constitution*, 3rd ed. (Cambridge University Press, 1950), p. 80.

66   See Norton, *Conservative Dissidents*, pp. 263—4, for comments on such instances in the 1970—4 Parliament.

67   Michael Stewart, MP, talking in 'The Parliamentary Process: Government and Opposition', BBC Radio 3, broadcast 19 February 1976.

68   Bernard Crick, 'Parliament and the Matter of Britain', in B. Crick (ed.), *Essays on Reform 1967* (Oxford University Press, 1967), p. 208.

69   See O. Hood Phillips, *Constitutional and Administrative Law*, 5th ed. (Sweet & Maxwell, 1973), pp. 96—9 and chs 5 and 6; also E.C.S. Wade and G. Phillips *Constitutional Law*, 8th ed. (Longman, 1970), p. 153.

70   O. Hood Phillips, p. 97.

71   *House of Commons Debates*, 443, c. 1195—8, 1221—2, and *The Times*, 1 November 1947.

72   *House of Commons Debates*, 936, c. 332—460, and Alan Doig, 'Self-discipline and the House of Commons', *Parliamentary Affairs*, 32 (3), Summer 1979, pp. 248—67.

5
Scrutiny and influence: the legislative process

Legislation is defined by various dictionaries as 'the act of making laws'. Unfortunately, such a definition does not take us very far. When we do seek to go further, the position becomes a complex one. For one thing, the term 'law' itself is not easy to conceptualise, and the process by which it is 'made' not easy to delineate. It is probably popularly assumed that Acts of Parliament constitute 'law', and that such law is 'made' by Parliament. In practice, there is more to law than Acts of Parliament, and whatever else it is, it cannot really be said to be made by Parliament.

A definition of the concept of law cannot be attempted with any precision. For example, the distinguished constitutional lawyer S.A. de Smith said of administrative law that:

> it is to be found in public and private acts of Parliament and subordinate legislation. Some is embodied in internal regulations for the civil service, some in departmental circulars, some in unwritten constitutional conventions. Some can be extracted from decisions of courts and statutory tribunals.[1]

Given the variety of sources from which it may emanate, an accurate conceptual definition, as S.A. Walkland has effectively argued, is not really possible.[2] Only by concentrating upon one particular and generally recognisable form of law is it possible to produce a definition which, though necessarily restrictive and arbitrary, can be viewed within a conceptual framework. For our purposes, it is probably most useful to take 'law', *for the moment,* as referring solely to statutory law – that is, Public General Acts of Parliament, Private (and hybrid) Acts of Parliament, and statutory instruments – which is popularly held to constitute legislation. A further advantage of this definition is that the end products of legislation, as Stuart Walkland has observed, are easily recognisable: they are Acts of Parliament as published in the *Statutes Revised,* and the contents of the collected annual volumes of statutory instruments.[3]

A case could be made for saying that prior to the Reform Acts of the nineteenth century, Parliament did 'make' law. In a still highly localised society, 'which wished to make marginal adjustments to the reigning state of affairs, but which could not conceive of consciously directed, broad social and economic reform',[4] it was individual Members of Parliament, conversant with local conditions and their personal interests, who could bring about piecemeal reform — be it the enclosure of land, the building of canals, the provision of local railways, or new powers for local authorities — through the procedure of the quasi-judicial Private Bill. Throughout the eighteenth century, most of the Commons' legislative work consisted of passing such private measures. 'Though much of this legislation', Ronald Butt has observed, 'was of national importance, it was not regarded in this light and was enacted with a view to the requirements of a private world — and by the initiative of private Members.'[5] The Government of the day played little part in this process — its chief duty, according to Dicey, was not the passing of laws, but the guidance of national policy — and even on those occasions when it considered it necessary to introduce a legislative measure of its own, it could not necessarily ensure its passage.

In the nineteenth century, this legislative function, as we have seen, was to be transferred effectively via party to the Cabinet. The growth of a mass electorate and the consequent growth of organised mass-membership parties, the demands of the growing electorate, the increased specialisation of an industrial society (with its increasingly specialised components forming pressure groups to protect their interests, especially towards the end of the nineteenth century), the nation's military and commercial commitments abroad — all contributed to the pressure for more legislation, measures of *public* policy, the initiative for which had, of necessity, passed to Government. In order to ensure the passage of such legislation, the Government needed not only an overall majority but precedence in the parliamentary timetable as well. As we have seen, the years following the Second Reform Act were to produce both increasingly cohesive party voting in the Commons — with Government defeats being few and far between — and parliamentary procedure re-organised in the Government's favour. Members of Parliament, now returned as representatives under the labels of political parties, were relegated to a secondary role. The initiative to introduce measures and the freedom of action to determine the fate of Bills largely, though not wholly, left them. They had neither the knowledge nor the facilities to prepare the increasingly technical and complex Bills that were becoming a feature of parliamentary life. 'Civil servants came increasingly to do for governments what Parliamentary clerks had formerly done for MPs, and the initiative for the introduction of all major legislation passed to the executive.'[6] Although some writers continue to list 'legislation' as one of the functions of the House of Commons, it is a function which for all intents and purposes has not been exercised by the House in the twentieth century. As a consequence of the developments of the last century, it is now, as some members of the Study of Parliament Group have baldly observed, 'pre-eminently a function of government'.[7] The Commons still has an important role to play in the legislative process, but it is not one associated with 'making' law.

Government Bills

What, then, is the House of Commons' role in the contemporary legislative process? Confining ourselves for the moment to Public General Bills introduced by the Government (which, compared with the amount of time spent on Public General Bills introduced by private Members and on Private Bills, dominate the parliamentary timetable), the process by which law is 'made' may be said to comprise a number of different stages, not all of which are simple or distinct: initiation (or input), formulation, scrutiny, legitimisation, application, and feedback.[8] Of these stages, the House of Commons plays a leading role in only two, those of scrutiny and legitimisation, and in the former (and more recently to some degree in the latter) its effectiveness has been much questioned. By the time both stages are reached, legislation has largely, though not fully, been 'made'.

The initiation of Government legislation may be the product of pressure from interest groups, or party promises (especially those contained in an election manifesto), of recommendations from Royal Commissions or committees of inquiry, of crises at home or abroad, or of what Ministers may perceive as being in the national interest or to their possible electoral advantage. A number of Bills (such as the Finance and Consolidated Fund Bills) have of necessity to be introduced each year as well.

Interest groups, especially sectional interest (or producer) groups, have regular, well-established contact with the relevant Government Departments; indeed, many have effectively been co-opted into the decision-making process through having been given representation (sometimes statutory) on various governmental or quasi-governmental bodies.[9] The groups are often dependent upon Government for various actions or measures that would benefit their members; the Government, for its part, is often dependent upon such groups for advice, information and help in implementing policies. Agreed legislative measures may be the result of bargaining between the two.

Each party fights a general election on a platform of promised actions as detailed in its election manifesto (actions which may be based upon party philosophy, promises to certain groups, or what is considered to be electorally popular, and often a blend of all three), and the early part of a Parliament is often devoted to giving legislative effect to such promises. (Indeed, Governments attach great importance to implementing manifesto promises, even though their successful implementation carries no guarantee of electoral success at the succeeding general election.)[10]

A number of important measures have been introduced as a result of the recommendations of various Royal Commissions or committees of inquiry; for example, the Family Law Reform Act of 1969, which lowered the age of majority to eighteen years, was the result of the Government's acceptance of the recommendations of the Latey Commission.

Economic or political crises at home or abroad may also motivate the Government to introduce emergency measures: for instance, the unilateral declaration of independence by Rhodesia in 1965 led the Government to introduce the Southern Rhodesia Bill in that year; the crisis in Northern Ireland provoked the Government of Mr Heath to bring in the Northern Ireland (Temporary Provisions) Bill in 1972; and the strike by executive and clerical staff in Scottish courts in March 1979 resulted in the introduction of the Administration of Justice (Emergency Provisions) (Scotland) Bill.

On occasion, a Government has been accused of introducing a measure for some clear partisan advantage over its opponents. For example, the Labour Government was much criticised for the introduction of the House of Commons (Redistribution of Seats) Bill in 1969, which sought to absolve the Home Secretary of the duty to give effect to the recommendations of the Boundary Commissioners (in the event, the Bill was emasculated in the House of Lords); a number of the Bill's critics contended that it amounted to an attempt to alter the electoral map of the country to the advantage of the Labour Party.

Some Bills may themselves originate as a consequence of previous legislation. Two measures introduced by the Government in 1972, enacted as the European Communities Act and the Northern Ireland (Temporary Provisions) Act, have in one form or another been the progenitors of much later legislation.

A number of other sources may be identified as being responsible for the Government's decision to introduce legislative measures. The House of Commons is rarely likely to be among them. Although the House can still exercise certain powers in the legislative sphere and can influence the early deliberations of Government, and although the Government may occasionally introduce legislation after accepting some of the recommendations of a Select Committee (though examples are not always easy to find), its power and influence are largely negative. It is difficult to recall any instance in recent years of pressure from the House resulting in the Government's introduction of a measure of any significance.

In the formulative stage, the Commons plays little formal role. A legislative proposal will be put forward by a Department following discussions between the Minister and his officials, and will be circulated to interested parties, including the Treasury, which to confirm its estimated cost. It will be considered by the Cabinet or relevant Cabinet Committee, and (essentially to ensure that the measure as drafted accords with the decision of the Cabinet, and to gain a slot in the legislative programme for the session or the Parliament) by the Legislation Committee of the Cabinet.[11] In this process, legislation can largely, if not wholly, be said to be 'made': it is drafted by Parliamentary Counsel, discussed, decided upon by Government, and put forward in the form that the Government hopes it will be enacted as an Act of Parliament. It may be later amended or even 'unmade', but if it does emerge as an Act, its substance may be said to have been determined largely, and often wholly, at this stage.

Although the House of Commons may play little formal part at this point, it is not altogether ignored. 'In considering projected legislation or policy', as Lord Morrison of Lambeth noted,

> a sensible Government will take all opinions into account before becoming committed, and so it is likely that modifications will have been made before the publication of Bills. This may be described as the process of concession in advance of parliamentary proceedings, though sometimes Ministers may prefer to save up concessions until Parliament is dealing with the matter.[12]

The means by which the opinions of the House are canvassed, as either a collective entity or its component parts, are varied. The Government Chief Whip, although not usually a member, attends meetings of the Cabinet and advises it of likely parliamentary reaction, especially reaction within the parliamentary party, to a proposed measure. If the reaction is likely to prove unfavourable, and perhaps to generate bad publicity, the Cabinet may decide to compromise or even not to proceed with a measure; for example, the Macmillan Cabinet decided on two occasions not to proceed with a measure to abolish resale price maintenance because of known hostility to such a move on the Conservative back benches,[13] and in 1969 the advice from the Chief Whip was one of the contributory factors (though by no means the sole one) to the Wilson Cabinet's decision not to proceed with its proposed Bill to reform industrial relations.[14] A Minister may also consult with the relevant parliamentary party committee or its officers before bringing a Bill before the House, or at least before it is discussed on Second Reading. Indeed, the party committees are usually the first forums within Parliament in which measures are discussed, and the views expressed there may be such as to influence a Minister to introduce amendments, or to demonstrate to the whip who attends that the Bill may not have a smooth passage when it does come before the House. Between them, the whips and the party committees (especially on the Conservative side of the House) provide a valuable early-warning system of possible trouble within the parliamentary party.[15]

In order to sound out the opinion of the House itself (as well as that of other bodies), the Government in recent years has made greater use of discussion papers (known as Green Papers) and papers outlining its proposals (White Papers). Debates on White Papers, though still few in number, provide Members with an opportunity to express their opinions in advance of the introduction of the proposed legislation, and take place usually on 'take note' or 'welcome' motions. Among important issues discussed in this way have been reform of the House of Lords (1968), industrial relations (the Government's White Paper *In Place of Strife* in 1969), Northern Ireland (1973), continuing membership of the European Communities (1975), devolution (1976),[16] and, annually, the Government's expenditure proposals. Another attempt to ensure that the House plays some role in the formulation (and indeed the initiation) of legislation has been the use of pre-legislative Select Committees, designed to examine subjects with a view to recommending legislation. However, the use of such committees has been comparatively rare. They were established to consider such issues as censorship of the theatre (1966–7, a joint committee with the Lords), corporation tax (1970–1), tax credit (1972–3), a wealth tax (1974–5), and, at the Government's request after a Private Member's Bill on the subject had already received a Second Reading, sex discrimination (1972–3), and have not achieved a great deal. As the First Report from the Select Committee on Procedure, 1977–8, put it, the experience of the committees 'has not been one of uniform success', and the Committee expressed the view that their value was 'probably greatest in areas outside acute party controversy and where there will not be a strong Government attitude towards the final Bill'.[17] In short, the House as a collective entity cannot expect to wrest domination of the initiative and formulative stages from Government and those co-opted into the decision-making process. The role of the House, collectively and individually, is essentially a reactive one, and its reaction is one among several that the Government will normally be concerned to consider.

Once the Government has decided upon a measure, it brings it before the House. The first stage is that of First Reading (see Figure 5.1). This is a formality, with the title of the Bill being read out; it is then automatically ordered to be printed, and the date for Second Reading appointed. (It is after publication and before Second Reading that party committees usually discuss it.) The Second Reading is the first occasion when a Bill is discussed on the floor of the House, and is reserved for debate on the principle of the measure. Although the debate is an

Stage	Where taken	Comments
First Reading	On floor of the House	Formal introduction only. No debate
Second Reading	On floor of the House (non-contentious Bills may be referred to a Second Reading Committee)	Debate on the principle of the measure
(Money Resolution)	(On floor of the House)	
Committee	Standing Committee (constitutional and certain other measures may be taken in Committee of the Whole House)	Considered clause by clause. Amendments can be made
Report	On floor of the House (no Report stage if Bill reported unamended from Committee of the Whole House)	Reported to the House by the Committee. Amendments can be made
Third Reading	On floor of House (no debate unless six Members table motion beforehand)	Final approval of the Bill. Debate confined to its content
Lords amendments	On floor of the House	Any amendments made by the House of Lords considered, usually on motion to agree or disagree with them

Figure 5.1 Legislative stages in the House of Commons

opportunity for the House as a collective entity to express its opinion, its structure is based on the existence of the component parts of the House, the Government and the Opposition, and, to a lesser extent, other Opposition parties. The Minister responsible for the Bill moves its Second Reading; his opposite number then rises to speak for the Opposition (and may move an amendment for rejection);[18] backbenchers are then called from each side of the House, usually alternately; an Opposition front-bench spokesman winds up for the Opposition; and a Minister winds up for the Government. If the Bill is opposed, a division then follows.

Although the Government is almost always assured of carrying Second Reading — since 1905 only two Government Bills (in 1924 and 1977) have been lost on Second Reading[19] — the debate and the vote are more than a mere formality. The Government has to explain the measure and defend it against any criticism levelled at it from the Opposition benches or (worse still, from the Government's point of view) its own back benches. Effective criticism by the Opposition, or a sizeable dissenting vote by a number of its own supporters, can result in embarrassing publicity for the Government, publicity which it would prefer to do without. The reduced majority of eight on the Second Reading of the European Communities Bill in 1972 was a serious blow to the Government and especially to the Prime Minister, Mr Heath; immediately following the vote, some observers considered the future of the Bill to be in doubt.[20] Speeches by Opposition MPs or Government backbenchers sometimes (albeit not often) influence Ministers to introduce subsequent amendments, either in order to dissipate criticism or, quite simply, because they have been persuaded by the force of the argument put forward;[21] as we noted in Chapter 4, Ministers do not always approach debates with closed minds. The chief value of Second Reading, though, probably lies in the fact that it constitutes the first public scrutiny of the measure, and knowledge of this operates in advance, contributing to 'the process of concession in advance of parliamentary proceedings'.

Almost all Bills go through this Second Reading procedure. The exceptions are some non-controversial Bills and exclusively Scottish Bills. When a measure which is essentially non-contentious has been printed, a Minister may propose to the House that it be referred to what is known as a Second Reading Committee. The purpose of the Committee is to consider a Bill and to recommend whether or not it should receive a Second Reading. When the Committee has reported to the House, a note of its recommendation is appended to the order for the Second Reading of the Bill, and the Second Reading taken without amendment or debate. (Similarly, a Bill which Mr Speaker certifies as relating exclusively to Scotland can, on the motion of a Minister, be referred to the Scottish Grand Committee.[22] The Committee considers the Bill in relation to its principle, and then reports this fact to the House. When the order for Second Reading comes up, a Minister may move that the Bill be committed to a Scottish Standing Committee, and, if agreed, the Bill is then deemed to have been read a Second time.) The use of Second Reading Committees helps to facilitate the passage of measures on which there is general agreement — a Bill can be blocked from being referred to a Second Reading Committee by twenty or more Members rising in their places (ten in the case of Bills certified as exclusively Scottish) — and the Procedure Committee in 1978 recorded that there appeared to be general satisfaction with the way the procedure was operating; it felt that more Bills might be recommended for such treatment, including Private Members' Bills,[23] a recommendation accepted (on an experimental basis for one session only) in October 1979.

After a Bill has received a Second Reading (and, in the case of Bills involving a charge on public funds, a Money Resolution),[24] it is committed as a matter of course to a Standing Committee,[25] unless a motion is tabled and passed to commit it to a Committee of the Whole House. Standing Committees each comprise between sixteen and fifty Members, the membership being commensurate with the party composition of the House. Each Committee is known by a letter (Standing Committee A, B, C, etc.), except for two Scottish Standing Committees, which deal with Bills relating exclusively to Scotland. Members are nominated to serve on a Committee to deal with each Bill (there is no permanent membership, and no specialisation by a Committee, except for the Scottish ones),[26] and the Committee of Selection which nominates them is required to have regard to the qualifications of Members in respect of the Bills to be considered. Each is chaired by a senior MP drawn from what is known as the Chairman's Panel,[27] and meets in a room on the committee corridor on the floor above the main floor housing both chambers; as a result, sending a Bill to Standing Committee is known as sending it 'upstairs'. It is at this stage that a Bill is supposed to receive detailed scrutiny. Amendments are considered (as long as they do not conflict with the principle of the measure, agreed to on Second Reading), and each clause has to be approved on a 'stand part' motion, that is, that the clause (or the clause as amended) stand part of the Bill. Discussion will usually be based upon the adversary relationship between the Government and Opposition; the relevant Minister or his deputy, his Parliamentary Private Secretary, and a whip, are as a rule among the Government members appointed to the Committee, with an official spokesman and a whip being among Opposition Members. The purpose of the whips is to maximise attendance of their supporters, to reason with possible dissenters on their own side, and to alert front-benchers to likely problems.[28] Voting is usually on party lines.

The effectiveness of Standing Committees in scrutinising Bills is a point of some debate. On the positive side, it has been pointed out that debate is less formal than on the floor of the House and is less well-publicised, arguably making Government supporters less inhibited in expressing criticism; debate is often on detail rather than principle, arguably making the divide between party philosophies less relevant; and the confines of a small Committee, meeting on multiple occasions helps to keep a Minister on his toes.

> For hour after hour and for week after week a Minister may be required to defend his Bill against attack from others who may be only slightly less knowledgeable than himself. His departmental brief may be full and his grasp of the subject considerable but even so he needs to be constantly on the alert and any defects he or his policy reveals will be very quickly exploited by his political opponents.[29]

The small size of the Committees may also make the Government vulnerable to defeat; this was to be the case especially in the 1970s, when intra-party dissent by Government backbenchers on some occasions, and a combination of opposition parties against a minority Government on others, resulted in multiple defeats, especially in the 1974—9 Parliament.[30] On the other side of the argument, critics point out that Standing Committees have limited information and resources and that the Government's ranks usually, if not always, hold firm, with the Government accepting but a small percentage of the amendments moved by Opposition spokesmen and backbenchers. As Professor John Griffith revealed in his work *Parliamentary Scrutiny of Government Bills*, only 171 of the 3510 amendments moved by private Members in the three sessions he studied were agreed to.[31] Though rarely employed, proceedings in Standing Committees may also be subject to guillotine motions. As a result of these factors, various proposals for reforming Committee procedure have been advanced. The most important recommendation has been that Standing Committees be given power to question witnesses and request the submission of written evidence. This found favour with the Procedure Committee in its 1978 Report, and, following a well-supported Early Day Motion on the subject tabled by Edward du Cann in July 1980, the Leader of the House, Mr St John-Stevas, recommended that it be tried on an experimental basis — Committees on certain Bills being given the power to summon witnesses and evidence — in the 1980—1 session. This was agreed to by the House in October 1980.[32]

Most Bills are considered in Standing Committee. A number, because of their importance, have their Committee stage on the floor of the House. Important constitutional Bills, such as the Parliament (No. 2) Bill in 1969, the European Communities Bill in 1972, and the Scotland and Wales Bill in 1976—7, are taken in Committee of the Whole House, as are the annual Consolidated Fund and Appropriation Bills. The annual Finance Bill is taken, in part, in Committee of the Whole, and, for the more detailed provisions, in Standing Committee. A number of important, politically contentious measures are sometimes taken in Committee of the Whole as well, the 1971 Industrial Relations Bill being a good example. On occasion, Bills which require speedy passage, and for which there is general support in the House, may also be taken on the floor of the House: the procedure saves time because a Standing Committee does not have to be appointed or to sit, and because a Bill taken in Committee of the Whole and reported without amendment does not have a Report stage. The 1972 Northern Ireland (Temporary Provisions) Bill, though a constitutional measure itself (imposing direct rule in Northern Ireland), completed its Committee stage and remaining stages in one all-night sitting.

The advantages and disadvantages of taking Bills in Committee of the Whole (the standard practice until 1907) are various. It has been argued that it is to the Government's advantage, since the majority of Members taking part in divisions are unlikely to have much interest in the business being divided upon and will hence be more responsive to the whips; Standing Committees, by comparison, often comprise Members with special interest in a measure, who may be prepared to pit their views against those of the Government. 'Though in the last resort the Government can always use the whip, either in committee or in the House, it is generally found that it has to give way to the "sense of the committee" more often than it would have to do if it had the docile majority of the House as a whole.'[33] If a Bill is opposed by some of the Government's own supporters, who may press to be represented on Standing Committee, the Government may opt to take it on the floor of the House to avoid the possibility of defeat, as happened, for example, with the 1964 Resale Prices Bill.[34] Conversely, it may on occasion be to the Government's disadvantage to take a Bill on the floor of the House, since such a measure receives greater publicity, and, more important, it eats into the Government's parliamentary time. If a measure runs into serious and prolonged opposition, the Government can move a guillotine motion. Such a move is usually politically contentious, and may attract adverse publicity. 'A guillotine both anticipates and invites trouble so a Government will not resort to it lightly.'[35] Without a guillotine motion, a measure can be lost. In 1969, the Government was not sure if it could carry such a motion for the Parliament (No. 2) Bill, and eventually abandoned the measure; it needed to clear the parliamentary timetable for other matters. In 1977, the Government lost a guillotine motion for the Scotland and Wales Bill and decided not to proceed with the measure in its original form. The experience of recent years has been such as to suggest that taking Committee stage on the floor of the House is far from trouble-free for the Government. From the point of view of Members generally, it gives more of them a greater opportunity to involve themselves in proceedings than is usually possible at Report stage.

When a Bill has completed its Committee stage, it is then reported to the House and has what is known as its Report stage. (The exceptions are Bills reported from Committee of the Whole without amendment; they proceed straight to their Third Reading.) At this stage, the House considers whether it wishes to make any further amendments. The Government often makes use of the occasion to introduce amendments promised during Committee proceedings. Indeed, Report stage bears many similarities to the Committee stage. The dissimilarities are that only amendments are considered on Report (there is no discussion of each clause on a 'stand part' motion); Members can speak only once on the same question (unlike in Committee, where multiple contributions are possible); and the Speaker may use his powers of selection to ensure that proceedings are not a repetition of what took place in Committee.[36] Report stage is useful to the Government, not only for introducing amendments promised earlier, but also for seeking to have reversed any defeats incurred in Standing Committee. Governments not infrequently accept defeats suffered in Committee,[37] but they may if they wish attempt to have them reversed, at least *de facto* if not *de jure,* on Report.[38] (In the 1970s, though, there were a number of occasions when Government attempts at reversal were unsuccessful.) Bills which have been considered by a Second Reading Committee or in the Scottish Grand Committee may have their Report stage taken in a Standing Committee or in the Scottish Grand Committee respectively rather than on the floor of the House (a motion so to commit a Bill can be blocked by twenty or more Members rising in their places), but this procedure is rarely employed.

When a Bill has completed its Report stage, it proceeds to its Third Reading. This is when the Commons gives its final approval to the measure. Except in the case of certain money Bills, Third Reading can be, and often is, taken 'forthwith' when Report stage is concluded.[39] As a result of a procedural change introduced in 1967, it is now taken formally, the question being put without debate unless six Members have tabled in advance an amendment (either a straightforward amendment to reject the Bill or a reasoned amendment for rejection) or a motion that the question 'be not put forthwith'. In order to ensure a debate, Members not infrequently employ this procedure.

If a Bill originates in the Commons, as most important and all money Bills do, it is sent upon completion of Third Reading to the House of Lords. In the Upper House, it passes through stages analagous to those in the Commons. If it is agreed with amendments, the Bill is returned to the Commons with a request that the Lower House concur in the changes. In the House, amendments to the Lords amendments may be tabled. If none is forthcoming, the Lords amendments are considered individually on a motion either to agree, or to disagree with them. If the House disagrees with a Lords amendment, it is unusual for the Lords to insist upon their amendment (though they may offer further or alternative amendments in the light of the rejection of the original one); if the Upper House persists in its amendment, and agreement between the two Houses cannot be reached, the Commons can make use of its powers under the Parliament Acts of 1911 and 1949 to present a Bill for Royal Assent after one year and in a new session without the concurrence of the Lords. Once a Bill has received the assent of both Houses, or is passed under the provisions of the Parliament Acts,[40] it receives the Royal Assent, in itself a formal procedure. The moment it receives the Royal Assent, it becomes an Act of Parliament, the law of the land.

The dispatch of a Bill for the Royal Assent after it has gone through the stages detailed in Figure 5.1 constitutes the completion of the Commons' most significant contribution to the legislative process. By assenting to a measure, the House, as a collective entity, is giving its approval on behalf of those whom it is elected to represent; it is the body with authority to give legitimisation to a Bill on behalf of the electors. (In practice, as we have seen in considering the Commons' representative function, the position is somewhat more complex than the formality implies.) Prior to giving its assent, the House is deemed to fulfil the function of scrutiny, examining through debate the principle of the measure (on Second Reading, and the final product on Third Reading) and its specific provision (in Committee and usually, though not always, on Report). The extent to which it can and does effectively fulfil this function — given the dominance of one of, and the competition between, the parties in the House — is a point of contention, one to which we shall have cause to return later.

Although this is the main stage at which the House exercises the functions of scrutiny and legitimisation, it is not the only stage, as we shall see. Nor is the House of Commons the only body which, in practice, exercises these functions. The House is the body formally responsible for scrutinising Bills, but once the Government has introduced a Bill, it comes in for scrutiny by interests affected by it (which are likely to have been consulted at the formulative stage, but are not usually made privy to the specific contents of the measure proposed); as it passes through the House, interested bodies will keep an eye on its progress, perhaps pressing the Government for its amendment, or responding to amendments that are introduced. Thus, while a Bill is going through the House, the Government may have to contend with pressure from both within and without Parliament, and, not infrequently, with an alliance of external interests and Members. For example, when the Heath Government introduced its Industry Bill in 1972, a number of the Bill's provisions were criticised strongly both by the Confederation of British Industry (CBI) and by a number of Conservative backbenchers, some of whom had connections with the CBI or close links with industrial interests. As a result of this pressure, public and private, from both the leaders of the CBI and some of its own supporters, the Government proved willing to amend the measure.[41]

The Government may also find itself cross-pressured as a result of the stands taken by interested parties within and outside the Commons. In 1976, the Labour Government's Dock Work Regulation Bill ran into trouble in the Commons: it was opposed by Opposition parties and by some of its own backbenchers, and this at a time when the Government had formally lost its overall majority. The Government, though, was widely believed to be under strong pressure to persevere with the Bill from the Transport and General Workers' Union, whose general secretary,

Jack Jones, was thought to have been responsible for its initiation. In the event, the Government proceeded with the Bill, only to have its central provision defeated when the Commons voted to uphold a Lords amendment to it.[42] Also, although the Queen-in-Parliament alone can legitimise a measure *de jure,* a number of observers now take the view that certain measures require what may be described as *de facto* legitimisation by various powerful groups. In particular, in a society viewed as increasingly corporatist, a Government will often be keen to seek the 'seal of approval' of the CBI and the Trades Union Congress (TUC), and sometimes of international bodies such as the International Monetary Fund, for its measures of economic management. In the various legislative stages identified, of initiation, formulation *et al.,* the Government will normally have more regular contact and engage in more serious bargaining with such interests than with the House of Commons.

Once a Bill has received the Royal Assent and has become the law of the land, it is applied and enforced. The manner of its application will vary from measure to measure. A large number of measures are given effect through the Civil Service. Acts regulating social security benefits, tax rates, eligibility for immigration, and the like, are administered by the various Government Departments or other public agencies. Others are applied and enforced through the police and the courts. Many, though legally binding, nevertheless require in practice the co-operation of groups affected by them if they are to work. The 1971 Industrial Relations Act, which changed the law affecting trade unions, is largely deemed to have failed as a result of the refusal of the TUC and individual unions to co-operate in its implementation. The legislation passed in 1973 providing for an elected assembly and a power-sharing executive in Northern Ireland was effectively to fail as a result of opposition from Protestant loyalist groups in the province. Hence the concern of Government to consult with interested groups at the earlier stages of initiation, formulation and scrutiny.

In this process of application, the Commons plays a role, albeit a limited one by comparision with that of interested groups, the Civil Service, the courts, and the like. In order to apply the principles established in various Acts, Departments are given power under the appropriate Act to promulage regulations — statutory instruments, known popularly as delegated legislation — which, in some instances, require the approval of the House. We shall consider the Commons' role in scrutinising delegated legislation in more detail below. In order to investigate cases of alleged maladministration by officials under powers granted to them, the Parliamentary Commissioner Act of 1967 was passed, creating the position of Parliamentary Commissioner for Administration, commonly called the Ombudsman. More recently, in 1979, in order to conduct a more effective and structured scrutiny of the conduct of Departments, a new series of Select Committees has been established, based on Departments rather than subject areas. While they are a major improvement on what went before, the new Committees (and the Ombudsman, for that matter) have limited resources and powers, and their scrutiny is of necessity selective rather than comprehensive; their interests extend beyond matters that may be deemed to fall in the application stage of legislation. We shall consider both the new Select Committees and the Ombudsman in more detail in the following chapter.

As the provisions of Acts of Parliament are applied, so a process of feedback (see Figure 1.3, p. 7) commences. The Government will start to receive some reaction to its measures. Are they achieving what was intended? Are there any unexpected side-effects? Are they well-received by the public and by those most directly affected by them? The answers to these questions will be determined, as appropriate, by the response of various sources. Answers may be provided by monitoring by Departments or communications from affected parties; by stories in the press or on television; by reports of officials or of inquiries of one sort or another. MPs play some part in this process as well. They may serve as channels through which the reaction of constituency interests and individual constituents is expressed; they will themselves read and interpret reports appearing in the press and elsewhere, and may press their leaders to respond to any disquiet on their own part. The House as a collective entity may be involved if Members raise on the floor of the House the question of the way in which a particular Act is working,[43] or if a Select Committee seeks to investigate it; a number of Acts have come in for such scrutiny.[44] However, the House remains but one of many channels through which this feedback takes place.

In response to the reactions it receives, the Government may determine that a measure is working well and leave it at that; it may decide that it is not working as well as anticipated, and introduce some amending measure; it may come to the conclusion that it is not working at all as was intended (that is, that it is dysfunctional rather than malfunctional) and decide to revise radically or even repeal the measure. The Government may come under pressure from interested bodies to introduce new legislation if Acts are not proving as successful as had been hoped. In short, new measures may be initiated, and the legislative process which we have identified may start over again. It is, in other words, a dynamic process. It is one in which the House of Commons clearly has a role to play, one which is necessary but by no means sufficient in achieving the making of law. The House is one of the many elements, and by no means the most important (at least not by itself), that contribute to law-making in Britain.

Delegated legislation

With the increased demands made upon Government, and the resulting increase in the size and complexity of legislation formulated and proposed to Parliament, it has become more difficult to include in Bills specific details for the implementation of the principles enshrined therein. The Bills cannot provide for every possible eventuality. Recognition of this fact has led to the development of what is essentially a twentieth-century phenomenon — delegated legislation. In a Bill, powers may be delegated for the promulgation of orders, regulations and rules designed to give effect to the principle or principles laid down in the measure. Under the Statutory Instruments Act of 1946, the comprehensive name of 'statutory instruments' is given to most, though not all, delegated legislation.

The advantage of delegated legislation is that it allows for speed, flexibility and adaptability in implementing the principles laid down by the parent Acts. The advantage for the House of Commons is deemed to be that, by withdrawing discussion of essentially minor, subsidiary or technical details from the floor of the House, more time is allowed for the discussion of general public policy.[45] However, a problem is created when one considers how the Commons might fulfil its function of scrutiny of such legislation. As the Procedure Committee recognised in 1978, the concept of delegated legislative powers involves an uneasy confusion between executive and legislative powers and the Commons retaining the power to scrutinise those powers and, in some cases, to withhold consent to their use.[46] The Committee argued that 'a balance must be struck between the desirability of effective parliamentary scrutiny, where there is statutory provision for it, and the executive's need to exercise the legislative authority delegated to it'.[47] In practice, there has tended to be something of an imbalance in favour of the executive, more even than exists in relation to primary legislation, with the Commons lacking the means of scrutinising effectively the volume of delegated legislation which is now a feature of British government. Although the number of statutory instruments made in recent years has shown no great increase, the length of instruments has. In 1947 the total length of all statutory instruments was 2678 pages; in 1955 it was 3240 pages, in 1965 6435 pages, and in 1974, no less than 8667 pages.[48] Nor has the position been helped by the fact that there are different procedures which may be stipulated for parliamentary scrutiny of an instrument, and at present there exists 'no consistent pattern or direct connection between the subject matter of any particular instrument and the procedure to which it may be subjected'.[49] An unwillingness on the part of Government (and apparently some private Members) to devote more parliamentary time to scrutiny of this legislation creates further problems. Whereas somewhere in the region of one-third of the Commons' time (on the floor of the House) is devoted to debate of Government Bills, less than one-tenth of its time is given to consideration of delegated legislation;[50] indeed, more time is devoted to Private Members' legislation and motions (most of which will never be passed) than to the statutory instruments being promulgated in Government Departments.[51] A number of Members also regard as unduly limiting the fact that statutory instruments cannot be amended: if an instrument comes before the House, it can only be approved or rejected.

The existing procedure for parliamentary scrutiny allows for instruments to be subject to Commons' approval through either the affirmative or the negative resolution procedure, depending upon the provisions of the parent Act, or to be made without even requiring any action by the House. An Act may stipulate that instruments made under it shall be subject to the affirmative resolution procedure, which means that they have to be approved by a resolution of both Houses (or the Commons only in certain cases); it may stipulate that they are subject to the negative resolution procedure, which means that they come into effect automatically unless a motion to annul them is tabled and passed (usually within forty days) by either House; or it may stipulate that they should be laid before both Houses, with no provision for Parliament to take any action, or even that they shall be statutory instruments with no provision for them to be laid before Parliament at all. In practice, few statutory instruments are debated in the House, and those that are (that is, those requiring an affirmative resolution and some of those 'prayed' against under the negative resolution procedure)[52] are subject to a time limit. Normally taken after 10.00 p.m., they are limited to one and a half hours at most.[53]

Given the inadequacy of the House itself to scrutinise the large number of statutory instruments made by Departments, a Select Committee on Statutory Instruments was established in 1944. This was replaced in February 1973 by a Joint Committee on Statutory Instruments. It consists of seven Members from each House, and is chaired by an Opposition MP. It considers instruments laid before both Houses (excluding certain instruments made under the 1974 Northern Ireland Act) and general statutory instruments not required by statute to be laid before Parliament. For instruments which are subject to Commons approval only, the MPs on the Committee meet separately. The purpose of establishing the Joint Committee was to remove the anomalies resulting from having similar Committees in both Houses, though the terms of reference of the Committee are similar to those of the Commons Committee which existed until 1973. The purpose of the Committee is to undertake technical scrutiny, and to determine whether or not the attention of the House should be drawn to an instrument in certain specified cases.

The specified grounds include if the instrument imposes a charge on the public revenue; gives rise to doubts whether it is *ultra vires* (that is, beyond the scope of the power granted by the parent Act); appears to make an unusual or unexpected use of the powers conferred by the Act; is made under an enactment excluding it from challenge in the courts; purports to have retrospective effect where the parent Act does not so provide; where there is an unjustifiable delay in publication or in being laid before Parliament; if it has not been notified in proper time to the Lord Chancellor and Mr Speaker where it comes into effect before being presented to Parliament; if it requires elucidation as to its form or purport; or if it is defective in drafting.[54] Such scrutiny, in itself, is obviously useful, and since its creation the number of instruments considered by the Committee has increased from fewer than 700 in the first session of its existence to over 1000 in the 1976–7 session.[55] However, there are serious limitations to the Committee's effectiveness. There is no procedure to ensure that the House takes note of its views. Indeed, an instrument may be considered on the floor of the House before the Committee has looked at it. In one recent session, this happened on more than twenty occasions, and the chairman of the Joint Committee complained that it often happened 'at a time when the Department concerned is well aware . . . that the Committee has queries on the instrument'.[56] Also, the Committee is confined to technical scrutiny. It cannot consider the merits of or policy behind an instrument. The job it performs is thus useful but very limited.

The Joint Committee was established on the recommendation of the Brooke Committee, whose brief was to consider delegated legislation. In order to permit more debate on the merits of statutory instruments, the Committee recommended the establishment of a Standing Committee on Statutory Instruments; the idea was that it would consider motions to annul instruments (under the negative resolution procedure) and some taken under the affirmative resolution procedure. The proposal was accepted by the Government, and standing order 73A, providing for the setting up of one or more Standing Committees to consider statutory instruments or draft instruments referred to them, was approved in 1973. Under the standing order, motions for annulment are referred, as are affirming motions if a motion to refer them is tabled by a Minister.

Although the use of such Standing Committees has meant that more instruments are debated than was previously possible on the floor of the House (in the 1976–7 session, 126 statutory instruments were referred to Standing Committees), and their use has helped to relieve some of the pressure on the floor, a number of criticisms of the new procedure have been voiced, not least by the Procedure Committee. In its 1978 Report it intoned: 'We believe that the system provides only vestigial parliamentary control of statutory instruments – particularly in the case of negative procedure instruments – and is in need of comprehensive reform.'[57] It recorded several drawbacks associated with the working of the Standing Committees, including the fact that they could only discuss instruments on a neutral motion – 'That the Committee has considered the instrument (or draft instrument)' – and could not make any recommendations to the House; that the subsequent effective motion in the House could be brought on by the Government for decision without debate at any time; that in the case of instruments subject to the negative resolution procedure the subsequent prayers were rarely brought before the House; and that the procedure could be used indiscriminately by the Government business managers as a means of unloading business from the floor of the House.[58] Indeed, the Government has tended to use the procedure to its advantage; over 60 per cent of its affirmative resolutions were dealt with in Committee in the 1974–5 session.[59] As Paul Byrne recorded in 1976, 'The Government have not hesitated to utilise this useful method of saving time on the Floor of the House by transferring some of their responsibilities to committee scrutiny; there has not, however, been any noticeable corresponding increase in the time available for prayers.'[60] The Procedure Committee also referred to the fact that debate in the Committees was subject to the one-and-a-half hour time limit, except when instruments for Northern Ireland were dealt with, when the time limit was two and a half hours. To overcome these drawbacks, and to achieve a more effective scrutiny of instruments on their merits, the Committee made several recommendations, including that the Standing Committees, in dealing with affirmative resolutions, should discuss instruments on motions recommending their approval, that they should be able to sit for up to two and a half hours, and that if a Committee failed to recommend the approval of an instrument, provision should be made for it to be debated in the House. These recommendations were viewed with some sympathy by the Leader of the House, Mr St John-Stevas, when he devised his third package of procedural reforms, which he put before the House in October 1980. However, allowing Standing Committees to debate instruments on substantive motions was known not to be popular with the whips (given that it would require them to extend their activities to such Committees), and Mr St John-Stevas decided with reluctance not to recommend this change to the House. Instead, he commended some minor changes – as, for example, the provision of information on instruments to Committees considering them – which did not require changes in standing orders.[61]

As a result of the procedural changes of recent years, the House of Commons exercises a slightly improved scrutiny of delegated legislation, but one which many feel still to be inadequate. The balance between the executive's need to exercise legislative powers granted it (effectively by itself in drawing up the parent Act) and the need for effective parliamentary scrutiny has yet to be achieved. Although, as the Study of Parliament Group commented with reference to the growth of primary and delegated legislation, 'this vast mass of legislation affects the lives of us all, our rights and expectations,'[62] delegated legislation remains a much neglected form of legislation (except by affected interest groups and the Departments that promulgate it). It receives little time and attention in the House[63] and little detailed treatment in works on Parliament (it is one area where *Erskine May* may be considered somewhat better than recent academic texts), and few proposals are put forward that would effect a significant shift in the relationship between the Commons and the Government to achieve the balance sought by the Procedure Committee. Indeed, even the Committee itself fought shy of recommending that statutory instruments be amendable by the House, clearly believing that such a power would lead to confusion. (It preferred that influence should be exerted before an instrument was formally laid, though how this could be achieved is far from clear.) The result, in practice, is that delegated legislation, even more than primary legislation, is the product of consultations between Government and outside interests,[64] and is 'made' before it reaches the House of Commons.

Private Members' Bills and Private legislation

The function of scrutiny and influence of Government in the process of legislation is exercised in respect of Government Bills and delegated legislation. However, the Commons also has a role to play in the formulation and approval of legislative measures which are not brought in on the initiative of, nor are the responsibility of, Government. The legislation involved is that brought in on the initiative, or at least the sponsorship, of private Members — Private Members' Bills which, like Government Bills, constitute Public General legislation — and measures which emanate from local authorities or private concerns, these latter Bills constituting a distinct form of legislation known as Private legislation.

Private Members' Bills, like Government Bills, are introduced to cover aspects of public policy. Unlike Government Bills, they are precluded from imposing a charge on the public revenue, though costs incidental to the main purpose of a measure are permissible. There are three separate methods by which a Private Member's Bill can be introduced.

First, a Member may simply introduce a Bill under standing order 37. By this procedure, the Bill is presented, given a First Reading, and put down for Second Reading on a Friday. On Second Reading, the question is put without debate at 2.30 p.m. (unless time unexpectedly becomes available for debate before this time, which hardly ever happens); if one or more Members shout 'Object', the progress of the Bill is effectively blocked. Bills rarely achieve passage by this procedure unless they are so uncontroversial that no Member is willing to turn up to object, or the Government provides time for them (again, a rare occurence). Not surprisingly, few Bills are introduced by this method, and of those that are, very few ever reach the statute book. In the 1971–2 session, for example, thirteen Private Members' Bills were introduced under standing order 37, and only three were passed.[65]

The second method is that known as the 'ten-minute rule'. Under this procedure, a Member, after giving notice, may move a motion at the commencement of public business on a Tuesday or Wednesday for leave to bring in a Bill. The Member is allowed to make a brief explanatory statement of ten minutes' duration in support of the measure he wishes to introduce, and another Member may then rise to speak for ten minutes against it. Opponents of the proposed measure may divide the House on the motion. If defeated, the Bill obviously cannot be introduced. If passed, it is given a First Reading and then joins the queue of Private Members' Bills awaiting Second Readings on Fridays. Again, unless time unexpectedly becomes available on a Friday, or the Government provides time, it is rare for such Bills to make progress. Of thirty-five Bills introduced under this procedure in the 1967–8 session, only three were passed; of thirty-nine introduced in 1971–2, forty-two in 1975–6, and thirty-eight in 1976–7, not one was passed.[66] In practice, the procedure tends to be utilised as a means of raising an issue and testing support for it at a time when many Members are normally present, waiting for the main business of the day. The issues raised are not infrequently controversial and partisan. In the 1978–9 session, for example, the subjects covered included the abolition of secondary picketing, the allocation of political funds by trade unions, workers' freedom, equal opportunities for men, protection of prostitutes, and restricted reporting of criminal proceedings in magistrates' courts. Voting is often on party lines even though the whips are not applied.

The third and most important method is that of introducing balloted Bills. At the beginning of each session, under the provisions of standing order 6, a ballot is held of all Members who enter their names. Up to twenty names are drawn (depending on the number of Fridays available to discuss Private Members' Bills) and these have priority in introducing their Bills, the first six or so normally being assured of their Bills having Second Reading debates. Whether they get much further will depend often on the subject of the measures and the attitude of the Government. Under the standing order, ten Fridays are available each session for Private Members' Bills (plus a further ten for Private Members' motions, and Bills, in that order), though this number is varied by sessional order. The later Fridays are devoted to the later stages of Bills, so sponsors have to bring up their Bills for Second Reading on one of the earlier Fridays. Unless they are uncontroversial measures, they may be subject to a full debate, and if no vote is taken by 2.30 p.m. (4.00 p.m. until 1980),[67] they are 'talked out'. To prevent being talked out, a Member may move the closure just before 2.30, but even if accepted by the Chair, it is rare for 100 Members to be present on a Friday to support such a motion. There is also the danger that the Government may advise against the measure. Although the whips are rarely applied in divisions on Private Members' legislation (unless the measure runs counter to Government policy), strong advice by a Minister against it may result in the so-called payroll vote of Ministers and whips entering the lobby against it. So, for a measure to be successful, it has usually to have widespread support within the House and the acquiescence of Government. If it is controversial, and has the benevolent but unofficial support of the Government, time may be made available, though instances of this in recent years are few. Even with extra time provided by the Government, the Bill still requires the support of a majority of Members in divisions. Nevertheless, balloted Bills are more likely to succeed than those introduced under standing order 37 or the 'ten-minute rule'. Of the nineteen balloted Bills introduced in the 1974–5 session, nine were successful; of the twenty introduced in 1975–6, eleven were successful, and of the twenty introduced in the following session seven were successful.[68]

Although the time devoted to Private Members' legislation is very limited, and only a small number of Bills promoted by backbenchers reach the statute book, this area of legislation is not an unimportant one. It provides individual Members with the opportunity to initiate legislation (the one occasion when they are involved in the initiative stage): if successful in the ballot, they may be approached by outside organisations, by the whips or by fellow Members, each with Bills they would like the Members to sponsor, or Members may already have measures of their own in mind. The choice is theirs. (In drafting measures, the first ten Members successful in the ballot now receive some financial assistance.) The areas covered by such legislation are many, as Peter Richards has noted,[69] and a number of important Bills have been enacted as Private Members' measures. Especially well-known are those passed in the 1966–70 Parliament covering important social issues, measures which aroused 'more public interest than the common run of legislation':[70] the Murder (Abolition of Death Penalty) Bill, the Sexual Offences (No. 2) Bill (legalising homosexual relations between consenting adults), David Steel's Abortion Bill, and the Theatres Bill (ridding theatres of censorship by the Lord Chamberlain) are probably the best-known.[71] They are by no means the only examples. For instance, those passed in the 1976–7 session covered the terms of unfair contracts, the control of food premises in Scotland, the housing of homeless persons, the registration of insurance brokers, the use of minibuses for educational purposes, rent charges, and an amendment to the Town and Country Planning Acts. Even if measures fail to reach the statute book, their introduction or the support for them in the lobbies may encourage the Government to introduce legislation of its own.

Although some criticisms can be levelled at Private Members' legislation, on balance it serves a useful purpose.[72] It could be argued that it is not really *Private Members'* legislation, given that controversial measures are dependent upon Government acquiescence and time (the 1964–70 Labour Government assisted no less than twenty-three Private Members' Bills). However, the Government can be pressured by its own backbenchers to provide extra time, as happened with the Divorce Bill,[73] and its acquiescence constitutes usually a necessary but not sufficient condition to ensure passage; only the votes of a majority of voting Members can ensure that.[74] Without the application of the whips, determined opponents of measures can delay and sometimes kill them.

Private legislation is a distinct form of legislation and should not be confused with that of Private Members. Private Bills, quite simply, are 'Bills for the particular interest or benefit of any person or persons': 'whether they be for the interest of an individual, of a public company or corporation, or for a county, district or other locality, they are equally distinguished from measures of public policy.'[75] Although many Private Bills are not measures of significance (though a number are, such as those promoted by British Rail or major authorities such as the Greater London Council), taken collectively they form a substantial body of law, between thirty and seventy-five such Bills passing each year.[76] They differ from Public Bills in two main respects. First, they differ *procedurally* in that, although required to pass through analagous legislative stages, the purposes and procedures of the stages differ. In agreeing to Second Reading of a Private Bill, the House is affirming the principle of the measure conditionally, subject to the case put forward by the Bill's promoters being proved in Committee. In Committee (comprising four Members in the case of opposed Bills, seven in the case of unopposed Bills),[77] promoters and objectors are represented by counsel, and witnesses are heard under oath; the job of the Committee is to act as judge and jury in assessing the promoter's attempt to prove the case stated in the Bill's preamble, while seeking to balance national interests with the private interests involved. Such Bills differ *politically* from Public Bills in that the whips as a rule are not applied and the Government contents itself with offering advice, which Members are free to ignore if they wish, and sometimes with offering no advice at all. The private interests concerned do not usually impinge upon matters of concern to national parties or central Government, and as Peter Bromhead has observed, the 'central Government can afford to leave its party members free because if a point should arise with serious political implications for national policy, the Government could protect its interests by other means.'[78] As a result, the Government itself pays little heed to Private legislation. The relevant Departments will consider the measure in order to determine what advice to offer (or what to include in their report to the Committee on the Bill), but otherwise the Government as such is little involved. The responsibility for the measures in the House and their timetabling rests with the Chairman of Ways and Means (the Deputy Speaker), not with the Leader of the House and the Government Chief Whip.[79]

As a result of the procedural differences, Members pay little attention to Private legislation. It does not usually affect national interests or, in the case of most Members, constituency interests, and is based normally on precedent. Members more often than not are willing to leave scrutiny of such measures to the Committee appointed for the purpose. As a result, most of the Bills receive unopposed Second Readings at the beginning of a day's sitting. However, on those occasions when Members do pay attention to particular measures, their influence is likely to be considerable as a result of the political differences. Promoters cannot rely on the strength of party loyalty to carry their measures through the House. Even if the Government advises in favour of Second Reading (which is the convention), there is no guarantee that the House will heed that advice. A number of Bills have been rejected against Government advice (as, for example, the 1969 Brighton Corporation Bill, the 1970 Calderdale Water Bill, the 1974 Clifton Suspension Bridge Bill, the 1974 Burmah Refineries Trust Bill, and the 1976 West Midlands County Council Bill), and on occasion some Ministers have actually voted against the advice of their own ministerial colleagues.[80] If a Member shouts 'Object' when the title of a Bill is read at the beginning of the day's sitting, the Second Reading has to be set for debate at 7.00 p.m. on a day selected by the Chairman of Ways and Means. The Parliamentary Agent for the Bill (the professional agent responsible for steering the measure through on behalf of the promoters) will note the name of any Member who voices objection in order to approach him subsequently to determine the nature of the objection and to ascertain if an agreed amendment can be secured. As one former Chairman of Ways and Means observed, 'The private Member plays an all important part in the discussion and voting on private bill legislation,'[81] and merely by objecting he is, as one former Local Government Minister conceded, 'bound to influence the bill one way or another'.[82] This is one very limited area of legislation in which Members can play a significant role, though, because of the nature of the measures, they are rarely concerned to do so.

There is also a Bill which falls between Public and Private Bills, known as a hybrid Bill. If a Public Bill affects a particular private interest in a manner different from the way in which it affects other private interests in the same category (technically, to which the standing orders for Private Business apply), then it is deemed to be a hybrid Bill. After Second Reading, a hybrid Bill is referred to a Select Committee (the procedure followed being similar though not identical to that of Private Bill Committees),[83] and after being reported from the committee is normally recommitted to a Committee of the Whole House. Following this, proceedings on it are the same as on Public Bills. Although the hybrid Bill procedure is not well-known, and not often employed, a number of important Bills have been passed as hybrid Bills, including the 1973 Maplin Development Bill and the 1974 Channel Tunnel Bill. A political controversy occurred in 1976, when a Conservative Member, Robin Maxwell-Hyslop (a procedural expert with an interest in Private and hybrid legislation), contended that the Aircraft and Shipbuilding Industries Bill, which had completed its Committee stage as a Public Bill, was in fact a hybrid Bill. The Speaker ruled that *prima facie* it was hybrid, and a political storm ensued when the Government sought to suspend the relevant standing orders for Private business in order to expedite its passage.[84] It is rare for hybrid Bills, and more especially hybrid Bill procedure, to be so much at the centre of the political stage in the Commons. Like Private Bills, they tend to form a small and little known part of the legislative process, though (unlike Private Bills) the rationale for them is no longer as clear as it might be.[85]

European Communities legislation

On 1 January 1973, the United Kingdom became a member of the European Communities (the EC). The Treaty of Accession had been signed in 1972, and the 1972 European Communities Act gave legal effect to the arrangements necessary for effecting membership. Under the Act, existing and future EC legislation was made applicable to the United Kingdom, with any conflict between the provisions of Communities' legislation and domestic law to be resolved in favour of the former. Although the power to repeal the 1972 Act remains, Parliament has no power over the regulations and directives emanating from the EC Council of Ministers or the Commission. As we shall see, there is some machinery through which it can consider and seek to influence the Government prior to decisions by the Council of Ministers upon recommendations submitted by the Commission, but it has no influence at all over legislation promulgated by the Commission itself. This is a very different legislative process from that which we have outlined for domestic law, and one in which the House of Commons is even less directly involved. The House has no control over EC legislation; it has but a very limited influence over it; and its legitimisation of it is already implicit by virtue of its having passed the 1972 Act. In 1979, it lost a channel of indirect influence when members of the European Parliament were directly elected, rather than being appointed by the national assemblies of the member states; from 1973 to 1979, Britain's members had been drawn from MPs and peers. Various suggestions have been made as to how the role of the Commons in scrutinising and influencing EC legislation might be improved. Given the distinct nature of this legislation, we shall consider these proposals, along with the existing machinery, in a later chapter. For the moment, we are concerned to note only the EC legislation, given effect in this country under the provisions of the 1972 European Communities Act, is distinct from domestic law and the process of law-making which we have identified above.

Conclusion

The process by which law is 'made' in Britain is complex. The role of the House of Commons in this process is a limited, though not altogether unimportant, one. It plays an important, though not exclusive, role in the stages of scrutiny and legitimisation of Government Bills, and can influence the Government at other stages, though its effectiveness at these stages is severely restricted by comparison with that of other bodies. Its ability effectively to scrutinise Bills is a question of some debate, and a number of proposals designed to increase its effectiveness have been put forward. Its ability to scrutinise statutory instruments promulgated under the provisions of Acts is seriously limited, and, as we have argued, is a cause for concern. The House plays a more central, though again not exclusive, role in the passage of Private Members' legislation and Private legislation. Though these two types of legislation are often, though by no means always, of less significance than Government measures, and take up little time in the House, they do provide a means by which Members can, individually and collectively, play a useful legislative role.

The House of Commons no longer 'makes' law, but without it the process of domestic law-making cannot be completed. However, the 1970s witnessed the advent of a new form of legislation (EC law), one beyond the confines of the domestic law-making process (though made possible by a piece of domestic legislation), and, for all intents and purposes, beyond the confines of the definition of legislation posited at the beginning of this chapter. Given the distinct character of this legislation, and the extent to which it is divorced from the relationship of the Commons to that part of it which forms the British Government, it will be considered in detail later.

NOTES

1 S.A. de Smith, *Constitutional and Administrative Law* (Penguin, 1971), p. 512.
2 S.A. Walkland, *The Legislative Process in Great Britain* (Allen & Unwin, 1968), pp. 9–10.
3 Walkland, p. 9.
4 Walkland, p. 14.
5 Ronald Butt, *The Power of Parliament* (Constable, 1967), p. 55.
6 Walkland, p. 71.
7 Some Members of the Study of Parliament Group, 'Parliament and Legislation', *Parliamentary Affairs,* 22 (3), Summer 1969, p. 210.
8 These distinctions draw to some extent on Gavin Drewry, 'Legislation', in S.A. Walkland and M. Ryle (eds), *The Commons in the Seventies* (Fontana, 1977), ch. 4. See also Figures 1.1 and 1.3 (pp. 4, 7) above.
9 As, for example, the TUC and the CBI through the National Economic Development Council and other bodies; the National Farmers' Union is well-represented on various agricultural advisory boards.
10 For example, both the Labour Government in the 1945–50 Parliament and the Conservative Government in the 1959–64 Parliament carried out almost all of their specific election manifesto promises, only to lose support in the next general election.
11 The tasks performed by the Committee used to be performed by separate Committees — the Legislation and the Future Legislation Committees — but these were combined in the mid-1970s. Sir Harold Wilson, *The Governance of Britain* (Weidenfeld & Nicolson/Michael Joseph, 1976), p. 129n.
12 Lord Morrison of Lambeth, *Government and Parliament,* 3rd ed. (Oxford University Press, 1964), p. 178.
13 See Butt, pp. 256–8, and also S.E. Finer, *Anonymous Empire,* 2nd revised ed. (Pall Mall, 1966), pp. 69–72, and J. Bruce-Gardyne and N. Lawson, *The Power Game* (Macmillan, 1976), pp. 80–117.
14 See John P. Mackintosh, 'Parliament Now and a Hundred Years Ago', in D. Leonard and V. Herman (eds), *The Backbencher and Parliament* (Macmillan, 1972), pp. 257–8.
15 See Philip Norton, 'The Organisation of Parliamentary Parties', in S.A. Walkland (ed.), *The House of Commons in the Twentieth Century* (Oxford University Press, 1979), pp. 7–68, and, by the same author, *Conservative Dissidents* (Temple Smith, 1978), *passim* and especially ch. 3, for a case study of the 1972 Industry Bill.
16 There was a four-day debate, the first three days being covered by adjournment motions and the fourth by a 'take note' motion on the White Paper *Our Changing Democracy.*
17 *First Report from the Select Committee on Procedure, 1977–8,* Vol. 1 (HC 588), p. xiii.
18 On Second Reading, the Opposition (or any Member) may table an amendment to reject the Bill. This may take the form of a straightforward amendment for rejection ('That the Bill be read a Second time upon this day six (or three) months', in effect rejecting it), or one in which a reason for rejection is outlined (for example, 'That this House declines to give a Second Reading to a Bill which will have the effect of . . . .'), commonly known as a 'reasoned amendment'. The

reasoned amendment is especially useful for the Opposition if it wishes to avoid outright rejection of the principle of a measure, allowing it instead to object to the method by which the Government seeks to achieve the principle.

19   The Rent Restrictions Bill in 1924, and the Reduction of Redundancy Rebates Bill in 1977.

20   See David Wood, *The Times,* 18 February 1972.

21   This was attested to by various former Ministers interviewed on the BBC Radio 3 series 'The Parliamentary Process', broadcast on 4 March 1976 ('The Making of laws') and, earlier, 19 February 1976 ('Government and Opposition'). The presenter was Professor G.W. Jones.

22   The Scottish Grand Committee consists of all Members sitting for Scottish constituencies, with a number of added Members for party balance.

23   *First Report from the Select Committee on Procedure, 1977—8,* pp. xiv-xv.

24   See Sir David Lidderdale (ed.), *Erskine May's Treatise on the Law, Privileges, Proceedings and Usage of Parliament,* 19th ed. (Butterworth, 1976), especially p. 769, and standing order 91, *Standing Orders of the House of Commons: Public Business* (HMSO, 1979), p. 81. The exceptions are Bills which are brought in on Ways and Means resolutions, especially the Finance Bills, the resolutions preceding introduction.

25   The annual Consolidated Fund and Appropriation Bills (as well as Bills confirming provisional orders) are excepted, and taken in Committee of the Whole House.

26   In addition, for Bills relating to Wales exclusively, the Committee includes all Members sitting for Welsh constituencies.

27   The Chairmen's Panel comprises Members appointed by the Speaker to act as temporary chairmen of committees (plus the Chairman and Deputy Chairman of Ways and Means). They are usually senior and well-respected Members with a knowledge of procedure.

28   See Philip Norton, 'Dissent in Committee: Dissent in Commons' Standing Committees 1959—74', *The Parliamentarian,* 57 (1), January 1976, p. 17, and above, ch. 3.

29   J.A.G. Griffith, 'Standing Committees in the House of Commons', in Walkland and Ryle, pp. 107—8.

30   See John Schwarz, 'The Commons Bites Back', *Financial Times,* 2 June 1978, and Norton, 'Dissent in Committee'.

31   J.A.G. Griffith, *Parliamentary Scrutiny of Government Bills* (Allen & Unwin, 1973), though note also the analysis of V. Herman, 'Backbench and Opposition Amendments to Government Legislation', in Leonard and Herman, pp. 141—55.

32   *HC Deb.* 991, c. 716—834. *First Report from the Procedure Committee 1977—8,* pp. xviii—xix. Though the proposal had been supported previously by various reformers, including Richard Crossman, one senior MP had expressed the view that power to summon witnesses was more appropriate for a pre-legislation committee. Fred Willey, MP, *The Honourable Member* (Sheldon Press, 1974), p. 132. Mr St John-Stevas was himself sympathetic to this view.

33   Sir Ivor Jennings, *Parliament,* 2nd ed. (Cambridge University Press, 1957), p. 271.

34   Walkland, pp. 75—6.

35   Peter G. Richards, *The Backbenchers* (Faber & Faber, 1972), p. 100.

36   On the Speaker's use of the power to select amendments for debate, see the comments of Selwyn Lloyd, *Mr Speaker, Sir* (Jonathan Cape, 1976), pp. 94—6.

37   See Norton, 'Dissent in Committee', pp. 17—18.

38   To reverse a defeat, the language of the new amendment has to be 'materially different' from the original that was defeated. A motion once defeated cannot be reintroduced (unless standing orders are suspended) in the same session.

39   Third Reading of money Bills cannot be taken forthwith. The Consolidated Fund and Appropriation Bills are excepted from this provision, and the House may vote to waive the rule on other money Bills in particular cases.

40   This includes not only Bills which can be passed after one year in a new session, but also Bills certified by the Speaker as money Bills under the provisions of the 1911 Parliament Act (that is, Bills containing *only* provisions dealing with taxation): if the Lords does not pass such Bills within a month they receive the Royal Assent without the Lords' consent. (The definition of a money Bill under the 1911 Act differs from that in general usage.)

41   Norton, *Conservative Dissidents,* pp. 90—8.

42   *Hou˙e of Commons Debates* 919, c. 581—92. The defeat was the result of Opposition parties combining against the Government and abstentions by two Labour MPs. See Philip Norton, *Dissension in the House of Commons 1974—1979* (Oxford University Press, 1980), p. 492.

43   For example, the workings of the 1957 Rent Act was a matter raised with some frequency in the late 1950s by Members on both sides of the House. See Butt, and on the passage of the Act see Malcolm J. Barnett, *The Politics of Legislation* (Weidenfeld & Nicolson, 1969).

44   For example, the Select Committee on Race Relations set up in 1968 had the task, among other things, of reviewing the 1968 Race Relations Act.

45   *Erskine May,* p. 573, and Sir Robert Speed, 'Parliamentary Scrutiny of Delegated Legislation', *The Parliamentarian,* 59 (4), October 1978, p. 266.

46   *First Report from the Select Committee on Procedure, 1977—8,* p. xxix.

47   *ibid.,* p. xxx.

48   'A Memorandum of Evidence' submitted to the Select Committee on Procedure by the academic members of the Study of Parliament Group (mimeo, 1976), p. 10.

49   *Erskine May,* p. 576.

50   See R.L. Borthwick, 'The Floor of the House', in Walkland and Ryle, p. 53.

51   The *Second Report from the Procedure Committee 1970—1* expressed the somewhat surprising view that the proportion of time spent on Public Bills was about right, echoing in so doing the view of the Leader of House and Government Chief Whip. See the comments of S.A. Walkland, 'Legislation in the House of Commons', in Walkland (ed.), *The House of Commons in the Twentieth Century,* p. 277.

52   Motions to annul statutory instruments are known as 'prayers' (though the term is now commonly applied to all motions to approve or annul orders of whatever sort); the name is derived from the fact that the House formally 'prays' the monarch to annul the order.

53   Under standing orders 3 and 4. A time limit was applied to debates on negative resolutions in 1954 and to debates under the affirmative resolution procedure in 1967.

54   *Erskine May,* p. 585, and Speed, p. 267.

55   In 1976—7, the Joint Committee considered 925 instruments (thirty-two of

which were drawn to the special attention of both Houses), and the Select Committee for the Commons alone considered 115 (one of which was drawn to the special attention of the House). Speed, p. 268.
56 Evidence to the Procedure Committee. *First Report from the Select Committee on Procedure, 1977—8*, p. xxxii.
57 *ibid.*, p. xxxiv.
58 *ibid.*, p. xxxiii.
59 Paul Byrne, 'Parliamentary Control of Delegated Legislation', *Parliamentary Affairs*, 29 (4), Autumn 1976, p. 377n.
60 Byrne, p. 373.
61 *House of Commons Debates*, 991, c. 727—8.
62 'Memorandum of Evidence', p. 10.
63 See Byrne, p. 375.
64 See Walkland, *The Legislative Process in Great Britain*, ch. 4.
65 Peter G. Richards, 'Private Members' Legislation', in S.A. Walkland (ed.), *The House of Commons in the Twentieth Century*, table IV.3, p. 308.
66 Richards, 'Private Members' Legislation', and Ivor Burton and Gavin Drewry, 'Public Legislation: A Survey of 1975/76 and 1976/77', *Parliamentary Affairs*, 31 (2), Spring 1978, table, p. 160.
67 Under standing order 25 — approved on 17 January, taking effect on 25 January 1980 — business on a Friday is now interrupted at 2.30 instead of 4.00 p.m., the sitting now commencing at 9.30 instead of 11.00 a.m.
68 Burton and Drewry.
69 Richards, 'Private Members' Legislation', pp. 313—14.
70 Peter G. Richards, *Parliament and Conscience* (Allen & Unwin, 1970), p. 215.
71 For a comprehensive study of these measures, see Richards, *Parliament and Conscience*.
72 See the points made in Richards, 'Private Members' Legislation', pp. 317—23.
73 Richards, *Parliament and Conscience*, p. 149; Leo Abse, *Private Member* (Macdonald, 1973), pp. 184—5.
74 See Philip Norton, 'The Influence of the Backbench Member', *The Parliamentarian*, 58 (3), July 1977, p.167.
75 *Erskine May*, p. 857.
76 Philip Norton, 'Private Legislation and the Influence of the Backbench MP', *Parliamentary Affairs*, 30 (4), Autumn 1977, p. 356.
77 The 'opposition' refers to objections lodged by petitioners against a measure and not to objections expressed on the floor of the House. (It is quite possible for a Bill to be 'opposed' without a Member having spoken against it.)
78 Peter Bromhead, *Britain's Developing Constitution* (Allen & Unwin, 1974), p. 132.
79 In practice, in order to arrange convenient times, there is contact between the Chairman's clerk and the clerk to the Chief Whip.
80 Norton, 'Private Legislation and the Influence of the Backbench MP', p. 359.
81 Lord Harvington (formerly Sir Robert Grant-Ferris) to author.
82 R. Graham Page to author.
83 See *Erskine May*, pp. 556—8.
84 See Burton and Drewry, pp. 151—6. (The Bill was subsequently lost because of disagreement with the Lords and had to be reintroduced in the following session.)
85 Burton and Drewry, pp. 155—6.

6

Scrutiny and influence: executive actions

The actions of the Government are not confined to formulating legislation and obtaining Parliament's approval of it. Ministers devote much of their time to deciding various courses of action (not requiring legislation) in connection with a wide variety of issues that come within their sphere of competence. Their decisions are reached and carried out either under existing statutory authority or under prerogative powers.

Although the Government relies upon Parliament for legitimisation of both itself and its measures, it derives also a separate legitimacy as Her Majesty's Government, and exercises prerogative powers on behalf of the Crown. The royal prerogative consists of those powers vested in the Crown before Parliament asserted its authority, and which, while lacking the authorisation now normally provided by Act of Parliament, are binding upon the courts by virtue of the royal authority from which they are derived.[1] A number of these prerogative powers are formal, but some are of great importance. Among the latter are the powers to declare war and to negotiate treaties. The declaration of a state of war with Germany in 1939 was an executive and not a parliamentary decision (in the United States, Congress alone has the formal power to declare war), and in 1972 Parliament was not asked to approve the Treaty of Accession to the European Communities.[2] Most executive decisions, though, are now taken and carried out under powers granted by statute. Ministers are vested with a wide range of powers: powers to render various definitive orders, instructions and directions; powers to give assent to recommendations of various bodies; and powers to appoint members to a variety of boards, committees, and official bodies. It was discovered in 1975, for example, that the Secretary of State for Health and Social Security had no less than 31,000 patronage appointments at his (then her) disposal.[3] Ministers, according to one critic, 'collectively and individually enjoy vast and virtually undiluted . . . executive power'.[4]

The scrutiny and influence of executive actions, or contemplated actions, is conducted by the Commons, individually and collectively, through various channels. These channels may be identified as: Question Time, private correspondence, Early Day Motions, debates (including adjournment debates), the Parliamentary Commissioner for Administration, and — of special contemporary interest and significance — Select Committees. Although, as we shall argue, such channels may be most effective when used in combination with one another, it is useful to commence by considering each in turn.

Question Time[5]

Although having its origins in the eighteenth century (the first recorded parliamentary question was asked, in the Lords, in 1721),[6] Question Time developed significantly in the nineteenth century and more especially in the twentieth. The popularity of Question Time with Members is such that, for over sixty years now, the demand to ask oral and follow-up (supplementary) questions has exceeded the supply of time available for them.

Though often referred to as Question 'Hour', Question Time occupies between forty-five and fifty-five minutes at the beginning of a day's sitting (from Monday to Thursday inclusively when the House is sitting), coming after prayers and Private business and not later than 2.45 and finishing at 3.30 p.m. Because of demand, a Member is restricted to tabling no more than eight questions for oral answer in any ten sitting days, and can ask no more than two questions on any one day. (And, if two are tabled for one day, they cannot both be directed to the same Minister.) Ministers answer questions on a rota basis, the more important and popular Ministries coming up more regularly than the minor and less popular ones. An exception applies in the case of the Prime Minister, who answers questions from 3.15 to 3.30 p.m. on each Tuesday and Thursday; an arrangement for questions to some of the smaller Departments to come on not later than 3.10, 3.15 or 3.20 on the day they appear on the rota has also been introduced. There is now also a separate slot in Foreign Office questions for questions about the European Communities, such questions coming on not later than 3.10 on days when the Foreign Office is top of the rota.

As well as tabling questions for oral answer, Members are free to table questions for written answers.[7] (Oral questions not reached also receive written answers unless those who tabled them request their deferment to a later sitting.) The answers to the questions are printed in *Hansard*. There is no limit to the number that can be tabled, and their use has gained in popularity among Members, in part because of the limitations placed on the asking of oral questions. Usually between one and two hundred written questions (sometimes more) appear daily on the order paper. It is common for such questions to be accompanied by the letter W, a relatively recent innovation which means that the questions have been set down for answer on that particular day; otherwise, a question is answered by the Department concerned if possible within three working days.[8] To take one parliamentary day: on 21 November 1979, no less than 213 questions appeared on the order paper for written answer; of these, eighty-eight were designated with a W.

In addition to these oral and written questions, there are what are known as private notice questions (PNQs). These are questions which are 'of an urgent character, and relate either to a matter of public importance or to the arrangement of business', are handed in for answer (as long as put in before noon) on the same day, are accepted at the discretion of the Speaker, and do not appear on the order paper. If accepted, they are answered orally by the relevant Minister after Question Time. About forty such questions are allowed each year, and cover matters requiring urgent Government comment, as, for example, disasters involving loss of lives, threats to British subjects abroad, or sudden actions that threaten Britain's defence or economic well-being.

The advantages and disadvantages of Question Time for the backbench Member have been variously debated. As a device for ensuring effective scrutiny of executive actions it has come in for increasing criticism. Members are restricted as to the number of oral questions (known as 'starred' questions because they have to be accompanied by an asterisk when submitted) that they can table. Because of the number of supplementary questions asked and the number and length of them in recent years, along with the length of Ministers' replies,[9] many of the questions on the order paper are not reached. Because of the increased pressure (demand exceeding the supply of time), there is believed by many to be insufficient time to penetrate a Minister's defences, especially given that the Minister comes well-briefed by his officials (not only on the answer to the question tabled but also on answers to likely supplementary questions), and, as Richard Crossman noted, in the last resort a Minister can always refuse to answer a question. A Minister is not required formally to answer, and it is far from uncommon for a Minister to reply that information requested is not obtainable or could be obtained only at disproportionate cost.[10] (There are also many subjects on which successive Governments have refused to answer questions; for example, details of arms sales, budgetary forecasts, tax affairs of individuals, and the existence of Cabinet Committees.)[11] In addition, the increasing involvement of Opposition spokesmen in asking questions (primarily supplementaries), and the use made of them by Opposition Members to harry Ministers, has reduced their utility as a back-bench device for eliciting information. Question Time is viewed increasingly as a part of the House's adversary proceedings, Ministers staving off with as little information as possible critical questions from the other side of the House. A number of Members now regard proceedings at Question Time as a farce, and Barker and Rush in 1970 found that about one-third of Members taking part in their survey never bothered to table starred questions at all.[12] In the 1977–8 session, over 150 backbenchers failed to table starred questions.[13]

Nevertheless, Question Time retains some advantages for private Members. It does provide an established procedure for asking questions of Ministers (and questions must be just that – questions, and must be concerned with matters for which the Minister has responsibility);[14] it comes at prime time in the parliamentary day, hence attracting publicity; and, despite the increasing involvement of Opposition frontbenchers, it remains basically a back-bench occasion for asking questions, back-benchers on both sides of the House being free to table whatever questions they like. Despite the criticisms of some participants, a case can still be made for the view that Question Time helps to keep Ministers on their toes. Priority is accorded to questions by officials in Departments who ensure that their Minister is well-briefed on the matter. A well-briefed Minister is arguably preferable to one who knows nothing about the matter, and by tabling a question a Member can ensure that a Minister has brought to his attention something that otherwise would not be put before him.[15] Although partisan questions can be parried by a Minister with an answer that attracts the cheers of those sat behind him, party loyalty is of little utility when answering questions based on constituency concerns. In answering questions, a Minister will wish to appear competent. An apparent inability to handle questions can affect adversely a Minister's career, and, however rare they may be, there is always the possibility of an incisive supplementary question to which a Minister may have no answer. The increased use of supplementary questions may actually have contributed to keeping Ministers under scrutiny. As Speaker, Selwyn Lloyd 'took the view that the number of questions reached was less important than a searching examination of a Minister's conduct'.[16] As a former Minister, he knew that several suplementaries created more problems for a Minister than getting through as many starred questions as possible.

Given the general nature of the questions addressed to the Prime Minister (who has few specific departmental responsibilities), and the partisan nature of Prime Minister's Question Time, the Prime Minister in particular seeks to be well-briefed in order to cope with questioners. Harold Macmillan is reputed to have felt physically sick before answering questions, and Sir Harold Wilson recorded that 'no Prime Minister looks forward to "PQs" with anything but apprehension; every Prime Minister works long into the night on his answers.'[17] Although the live radio broadcast of Prime Minister's Question Time was not a success (and was discontinued in the summer of 1979), the institution of Prime Minister Question Time is nevertheless valuable in itself. Few political systems provide for the head of Government to face his or her political opponents twice weekly to answer critical, and unknown follow-up, questions.

Various proposals designed to overcome some of the perceived limitations of Question Time have been put forward. Foremost among these is a recommendation to extend the length of Question Time, though it seems unlikely that such a recommendation will be implemented in the foreseeable future.[18] Question Time, warts and all, is likely to continue in its present form for some time.

Private correspondence

A much used, though widely overlooked, means of seeking information or action from Ministers is that of corresponding with them. Any Member, including Ministers and the Speaker, can write to a Minister on a matter within the Minister's sphere of competence. The expedient is specially popular in dealing with constituency matters (and Ministers and the Speaker, it should be remembered, retain constituency responsibilities).[19] A constituent raises a matter with his local MP, often through writing to him; the Member sends the letter to the relevant Minister with a covering note (there is a printed one available for the purpose); the Minister replies; and the Member sends on the Minister's reply to his constituent. In cases in which a Member takes a personal interest, several letters may be written, and the Member may threaten other action if the case is not dealt with satisfactorily.[20]

Because such correspondence is conducted away from the floor of the House and in private, it is difficult to quantify, and it receives little attention in the literature on the House. In practice, it constitutes an important element of Members' individual fulfilment of the role of scrutiny and influence, especially in order to represent the interests of their constituents. It can claim a number of advantages over Question Time as well as over correspondence written to Ministers by those outside the House. It has the advantage over Question Time in that it takes place in private, hence making less relevant an appeal to party loyalty by the Minister (and probably encouraging greater frankness); there is obviously no limit on the number of 'supplementary' letters that can be written; and a Member can send, and expect to receive, a detailed and reasoned letter, one which can be made public. These points are borne out by the experience of the Department of Health and Social Security: the five Ministers in that Department currently receive over two thousand letters a month from Members, and the complexity of some of the matters raised is such that Ministers' replies sometimes run to three or four A4 pages in length.[21] The value of such letter writing has been attested to by Richard Crossman. Writing as a Minister, he noted in his *Diaries*: 'If a letter is sent to me by an MP or ex-Minister, I have to take great care because I have to answer it in writing and make a considered reply which could be published in the press. So in my view letters are a greater check on the executive than Questions.'[22] This view has been supported by a number of other sources.[23] A Member, according to one informed source, may get a favourable response to a letter if he has built up good personal relations with Ministers (regardless of party) and is not one of the Members well-known as publicity seekers.[24] And, if a Member does not get a satisfactory response, a Minister knows a question may be tabled, with the Member airing his grievance about the reply in a supplementary. A letter from a Member also has an advantage over letters written by ordinary citizens in that it is dealt with at a higher level. A letter from a member of the public will be dealt with at a level probably no higher than that of an executive officer, and a stock reply sent on the basis of existing rules or guidelines applicable to the case raised. A letter from a Member will reach the level of an Assistant Secretary, and then be submitted to the Minister for approval and signature. Thus, a Member's letter (like a parliamentary question) may serve to draw a Minister's attention to a matter of which he might otherwise not be aware. Although a Minister's letter should not call for a decision different from that which would be given in analogous cases, it is possible that in rare cases he may be persuaded to change his mind; generally, though, 'possibly the greatest advantage of a Member's letter is that it suffers no danger of receiving a stock answer that is inappropriate to the case.'[25]

Though the value of correspondence with Ministers has been questioned by some sources — on the grounds that it places too great a burden on Departments,[26] that it has no appreciable effect upon Ministers' decisions,[27] and that the pressure of constituency work is now such that a Member cannot hope (through writing to Ministers) to do justice to the number of appeals he receives from constituents[28] — it nevertheless remains a useful weapon in a Member's arsenal, one that can be exercised without formal limitations and without formal party control, and one that can be used effectively, like questions, as part of a wider strategy.

Early Day Motions

The amount of time available on the floor of the House for private Members is limited. A Member who wishes to draw a matter to the attention of the House and the Government, but who is unable to obtain parliamentary time, may table an Early Day Motion (EDM). Such motions, tabled formally 'for an early day', stand a negligible chance of being debated. They are, though, published in the daily Votes and Proceedings. Members who support them may add their names. There is no limit to the number of motions a Member may table, nor to the number he may sign; if a Member was so minded, he could add his name to all the motions tabled. One or more EDMs is usually tabled on each sitting day, and the number tabled each session is normally a substantial three-figure one; over eight hundred were tabled in the first session of the current Parliament. The matters covered by such motions are varied: a few are essentially frivolous, a number comment on the conduct of other Members or on procedural issues, some ask for Government action on certain national problems, some call for Government action on specific regional or constituency problems, a number express anxiety about international or domestic events, and others constitute statements, for example, congratulating a public figure upon a recent achievement. The most important from the Government's point of view are those which call for action or touch upon Government policy.

The value of tabling Early Day Motions in order to try to influence Government is limited. Given the number tabled, the chance of any one having an impact upon Government consciousness is limited; it becomes difficult to see the wood for the trees. The motions attract little public attention. The only time they tend to be referred to on the floor of the House is on Thursdays when the Leader of the House is questioned on the business for the next week. The sponsor of a motion will rise to draw attention to it and ask if time can be found for it to be debated. Though sometimes expressing sympathy with the content of the motion, the Minister's response is invariably in the negative.

The tabling of EDMs does have some uses. Such motions allow the Government's business managers and whips to gain a rough indication of what issues are exercising the minds of the Members. A motion carrying a great many names, especially if the names of Government backbenchers predominate, may cause the Government to take notice. Government supporters may table a motion as a means of giving public warning of their disquiet on a particular issue. The Government may then respond in order to deter the Members from taking action on the floor of the House. There are various instances of EDMs being used as a means of putting warning shots across the bows of the Treasury bench. In the 1970–4 Parliament, for example, the Government appeared to moderate its policy on the sale of arms to South Africa in response to a critical motion signed by 40 of its own backbenchers. (The Government could also have avoided the embarrassing defeat of its immigration rules in 1972 had it responded to a motion tabled earlier expressing the opposition of over 40 Conservatives.) The list of Early Day Motions in the Votes and Proceedings thus serves both as a noticeboard and a source of political intelligence.

The number of EDMs which have an impact upon Government policy, or which cause concern to the whips, is a very small one. Nevertheless, each motion receives attention. A motion covering a matter within the competence of a particular Department is sent to the parliamentary office of the relevant Minister. The response of the Department to the motion is prepared and submitted to the Minister for approval and then forwarded to the Leader of the House. As a result, the Leader is prepared with the Government's reply should one of the motion's supporters draw attention to it during the Thursday business questions. Even though a sponsor may not achieve a positive response, the tabling of a motion ensures that the Government's position is considered.

Debates

Debates on the floor of the House constitute one of the best-known devices for seeking to scrutinise and influence Government. In practice, there are different types of debate. In addition to the debates which take place at the various stages of a Bill's passage (as outlined in the preceding chapter), there are general and adjournment debates:

General debates

This constitutes an umbrella category, and comprises those debates which take place on substantive (as opposed to adjournment) motions. These include motions tabled by the Government for debate during Government time, by the Opposition for debate on one of its Supply Days, Private Members' time, as well as the annual debate on the Address, and on the Consolidated Fund Bill, the Second Reading debate of which constitutes Private Members' time. The motions themselves take various forms – expressing opinions ('That this House supports . . . '), just 'taking note', or even, on some Opposition Supply Days, calling for a reduction in a Minister's salary (the formal method of censuring a Minister). Except for debates in Private Members' time, the format of these debates is based on the adversary relationship between Government and Opposition. Indeed, the format is basically the same as that of Second Reading debates. About a quarter to a third of the time of the House is occupied each session by such general debates.[29]

The extent to which such debates help private Members to fulfil the function of scrutiny and influence has been questioned, even by Members themselves. The rationale for debate is that it enables the House collectively to debate a motion, and then decide upon it, the Government and its policy being the subject of the House's scrutiny and being influenced by its deliberations. It would be misleading to assume that this is what actually happens. Formally, the House debates motion, but during the debate the 'House' may constitute but a handful of Members. Though traditionally the relevant Ministers (usually the two taking part) remain throughout or for most of the debate, few Members stay after the front-bench speeches; a Member may find himself addressing one or two frontbenchers and half-a-dozen or more backbenchers, who themselves are present for the purpose of speaking rather than listening. The House occasionally fills up for a well-known and effective speaker, such as Enoch Powell or nowadays Edward Heath, or an important dissenting speech, but few Members regularly enter the chamber to listen to the speeches being made; only one in six of respondents in the survey by Barker and Rush said that they often listened to backbenchers speaking.[30] Also, in many debates the number of Members wishing to speak exceeds the number that the Chair is able to call; this, coupled with the fact that those wishing to speak may have decided views on the topic not shared by their less interested colleagues, can produce debates in which the views expressed are not a fair reflection of the views of the collectivity of Members.[31] In many, though not all, cases it is inaccurate to refer to them as *debates*; Members do not debate with one another, but tend rather to rise to deliver prepared texts, with which they proceed regardless of what has gone before. One could contend that there is something of a debate between parties (to influence not the opposite side but those outside the House), but this tends to take place most effectively during the front-bench speeches at the beginning and the end of proceedings, when the House is fairly well-attended. The explanation for the poor attendances and non-debate is largely, though not wholly, the fact that on most occasions everyone knows in advance how the vote is going to go at the end of the debate. The Government's supporters are usually prepared to support it in the lobbies, and will do so without many of them having listened to the debate; they are prepared to accept the guidance of the whips, and as a result normally provide the Government with a majority. Although the 1970s witnessed an increase in the willingness of backbenchers to engage in more independent voting than before — the result of certain divisions ceased to be foregone conclusions — this did not necessarily produce a commensurate increase in attendance or in meaningful debates on the floor of the House. The reason for this was (and is) that the important relationship was not the one between the debate in the chamber and the division, as presumed by the rationale for debates, but the one between what happened privately outside the chamber and the division. Because of the likelihood of its carrying the division, and the awareness that the debate—vote relationship is not as important as the intra-party discussion—vote relationship, the Government is generally believed to be not much influenced by views expressed in debate. Its position is further strengthened by the fact that most motions discussed in such general debates are declaratory rather than (as on legislation) binding. While naturally preferring to carry them, the loss of such motions — except confidence motions and those covering matters at the heart of Government policy — creates fewer headaches for the Government than the loss of legislation or important parts of legislative measures.

Such general debates are nevertheless not without some uses in helping to ensure a measure of scrutiny and influence, however limited. A debate prevents a Government from remaining mute. Ministers have to explain and justify the Government's position. They may want to reveal as little as possible, but the Government cannot afford to hold back too much for fear of letting the Opposition appear to have the better argument. The involvement of Opposition spokesman and backbenchers ensures that any perceived cracks in the Government's position will be exploited. If it has failed to carry its own side privately, the Government may suffer the embarrassment of the publicly expressed dissent of some of its own supporters, dissent which provides good copy for the press. On some occasions, Ministers may even be influenced by comments made in debate. They will not necessarily approach an issue with closed minds, and will normally not wish to be totally unreceptive to the comments of the Opposition (whose co-operation they need for the efficient despatch of business) or of their own Members (whose support they need in the lobbies, and among whom morale needs to be maintained); a Minister who creates a good impression by listening attentively to views expressed by Members may enhance his own prospects of advancement. The likelihood of a Minister's being influenced may be greatest when he is at the despatch box. Though the House may be nearly empty for much of a debate, it fills up during the front-bench speeches, and this is when the atmosphere of the House becomes important. A Minister faced by a baying Opposition and silence behind him may be unnerved and realise that he is not carrying Members on either side with him, and in consequence may moderate or even, in extreme cases, reverse his position. On such an occasion, the debate—vote relationship may become important, the fear of defeat concentrating the minds of Ministers. A recent example of such a debate was that on Members' pay in 1979, when the Leader of the House, Norman St John-Stevas, received such a rough reception at the despatch box that the Cabinet realised it did not have the support of the House and changed its previous decision.[32]

In addition, debates may act as useful channels for the expression of views held by the general interests and specific bodies represented by Members. If a Member with a known constituency interest in a certain subject rises to speak, he will invariably be listened to with greater respect than one who seeks solely to score party political points, and may even have some influence on the Minister's thinking; all MPs — Ministers and backbenchers — represent constituencies, and will normally have at least a degree of empathy for a Member seeking conscientiously to defend the interests of his constituents. (Some Members also make regular use of debates to convey opinions on Government policy expressed to them in letters from individual constituents, regardless of any special knowledge or interest in the subject.) If a Member known to have a close association with an important body rises to speak — interests have to be declared — the Minister may be more inclined to listen than might be the case if the Member were expressing a personal and not well-researched view. Such debates may be especially useful for the expression of views held by bodies which do not have the regular and well-established contact with Government Departments enjoyed by the influential sectional interest groups. Debates on Private Members' motions in particular may give an airing to subjects for which the Government might otherwise have little time. Thus, though general debates may be of limited value, they are not without their uses. Indeed, merely by being held they serve an important symbolic function, and, to some extent, do help Members to fulfil the functions for which they are returned.

Adjournment debates

In addition to the debates on substantive motions, there are debates on adjournment motions. Though, strictly speaking, each adjournment motion is the same, in that it calls for the adjournment of the House, there are, in practice, four types of debate which take place on the motion: general adjournment debates, the half-hour adjournment debates, emergency debates under standing order 9, and recess adjournment debates.

Debates similar to general debates on substantive motions (in terms of length and format) take place occasionally on adjournment motions. The advantage of tabling an adjournment rather than a substantive motion is that it can allow a wide-ranging debate on a topic, one on which the Government has no decided policy and/or on which it wishes to assess the views of Members. For example, in November 1979, following the Prime Minister's revelation (in reply to a written question) that Anthony Blunt had engaged in spying activities and had later been granted immunity from prosecution in return for information,[33] pressure built up in the House for a detailed Government statement and a debate on the matter. The Government conceded the case for a debate and tabled an adjournment motion for debate on 21 November.[34] Given that the matter had little to do with the policies of Government (Blunt had ceased his activities in the 1950s and had been granted immunity in 1965), and the number of issues raised by the case which MPs wished to comment upon — whether previous Prime Ministers had been informed, why immunity had been granted, whether other names were still being concealed, the implications for security and for the proposed reform of the Official Secrets Act,[35] among others — an adjournment debate seemed most appropriate; as the Government had nothing that it wished the House to 'take note' of or 'support', it is not at all clear what substantive motion could have been tabled. On occasion, the Opposition itself will table an adjournment motion for one of its Supply Days.[36] If critics of the Government's stance on the matter being debated wish to oppose the Government in the lobbies, they traditionally divide the House in support of the motion; that is, those opposed to the Government's position vote for the motion, the Government and its supporters vote against, regardless of who tabled the motion. On rare occasions, the Government has sought a confidence vote on an adjournment motion, as happened in the May 1940 debate on the Norwegian campaign, and on 11 March 1976 following the Government's defeat the previous day on its Expenditure White Paper.

The half-hour adjournment debate takes place at the end of each day's sitting, including Friday. At 10.00 p.m. (or 2.30 on Fridays),[37] or when exempted business is completed, a Government whip moves formally a motion for adjournment. A Member rises to discuss a topic, usually of constituency interest, for about ten or fifteen minutes, perhaps allowing another interested Member to intervene for a few minutes; a junior Minister then rises to reply for about ten or fifteen minutes. Half an hour after the adjournment motion has been moved, the Speaker adjourns the House.[38] There is a weekly ballot to determine which Members shall have four out of the five adjournment slots each week; the exception is on Thursday, when the Speaker chooses the Member. These debates are popular for raising matters of constituency or regional interest (especially as a follow-up to constituency matters raised at Question Time to which unsatisfactory responses were given) and for raising general, non-partisan issues in which Members take an interest. In the 1978–9 session, for example, topics which fell in to the former category included the casualty service in Redditch, the rebuilding of the Flixborough chemical plant, employment and industry in Hucknall, flooding in Faversham, the fishing industry in Hull, and housing, rates and employment in Lambeth (in each case raised by the or a local Member); topics falling into the latter category included tinkers, fluoridation, the Royal Commission on Gambling, glue sniffing, agoraphobia, transferability of pensions, export of drugs, footpaths, and lighthouse service pay. A Member may use the occasion to raise a national issue of some contention – in the 1978–9 session, Miss Jo Richardson raised the issue of immigration procedures, and Nigel Spearing that of European Communities' treaties – but such occasions are not common. Given the domestic nature of most of the issues raised, it is not surprising that the Ministries most involved in replying to adjournment debates are usually the Departments of Health and Social Security, Environment, Transport, Education and the Home Office. In the 1966–7 session, the Transport Ministry was responsible for replying to more than twice as many debates as the Treasury, and four times as many in the 1978–9 session.[39]

The timing and content of the half-hour adjournment debates results in their receiving little attention, either from the press or from most Members; it is not uncommon for a Member to raise a topic on adjournment and find himself with an audience comprising the occupant of the Chair, the junior Minister who is to reply, the Government whip present for procedural purposes, and if he is lucky, one or perhaps two other Members interested in the subject he is raising. Again, 'debate' is a misnomer. A Member delivers usually a prepared text, about the main points of which he will have advised the Minister in advance; the Minister then replies with a prepared brief on the points he knew would be raised. And when the half-hour is up, that is the end of it; no vote is taken, and the House rises. Nevertheless, these debates are not without value. Coming at the end of the day they do not impinge on other business, and they provide Members with thirty minutes in which to raise matters of interest usually to their constituents;[40] a Member has the opportunity to develop his case, and the Minister has time to give a considered reply, one which will have been well-researched. Having had the matter drawn to the Ministry's attention, the junior Minister replying may announce that his Department is prepared to accede to the Member's request;[41] if instead his reply is a negative one, he still has to justify that response. The Procedure Committee in 1978 felt that the debates were regarded by Members 'as a valuable opportunity to raise matters of concern, particularly to their constituents', and rejected the idea that the debates should be transferred from the floor of the House to committee.[42]

Another but very dissimilar form of adjournment debate is that which may, but rarely does, take place under standing order 9: the emergency adjournment debate. At the beginning of public business (except on Fridays) a Member may rise to ask for leave to move the adjournment of the House 'for the purpose of discussing a specific and important matter that should have urgent considerations'.[43] The Member briefly outlines the matter he wishes to have debated, and why he thinks it merits attention. If the Speaker is satisfied that the matter should be the subject of an emergency debate (in giving his decision he no longer has to give his reasons) and the leave of the House given (that is, no Member objects), the debate is granted. If objection is made, those who support the request rise in their places, and if forty or more Members rise, the debate is granted; if more than ten but less than forty rise, the matter is determined on a division. If an emergency debate is granted, it takes place the following day at 3.30 p.m. (or the following Monday if granted on a Thursday) or, if the Speaker decides the urgency of the matter justifies it, at 7.00 p.m. the same day. In deciding whether to accede to a Member's request for debate on a particular matter, the Speaker has to consider

> the extent to which it concerns the administrative responsibilities of Ministers of the Crown or could come within the scope of ministerial

action. In determining whether a matter is urgent Mr Speaker shall have regard to the probability of the matter being brought before the House in time by other means.[44]

Few such debates are granted: the Government, in large part the official Opposition, and the Speaker generally dislike the interruption to arranged business that emergency debates entail. Only about one to four such debates are granted each session. Examples included John Mendelson's successful request for a debate on the Crown Agents' affair in 1977 (in the division at the end of the debate the Government was defeated); Patrick Cormack's application for one in 1978 on the closure of *The Times* newspaper, and Tam Dalyell's request in 1980 for a debate on the Government's decision to apply economic sanctions against Iran retrospectively (between the granting of the debate and its taking place, the Government reversed its decision). Although few requests are granted, applications for emergency debates are many, and reached something of a peak in late 1978 and early 1979, when Conservative Members regularly sought such debates on the industrial disputes that were then current. Between 29 November 1978 and 21 March 1979 no fewer than sixty-nine applications were submitted to the Speaker, over fifty of them dealing in one form or another with industrial disputes or their consequences. Mr Speaker allowed three debates, one on *The Times's* closure and two under the general heading of the 'industrial situation'. The use made of the procedure by Conservative MPs was such that one Labour Member, William Molloy, actually sought an emergency debate to discuss 'the possible abuse by hon. Members in making applications to Mr Speaker under Standing Order No. 9 which brings this House into disrepute'; his request was refused by Mr Speaker.[45] The period was somewhat atypical, the other applications made during this period being more typical (in number and content) of those usually made. These covered the subjects of Vietnamese refugees, a radio interview with the Northern Ireland Secretary, an air crash in Rhodesia, the 1977 Aircraft and Shipbuilding Industries Act, the sale of harrier aircraft to China, a leaked Treasury memorandum on employment projects, national savings certificates, income tax, and an interview on a television programme with a doctor about the torture of suspects in Northern Ireland. None of these requests was granted. Despite this low success rate, the procedure has certain attractions to Members. It is essentially a backbenchers' weapon (though Opposition frontbenchers occasionally make use of it); it allows a Member to state briefly the case for a debate at prime time in the parliamentary day (an attempt to have requests for emergency debates treated in the same way as applications for private notice questions was rejected by the House in October 1979);[46] and there is always the chance that Mr Speaker may allow the application; if he does, the Government is forced to respond quickly. It is a useful backstop to prevent the Government from avoiding comment or debate on an urgent matter of public importance.

The final category is that of the recess adjournment debate. The final day before each recess is given over to discussion on an adjournment motion of topics raised by private Members. The topics to be raised are pre-arranged, and the debate takes the form for all practical purposes of a series of half-hour adjournment debates, the only difference being that on this occasion discussion of each topic tends to last a little, and sometimes a lot, longer than thirty minutes. Roughly eight topics are covered in each of these debates. The advantages and disadvantages of the recess debates are essentially the same as those of the half-hour adjournment debates. Though attracting little attention, they allow Members to raise subjects in somewhat more detail than would otherwise be possible on the floor of the House and to obtain a considered public response from the Government.

In proportion to the time it spends sitting, the House does not spend much time on the latter three types of adjournment debates (half-hour, emergency and recess) − only about 5 per cent of its time each session[47] − but the time that is so spent may be described as generally of value to the private Member. The debates do not impinge much upon other business, and they allow Members the opportunity to pursue (usually free of party influence) their task of representation, especially of constituency or regional interests.

The Parliamentary Commissioner for Administration

Although the use of Question Time and half-hour adjournment debates is valuable for questioning publicly Government decisions, they are not devices for investigating thoroughly the way in which certain decisions are made. This is a point of particular importance where administrative decisions are made that affect individual citizens. The influential Report published by the organisation Justice in 1961, *The Citizen and the Administration*, known as the Whyatt Report, commented upon the likelihood that proceedings between a Department and an MP would develop into a contest, one which was likely to be uneven, given the Minister's access to documents and information not freely available to Members.[48] In order to remedy this, and to provide the citizen with some more effective form of redress against injustice by Departments, it recommended the creation of a Swedish-style Ombudsman to investigate such cases. Although not acted upon by the then Conservative Government, the subsequent Labour Government responded to the Report and introduced a measure which was passed as the Parliamentary Commissioner Act and became effective on 1 April 1967.

The Act brought into existence an Ombudsman, known formally as the Parliamentary Commissioner for Administration (PCA), with power to investigate complaints of maladministration brought to his attention by MPs acting on behalf of members of the public. His powers of investigation extended to any action by a Government Department in the exercise of its *administrative* function, but not to policy decisions, which were the concern of the Government (it was, after all, the Government that introduced the measure), nor to matters affecting relations with other countries or the activities of British officials abroad. He was to consider the *way* in which decisions had been reached and not the merits of decisions reached without maladministration. He was precluded from investigating cases concerned with nationalised industries, the police, and the army, among others, though the Ombudsman procedure has subsequently been extended to encompass the National Health Service, local government, and Northern Ireland. Certain other matters were excluded from the scope of his investigations; also he does not normally intervene in cases where a complainant has an alternative remedy available, though he has discretion to do so if the complainant has not pursued such a remedy.

Since the creation of the post, the Ombudsman has had some success in obtaining the redress of grievances in a number of cases where maladministration has been found, and in a few cases his reports have attracted attention by the news media.[49] The definition of maladministration has been broadened somewhat as well. The main advantage accruing from the creation of the post, though, is probably its deterrent effect. It can be seen as helping to obviate cases, certainly deliberate cases, of maladministration by officials both now and in the future.

Nevertheless, there are clearly serious limitations to the Ombudsman's ability to function effectively to ensure the redress of grievances in cases of maladministration. He is excluded from investigations in certain areas; he has limited resources, and tends to rely for legal advice upon the Departments concerned; he has limited access to files (although he has access to all Departmental papers, he can under the terms of the 1967 Act be precluded from seeing Cabinet papers, as happened in the Court Line case); most of his work receives little public attention; he cannot undertake investigations on his own initiative; and he is precluded from considering the merits of decisions taken by Departments in the exercise of their discretionary powers. The method of referring cases to him has also been criticised, as has the fact that he has no powers of enforcement. Amending the method of referring cases to allow the citizen direct access, and giving the Ombudsman powers of enforcement, would arguably impinge upon the powers of the Commons.

Already, the PCA's relationship with the Commons is not a well-defined one. 'The Commissioner was brought into existence as a piece of parliamentary machinery. As Sir Edmund Compton used to emphasize, he is a *parliamentary* Commissioner.'[50] The creation of the Select Committee on the Parliamentary Commissioner for Administration acted and acts as a useful complement to his work, considering and pursuing with Departments some of his reports.[51] However, the Ombudsman himself is not appointed by the Commons — he is, in effect, a parliamentary official appointed by the Government. When Sir Idwal Pugh was appointed as the third occupant of the post in 1976, the Prime Minister admitted that he had not consulted MPs before making the appointment. The only direct contact Members (other than members of the Select Committee) have with the PCA is through referring cases to him and receiving his replies. Given that he is a Parliamentary Commissioner, and relies upon the House to take action on his reports when Departments are unresponsive to his findings, there is clearly some *prima facie* justification for MPs alone having power to refer cases. Removing that power would remove what little contact Members have with the PCA, and would arguably reduce even further their interest in his activities. Some writers have argued in favour of complainants having direct access, contending that this would not be inconsistent with the concept of a Parliamentary Commissioner. 'It would not deprive any Member of his right to invoke the Commissioner's assistance. It would both cheer the citizen and stimulate the machinery of administrative justice. Like a Bill of Rights, it would add a new and entertaining dimension to political life.'[52] However, as the same writer noted, the concept of maladministration by officials was not one that had much impact upon public consciousness.[53] Allowing the public direct access would, in practice, achieve little (the citizen, one suspects, would be unknowing rather than cheered), other than probably increasing significantly the amount of time spent by the Ombudsman's staff in rejecting complaints for want of jurisdiction. Using MPs as a filter helps to deter the more frivolous complaints, ensures that a Member is forewarned of cases that may become important later, and serves an important symbolic function.

A more difficult question is that of the PCA's lack of enforcement powers. Relying upon the Commons to act on his reports where Departments fail to heed his warnings has had obvious drawbacks, not least that of parliamentary time and, in certain cases, the ability of the Minister concerned to appeal to party loyalty (in the Court Line case, for example, the Minister had the support of the Cabinet). Giving the Parliamentary Commissioner enforcement powers of his own could raise certain questions about his role, and would probably be difficult to achieve: the powers would have to be granted by statute, and Ministers, encouraged by their officials, are unlikely to be enthusiastic about introducing such a measure. Either such a Bill would have to go through against the Government's wishes (which is improbable), or the House itself have to increase its interest in pursuing the Commissioner's reports. The latter would appear to be the more practical approach.

In its 1978 Report, the Procedure Committee recommended that the cases reported by the PCA should be the responsibility of the proposed Department-related Select Committees, with the residual functions of the Select Committee for the PCA allocated to the Treasury Committee.[54] However, the recommendation was not implemented. In the debate on the Committee's Report on 25 June 1979, the Leader of the House expressed the view that the PCA Committee could keep the system as a whole under review, and consider cases on the basis of principles common to every Department. 'The Government believe that this work would be a valuable complement to the work of the departmentally related Committees in relation to their own Departments.'[55] This view was not seriously challenged, and under the terms of the new standing order approved by the House, the Committee was retained.

Select Committees

There are essentially two types of Select Committee in the House of Commons, those that might fairly be described as domestic committees and those that may be described as scrutiny committees. The domestic committees are those concerned primarily with the internal administration of the House and its privileges, and comprise the Committees of Privilege (appointed regularly since the seventeenth century), Selection, House of Commons (Services), Register of Members' Interests, Broadcasting, and (as and when appointed) Procedure.[56] More important for our purposes are the scrutiny committees. Occasionally an *ad hoc* committee is appointed to consider a particular subject of a legislative or a pre-legislative nature (see Chapter 5), but the more numerous and important are the regular scrutiny committees appointed by standing order.

Although scrutiny committees constitute a topic of contemporary importance, with most of the now existing committees being of very recent creation, the House has boasted two long-standing committees, of which one still remains and the other is defunct.

The extant committee is the Public Accounts Committee (the PAC) which was first appointed in 1861 to ensure that public expenditure was properly incurred for the purpose for which it had been voted and in conformity with the relevant Act. Over time, the Committee has interpreted more widely its terms of reference, and has investigated cases to see whether a Department could have achieved better value for the money spent and whether or not there was any negligence involved. The Committee itself does not carry out departmental audits. This task is fulfilled by the Comptroller and Auditor General — though described by various sources and by certain Acts as an official of the House, his status is not as clear as it might be[57] – assisted by a staff of over six hundred. Both the PAC and the Comptroller and Auditor General perform a valuable, though increasingly limited,[58] role of *post hoc* scrutiny, and both make reports to the House, the PAC's report being debated each session. The PAC can make recommendations which are considered by the Treasury in consultation with Departments, and which, if accepted, are put into effect according to Treasury instructions. If the recommendations are not accepted, a reasoned reply has to be submitted to the Committee, which may either accept the reply or renew its recommendations in a later report. In 1978, the Procedure Committee recognised that the PAC had an 'indispensable, specialised role', and, while making some proposals to strengthen the effectiveness of the Committee and the Comptroller's audit functions, recommended that the Committee be retained.[59]

The other committee of long standing was the Estimates Committee. It was first appointed in 1912, but went into abeyance for the period from 1914 to 1921 and during the Second World War, and lasted until 1971. Its main functions were to consider the presentation of the Estimates and to look at ways in which policies could be carried out more cost-efficiently. It was not permitted to consider the merits of the policies. However, the dividing line between policy and administration was not always clear, and the Committee, especially in the post-1945 period, ventured into areas that could not be described as solely administrative.[60] It established itself as a useful surveyor of how effectively policy and expenditure programmes were implemented, and it helped accustom Departments to the dissemination of a great deal of information about their activities.[61] Nevertheless, it suffered from a number of drawbacks: its role was not clearly defined; its terms of reference were restricted; and its subcommittees tended to avoid any systematic scrutiny of departmental Estimates.[62] It was also hampered by the financial information presented to it by the Government, which tended to be inadequate for it to do a really effective job, and by the absence of a supporting official analagous to the Comptroller and Auditor General. The creation of new Select Committees in the 1966–70 Parliament helped to deplete membership of the Committee and to reduce the scope of its examination of departmental spending. In addition, there was some duplication between its subcommittees and some of the new committees, as, for example, between its Technological and Scientific Affairs subcommittee and the Select Committee on Science and Technology. The Procedure Committee, in its 1969 Report on the scrutiny of public expenditure and administration, drew attention to these problems, and recommended that the Estimates Committee be replaced with a new Expenditure Committee with wider terms of reference. The recommendation was accepted, and implemented in early 1971.

Although the use of Select Committees by the House is a well-established one, what may be described as the modern Department-related or subject-based Select Committees are essentially of recent origin. 1944 saw the creation of the committee to scrutinise statutory instruments (see Chapter 5), and, more important in this context, the 1950s witnessed the creation of the Select Committee on Nationalised Industries. Following disquiet expressed by Members on both sides of the House about the lack of accountability of nationalised industries, a Select Committee appointed to consider the relationship between the industries and the House recommended in 1953 that a Select Committee be appointed (with powers similar to the Public Accounts Committee) to consider the industries. In 1955, with customary caution, the Government moved the appointment of such a committee. However, the terms of reference of the committee were so limited that its members pressed the Government to widen them, and this was done in 1956. The committee was given power, almost a free reign, to examine the 'reports and accounts of the nationalised industries'. In terms of conducting incisive investigations and influencing and informing both the Government and the House, the success of the committee was limited. A number of industries under public ownership did not fall within its jurisdiction (only later did it acquire jurisdiction over the Post Office, Cable and Wireless Limited, the Independent Television Authority, and certain functions of the Bank of England); its resources were very limited: it had no full-time permanent advisers, acquiring only an additional clerk in 1959 and the power to appoint part-time outside advisers for particular inquiries in 1967 (the committee itself in 1959 had rejected the idea of having an official analagous to the Comptroller and Auditor General);[63] its reports were rarely debated by the House, and one chairman of the committee believed that few Members read them;[64] and its reports often failed to elicit positive responses from the Government. Furthermore, on occasion, Ministers appointed committees to investigate matters already under consideration by the committee.[65] Nevertheless, it did achieve some modest success. Despite limited resources, it managed by 1971 to investigate every industry within its jurisdiction, bar that of steel, and from 1966 to 1968 went beyond its normal scope of activity to conduct an across-the-board inquiry into the industries' relations with Departments and with Parliament. It saw *some* of its recommendations accepted by the Government (as on British Railways, the gas industry and the Post Office), and it developed a bipartisan approach that was to be much admired by parliamentary reformers. It was to serve as a useful precedent for those wishing to extend the House's role of scrutiny through committees.

The belief that the Commons should extend its scrutiny function through the wider use of investigative Select Committees was much in vogue in the 1960s, especially among academic reformers such as Bernard Crick and many newly returned Labour Members in the 1964–6 and 1966–70 Parliaments. Their calls for the setting up of such committees were to receive a warm reception from Richard Crossman, who became Leader of the House in 1966. In December 1966 he announced the establishment of two specialist Select Committees, one to cover the Ministry of Agriculture and the other to cover the subject of Science and Technology. The purpose of the committees, it was explained, was to make the executive more accountable to Parliament through eliciting information which previously had remained within the Government machine.

> This it was hoped would enable members of a Select Committee to formulate pertinent questions about policy before decisions had actually been made, and also it would result in the building-up within the House of Commons of a body of members with greater knowledge and experience of particular fields of Governmental activity.[66]

For the Agriculture Committee the reality was to be somewhat different. It chose for investigation the adequacy of the Ministry's study of the effects of EC entry on agriculture, and wanted to go to Brussels to pursue its inquiries. Its plans to do so ran into opposition from the Foreign Office, and it was able to go abroad only after a compromise was reached with the Government. In its first report, the committee gave the background to this dispute and criticised the Government. As the Procedure Committee was tactfully to put it in 1978, it was a committee which 'experienced some difficulty in establishing a *modus vivendi* with the relevant Government Departments'.[67] The Government responded by increasing the size of the committee the following session, in what appeared to be a none too subtle attempt to pack the committee,[68] and when this failed, announced the following session that the committee was not to be reappointed. It ceased to exist in February 1969. During its two-year existence, the Government replied officially to none of its reports, and the committee itself expressed the view that 'there is no evidence that the Government did consider the opinion of the Committee.'[69]

The Science and Technology Committee fared somewhat better. Its reports were better received; it fulfilled a useful informative function; and it had an occasional recommendation accepted by the Government (as, for example, that the Atomic Energy Authority should retain only the function of research and development);[70] it covered a subject that in party political terms was fairly neutral; and it achieved a relatively high stability in its membership, a number of its members having some technical or scientific background. In 1967, Richard Crossman commented that the committee satisfied an important need, and it survived until the reorganisation of 1979.

These two committees were followed by others: these comprised two committees set up to consider the work of particular Departments (Education and Science, and Overseas Development), one to consider a specific subject (Race Relations and Immigration), and one that could be described as a hybrid between the two (Scottish Affairs), as well as the committee on the Parliamentary Commissioner. Although these new committees performed a useful role in providing information, it was clear by 1970 that they were not proving very successful in their task of scrutiny and influence. 'Specialist Committees', as Donald Shell has noted, 'have so far exerted only the most minor influence on policy-making and administration.'[71] Even the leading proponent of reform, Professor Crick, had by the beginning of the 1970s begun, on his own admission, to 'blow hot and cold' about them.[72] In 1969 the Procedure Committee, as we have noted, drew attention to the problems the new committees were creating for the Estimates Committee; it recommended the creation of a new Expenditure Committee with wider terms of reference than the existing committee and eight functional subcommittees (and a general subcommittee) to cover the whole field of Government activity: it was envisaged that each subcommittee would be empowered to consider the activities of the Department within its given field as well as the Estimates of that Department. The incoming Conservative Government of Mr Heath accepted the principle of the recommendation, but proposed an Expenditure Committee of forty-nine Members, an insufficient number to man the proposed eight subcommittees. The result was an Expenditure Committee appointed with general terms of reference[73] and six subcommittees (covering Defence and External Affairs; Environment; Trade and Industry; Education, the Arts, and the Home Office; Social Services and Employment; and a general subcommittee); its first chairman was Edward du Cann. In the wake of the establishment of the new committee, the department related Education and Science Committee was wound up; the Scottish Affairs Committee suffered a similar fate a little later. There thus remained, in addition to the PAC and the new Expenditure Committee, the Committees on Statutory Instruments, Nationalised Industries, the Parliamentary Commissioner for Administration, Science and Technology, Overseas Development, and Race Relations and Immigration. The list was subsequently added to by the creation of the Committee on European Legislation.

The experience of the Select Committees in the 1970s was not a glorious one. They suffered from limited resources (being able to appoint only part-time specialist advisers), from doubts about their roles, from the absence of a coherent approach to scrutinising the executive (a lack of coherence which applied not only between committees but also between the subcommittees of the Expenditure Committee), from a lack of interest on the part of the Government and the House in their reports — few were debated on the floor of the House and when they were, it was committee members who tended to speak; and from an unwillingness on the part of the Government and reformers to concede to them the powers that could make them effective, powers which of necessity would detract from the powers of the Government.[74] The Expenditure Committee itself proved something of a disappointment. As Nevil Johnson has observed, it proved eclectic in its choice of topics, with little evidence of a desire to cover particular sectors of Government activity systematically or to stick closely to 'value for money' questions.[75] Though productive in output, its reports did not differ that substantially from those of its predecessors.[76] The committees did perform a useful function of providing information, but the release of 'several useful reports', some of which received 'favourable comments in editorials',[77] did not result in much Government action. One critic went so far as to claim that the work of the Expenditure Committee had not resulted in one penny of public money being allocated differently.[78] By the latter half of the decade, it was apparent that 'the expanded activity of Select Committees had brought little genuine change in the manner in which Parliament operates and in its relations between it and the Executive.'[79]

On 9 June 1976 a Select Committee on Procedure was appointed for the duration of the Parliament to 'consider the practice and procedure of the House in relation to public business and to make recommendations for the more effective performance of its functions'. In its First Report, released in August 1978, it directed its attention especially to the Select Committees of the House. Recognising the problem associated with the existing committees, it declared:

> The House should no longer rest content with an incomplete and unsystematic scrutiny of the activities of the Executive merely as a result of historical accident or sporadic pressures, and it is equally desirable for the different branches of the public service to be subject to an even and regular incidence of select committee investigation into their activities and to have a clear understanding of the division of responsibilities between the committees which conduct it. We therefore favour a reorganisation of the select committee structure to provide the House with the means of scrutinising the activities of the public service on a continuing and systematic basis.[80]

It recommended the creation of twelve small department-related Select Committees, with widely drawn terms of reference, and appointed (like the PAC and Expenditure Committee) by permanent standing order. It wanted the proposed committees to be able to appoint whatever specialist advisers they needed for their work and to have the power to summon Ministers, the members of the committees to be nominated by the

Committee of Selection, considerations to be given to paying committee chairmen a 'modest additional salary', and for eight parliamentary days to be set aside each session for debates on committee reports. Each committee was to be charged with the examination of all aspects of expenditure, administration, and policy within the responsibilities of a single Government Department or two or more related Departments. Between them, the committees were designed to cover the activities of all Government Departments, as well as the nationalised industries and other quasi-autonomous Government organisations within the responsibilities of the relevant Departments.[81] The Expenditure Committee, it recommended, should disappear, along with the Committees on the Parliamentary Commissioner, Overseas Development, Science and Technology, the Nationalised Industries, and Race Relations and Immigration, their tasks to be absorbed by the new committees. Only the PAC, the Committee on European Legislation, and the Statutory Instruments Committee, along with the Joint Committee on Consolidation Bills,[82] were marked down for retention. The Procedure Committee's Report was viewed by some observers as being both substantial and radical,[83] *The Times* going so far as to describe it as an 'historic document in British parliamentary history'.[84]

Initially, it looked as if the Report might go the way of other reports from Procedure Committees – ignored by the Government and undebated in the House. Working against its possible implementation was the fact that the Leader of the House, Michael Foot, was known to be unsympathetic to its proposals. However, interest in the Committee's Report began to grow among backbenchers on both sides of the House and also to find favour with the Opposition leadership through the Shadow Leader of the House, Francis Pym, and his successor, Norman St John-Stevas. The pressure for a debate built up, and eventually Mr Foot conceded that one should be held. The debate took place in February 1979, with the Opposition leadership combining with Conservative and Labour backbenchers to press the view that the House should be given the opportunity to vote on the Report's recommendations. Mr Foot sought to resist this demand, but the pressure from both sides of the House was such that he reversed his position and agreed to it. The general election of May 1979 then intervened. In the election campaign, the Conservative manifesto contained a pledge to 'give the new House of Commons an early chance of coming to a decision' on the Procedure Committee's recommendations (a promise previously voiced by Francis Pym at the 1978 Conservative Party Conference), and the new Government – on the initiative of the new Leader of the House, Norman St John-Stevas (see Chapter 9) – honoured that pledge, shortly after taking office, on 25 June 1979. After a full debate, the House approved the setting up of the new committee structure (voting was 248 to 12),[85] the

new committees being established to 'examine the expenditure, administration, and policy of the principal Government Departments . . . and
associated public bodies'.[86] In addition to the twelve new committees
(with some modification) recommended in the Report,[87] it was subsequently agreed to establish a Committee on Scottish Affairs and another
on Welsh Affairs (the Procedure Committee having avoided recommending
such committees until the outcome of the then Government's devolution
proposals was known); the Committee on the Parliamentary Commissioner was also retained. The new committees are listed, along with the
remaining committees, in Table 6.1. Although the Procedure Committee
also got its way on the selection of members (by the Committee of
Selection) and the size of committees (to be kept small), the House
failed to approve the recommendations that eight days should be set
aside each session for debates of committee reports and that the committees should have the power to compel the attendence of Ministers
(the committees retain the usual power to send for 'persons, papers and
records'); the Leader of the House, Mr St John-Stevas, did promise in
the debate, though, that Ministers would do all in their power to
co-operate with the committees. The membership of the new committees
was, after a delay, agreed to on 26 November 1979, each committee
then electing its own chairman (see Table 6.1). The calendar year 1980
marked the first full year of the committees' activities.

   Although it is still too early to evaluate the new committees, it is
possible to contend that they constitute a considerable improvement on
what went before. Their coverage of Government Departments can now
be described as comprehensive (in terms of what may be covered); they
have broad terms of reference; and they were set up with a fair degree
of enthusiasm on the part of those involved. They are more identifiable
as units than their predecessors, attract more publicity, and are increasingly the target of representations from outside interests; pressure groups
worried by some aspect of Government policy now approach the relevant
committee, something which never happened before. To ensure some
albeit limited co-ordination, the previously informal Liaison Committee,
comprising the committee chairmen, has now been formalised; in January
1980 it was established as a Select Committee.[88] However, the investigations undertaken by the committees and their effectiveness in fulfilling
the function of scrutiny and influence will not be, and already are not,
uniform. Each committee is free to choose the topics for investigation,
and each of necessity has to be selective rather than exhaustive in its
choice; Table 6.2, listing Select Committee meetings on an average
parliamentary day, reflects the range of committee interests, as does the
variety of reports already issued. (Up to the 1980 summer recess, almost
fifty reports had been issued, somewhat disparate in nature and content.)
Much depends not only on the use made of specialist advisers – and

TABLE 6.1

SELECT COMMITTEES OF SCRUTINY, 1979–80

Committee	Chairman	Number of members[a]	Number of specialist advisers[b]
New committees (established 1979)			
Agriculture	Sir William Elliot (Con.)	9	4
Defence	Sir John Langford-Holt (Con.)	11	4
Education, Science and Arts	Christopher Price (Lab.)	9	4
Employment	John Golding (Lab.)	9	4
Energy	Ian Lloyd (Con.)	11	9
Environment	Bruce Douglas-Mann (Lab.)	11	7
Foreign Affairs	Anthony Kershaw (Con.)	11	4
(Overseas Development subcommittee)	(Kevin McNamara (Lab.))	(10)	(5)
Home Affairs	Sir Graham Page (Con.)	11	2
(Race Relations subcommittee)	(John Wheeler (Con.))	(5)	(1)
Industry and Trade	Sir Donald Kaberry (Con.)	11	2
Social Services	Mrs Renee Short (Lab.)	9	5
Transport	Tom Bradley (Lab.)	11	2
Treasury and Civil Service	Edward du Cann (Con.)	11	7
(Treasury and Civil Service subcommittee)	(Robert Sheldon (Lab.))	(7)	(3)
Scottish Affairs	Donald Dewar (Lab.)	13	1
Welsh Affairs	Leo Abse (Lab.)	11	3
Liaison (est. Jan. 1980)	Edward du Cann (Con.)		
Previously established committees			
Parliamentary Commissioner for Administration	Anthony Buck (Con.)	8	
Public Accounts	Joel Barnett (Lab.)	15	
Statutory Instruments	Bob Cryer (Lab.)	7[c]	
European Legislation	Julius Silverman (Lab.)	16	
Consolidation Bills (Joint Committee)	(Lord Keith of Kinkel)	12[c]	

Notes: 'Domestic' committees excluded.

a Maximum number of members for department-related Select Committees (standing order 86A (2)).

b As at June 1980. Based on written answer, *House of Commons Debates*, 986, c. 272–4 Specialist advisers are not paid salaries, but are paid on a 'per diem' basis on production of evidence of work done.   c Number of Commons Members.

TABLE 6.2
MEETINGS OF SELECT COMMITTEES, 7 MAY 1980

Committee	Meeting	Subject	Witnesses
Education, Science and Arts	9.30 a.m. (private) 10.30 a.m. (public)	Funding and organisation of courses in higher education	Standing Conference of Principals and Directors of Colleges, and Institutes in Higher Education
Defence	10.00 a.m. (private)		
Scottish Affairs	10.00 a.m. (private) 10.30 a.m. (public)	Co-operation and overlap among the agencies, etc., responsible for attracting inward investment to Scotland	Scottish Economic Planning Department, Scottish Development Agency and Department of Industry
Energy	10.30 a.m. (private) 10.45 a.m. (public)	Government's statement on the New Nuclear Power Programme	Babcock Power Ltd
Industry and Trade	10.30 a.m. (private) 10.45 a.m. (public)	Import and export trade	British Paper and Board Industry Federation and Metal Trades Organisation
Agriculture	2.30 p.m. (public) (in Edinburgh)	Economic, social and health implications for the UK of the Common Agricultural Policy on milk and dairy products	Scottish Trade Union Congress and Scottish Grocers Federation
Social Services	4.30 p.m. (private)	To consider draft Report	
Welsh Affairs	6.15 p.m (public)	The role of the Welsh Office and associated bodies in developing employment opportunities in Wales	Development Board for Rural Wales

Other Select Committees meeting the same day: Public Accounts Committee, European Legislation, Joint Committee on Consolidation Bills, and one of the domestic committees, the House of Commons (Services) Committee.

committee approaches to their use vary already (see, for example, Table 6.1) — but also upon the committee members themselves. In terms of knowledge and competence in the fields covered, one or two committees have powerful memberships (the Treasury and Civil Service Committee being a case in point);[89] a number of others have not. (The chairmen in particular now play an important role, though the manner in which a number of them reached their positions does not augur well for the future.)[90] Some committees are more enthusiastic than others. For part of 1980, the Defence Committee was actually conducting three investigations simultaneously. The Overseas Development subcommittee of the Foreign Affairs Committee, by contrast, has experienced difficulty in generating interest among Conservative Members.[91] The lack of any guaranteed linkage between committee activities and the floor of the House creates problems: depending upon the Government to provide time to debate reports which may be critical of Government Departments is not the best way to proceed. (Only one of the first thirty reports emanating from the new committees was debated on the floor of the House.) As we shall argue in Chapter 9, in so far as the House retains power, it does so through the division lobbies on the floor of the House, and if committees are divorced from the floor of the House, from the interests of the collectivity of Members, then the danger remains of their existing and operating, like their predecessors, 'in a sort of bipartisan limbo, remote from the main House, unconnected with its procedures and deeply unsure of their role'.[92] The potential for the committtees to be effective exists, but it does and must depend largely upon the willingness of Members themselves, the collectivity of Members not in the Government, to make them so.

Conclusion

Various means exist by which Members may seek to scrutinise and influence the actions of Government. Question Time, private correspondence, the Parliamentary Commissioner for Administration, and half-hour adjournment debates are especially useful to Members wishing to scrutinise and influence Departments as part of their role of specific representation (primarily looking after the interests of constituents); debates are useful to one element in the House in particular, the Opposition, to exercise its critical scrutiny of Government; and Select Committees provide the House, working through subunits, with the opportunity to keep under more sustained scrutiny the work and expenditure of each Department. Each of these devices has its advantages and disadvantages, as we have seen.

However, the use of these means is not mutually exclusive. Members wishing to keep under observation a particular area of Government

activity or to influence a Department to take certain action may maximise the usefulness of these devices by employing not one but most of
them. A Member on the Government side of the House may first of all
make use of the intra-party channels available to him (see Chapter 3); if
those fail to produce the desired results, he can write privately to the
Minister, if necessary several times. He can then table a parliamentary
question, or as many as he likes if put down for written answer (in 1969,
for example, Ernest Marples tabled sixty-eight written questions to eight
Ministers about their Department's procurement arrangements).[93] He
may seek a half-hour adjournment debate; depending on the subject
involved, he may introduce a Private Member's Bill of his own (see
Chapter 5) or take part in the relevant Government debate, if there is
one, on the floor of the House and possibly vote against his own side in
the division. If a member of a Select Committee, he may utilise various
of these means to pursue the Government recommendations made by
his committee.

    Though the ability of individual backbenchers is limited by the nature
of the relationship between the House and that part of it which forms
the Government, the use of these means of scrutiny and influence can
be effective. Much depends on the subject involved (an individual
Member is unlikely to have much success in seeking to change the
Government's main economic policy) and also upon the Members
concerned. Persistence often pays. The greater the number of Members
seeking change, the greater the chances of success. A persistent Member
who is prepared to pursue a matter, and if necessary lobby like-minded
Members for support, can have some effect on a Minister's intentions, a
fact variously attested to by a number of MPs.[94] As one observed, 'if a
backbencher applies himself to the rules, procedures and the encouragement of his colleagues to assist him in using the Chamber of the House
of Commons, a great deal can be achieved.'[95] An excellent example is
the case of Sir Bernard Braine, the Conservative Member for Essex
South-East, who in recent years has, among other things, fought vigorously to defend a number of constituents against injustice on the part
of the Ministry of Housing, 1967—8 (use of the Parliamentary Commissioner for Administration and the Select Committee on the PCA);[96] to
defend part of his constituency, Canvey Island, from further proliferation
of oil refineries (use of the floor of the House, including making a mara-
thon speech lasting three hours and sixteen minutes in 1974);[97] to defend
his area against the proposed Maplin airport (use of intra-party forums,
correspondence and meetings with Ministers, adjournment debates, and
speaking and voting against the Maplin Development Bill);[98] to protect
the rights of entry into Britain of Commonwealth citizens (use of intra-
party forums, and speaking against and rounding-up like-minded
Members to vote against the 1972 immigration rules — as a result of

which the Government lost the division);[99] and to support the pleas of the Banaban people not to be part of the new independent state of Kiribati (use of lobbying like-minded Members and speaking and voting against the Kiribati Bill in 1979).[100] Sir Bernard's efforts have had mixed results, but clearly much more success than those of Members with less aptitude for persistence. Unfortunately, Sir Bernard and Members like him appear not to be in a majority in the House. A combination of the belief that backbenchers cannot be effective against the Government (given the resources at its disposal), a concern that the various devices for scrutiny, such as Question Time, are themselves defective, possibly compounded by a belief that advancement to office is achieved by not creating difficulties for one's own Ministers, and, on the part of some Members, the ability or unwillingness to expend the necessary effort, has resulted in the failure of a great many Members to utilise the means available to them to have some influence on Government. As we shall argue later, if the Commons is to be effective in fulfilling the functions of scrutiny and influence, a change of attitude on the part of many Members is a necessary prerequisite. Fortunately, there are signs that such a change may be coming about.

NOTES

1   D.C.M. Yardley, 'The Primacy of the Executive in England', *Parliamentary Affairs*, 21 (2), Spring 1968, p. 156.
2   The Chairman of Ways and Means ruled that the European Communities Bill was one to provide the 'legal nuts and bolts' necessary for UK membership of the Communities, and not one to approve the Treaty of Accession or any of the treaties basic to membership.
3   See Maurice Edelman, 'The Patronage State', *New Statesman*, 11 April 1975, pp. 470–1.
4   S.E. Finer, introduction to S.E. Finer (ed.), *Adversary Politics and Electoral Reform* (Anthony Wigram, 1975), p. 4.
5   The main work on Question Time is D.N. Chester and N. Bowring, *Questions in Parliament* (Oxford University Press, 1962); recent articles include R.L. Borthwick, 'Questions and Debates', in S.A. Walkland (ed.), *The House of Commons in the Twentieth Century* (Oxford University Press, 1979), pp. 479–507; John Rose, 'Questions in the House', in D. Leonard and V. Herman, *The Backbencher and Parliament* (Macmillan, 1972), pp. 89–107; and Sir Norman Chester, 'Questions in the House', in S.A. Walkland and M. Ryle (eds), *The Commons in the Seventies* (Fontana, 1977), pp. 149–74.
6   The first printed notice of questions to Ministers was issued in 1835. For a historical note, see K.A. Bradshaw, 'Parliamentary Questions: A Historical Note', *Parliamentary Affairs*, 7 (3), Summer 1954, pp. 317–26.
7   In May 1980, it was estimated that the average cost of answering an oral question was £50 and for answering a written question £30. Parliamentary written answer, *House of Commons Debates*, 985, c. 378–9.

8   Borthwick, 'Questions and Debates', pp. 489—90.

9   See Borthwick, 'Questions and Debates'. pp. 487—9.

10   Thus, among the answers given by Ministers from the Employment Department to questions on 18 March 1975 were: 'My Department keeps no records of this kind' (Michael Foot, c. 1430); 'We do not have comprehensive information of this kind which would make possible sufficiently precise answers to these questions' (Mr Foot, c. 1432); 'This is a matter for the Health and Safety Commission and executive and I am asking the chairman of the Commission to write to my hon. Friend' (Harold Walker, c. 1439); 'The matter is still being considered' (Mr Foot, c. 1440); 'I regret that the information is not available' (Albert Booth, c. 1443). Two other questions also received essentially non-committal replies. ('still under consideration'; 'not yet able to say'). *HC Deb.* 888, c. 1430—48.

11   A list of subjects on which Governments had refused to answer parliamentary questions was given in the Report of the Select Committee on Parliamentary Questions 1971—2, and is given in Brian Sedgemore, *The Secret Constitution* (Hodder & Stoughton, 1980), pp. 184—7; see also appendix 3, pp. 242—9.

12   Anthony Barker and Michael Rush, *The Member of Parliament and his Information* (Allen & Unwin, 1970), pp. 141—2.

13   Figure derived from F.W.S. Craig and E.P. Craig (eds), *The Political Companion*, No. 28, Winter 1978.

14   'Questions addressed to Ministers should relate to the public affairs with which they are officially concerned, to proceedings pending in Parliament, or to matters of administration for which they are reponsible.' Sir David Lidderdale (ed.), *Erskine May's Treatise on the Law, Privileges, Proceedings and Usage of Parliament*, 19th ed. (Butterworth, 1976), p. 326. Questions must not be 'tendentious, controversial, ironic, vague, frivolous or repetitive', must be framed as genuine questions, must not seek interpretation of a statute or legal opinion, and must not ask for information already published.

15   See Chester, 'Questions in the House', pp. 162—3.

16   Selwyn Lloyd, *Mr Speaker, Sir* (Jonathan Cape, 1976), p. 87.

17   Sir Harold Wilson, *The Governance of Britain* (Sphere Books, 1977), p. 163.

18   It has been recommended in one form or another by a number of Select Committees, as in 1966—7, 1969—70, and 1971—2.

19   One survey found that Ministers spent as much time on constituency business (outside the House) as did backbenchers. *Review Body on Top Salaries. First Report*, Cmnd. 4836 (HMSO, 1971) p. 5. See also Roy Gregory, 'Executive Power and Constituency Representation in United Kingdom Politics', *Political Studies*, 28 (1), March 1980, pp. 63—83.

20   For an analysis of an MP's correspondence (for 1972—3), and how he dealt with it, see Frances Morrell, *From the Electors of Bristol*, Spokesman Pamphlet No. 57 (Spokesman, n.d.).

21   Mrs Lynda Chalker, Under Secretary of State for Health and Social Security, to author.

22   Richard Crossman, *The Diaries of a Cabinet Minister*, Vol. 1 (Hamish Hamilton/ Jonathan Cape, 1975), pp. 628—9.

23   For example, by Chester and Bowring, and by various MPs to the author.

24   Keith Stainton, MP to author.

25   Peter G. Richards, *The Backbenchers* (Faber & Faber, 1972), p. 168.

26 Note the comments of the Fulton Committee that Parliament should 'take fully into account the cumulative cost (not only in time but in the quality of the administration) that the raising of minutiae imposes'. Quoted in Barker and Rush, p. 204. However, the junior Minister in the Department of Health and Social Security, Mrs Lynda Chalker, has recently expressed the view that the number of letters from MPs to Ministers in the Department of Health and Social Security — the busiest Department — 'on the whole is not unreasonable'. Mrs Chalker to author.

27 For example, John Page, MP, to author. Note also the comments of the ex-minister quoted in Barker and Rush, pp. 202–3.

28 Conservative MP to author. The Member went so far as to suggest that MPs should be statute-barred from having responsibility for raising matters in certain areas.

29 Calculated from the figures in R.L. Borthwick, 'The Floor of the House', in Walkland and Ryle, p. 53.

30 Barker and Rush, p. 133.

31 In some debates, for example, it is not unknown for two or three Government backbenchers to express disagreement with Government policy, those two or three constituting about a third of Government back-bench speakers, with the division revealing that they were the only ones disagreeing out of over 200 Government MPs voting. Conversely, it is possible for no Member to speak in dissent, yet for the division to produce a large dissenting vote.

32 See, for example, *Daily Telegraph*, 22 June 1979. For an example of another debate important in this context, see Philip Norton, 'Intra-Party Dissent in the House of Commons: A Case Study. The Immigration Rules 1972', *Parliamentary Affairs*, 29 (4), Autumn 1976, pp. 404–20.

33 *House of Commons Debates*, 973, c. 679–81.

34 *ibid.*, 974, c. 402–520.

35 The Government had introduced a Bill, the Protection of Information Bill, but decided not to proceed with it when it was realised that under its provisions the book which led to the identification of Blunt could not have been published.

36 For example, in February and March 1979, the Opposition tabled adjournment motions on three of its Supply Days to debate respectively education (industrial disputes) on 6 February, Employment Protection Acts on 8 March, and Scotland (courts) on 13 March.

37 Under standing order 25, the Friday half-hour adjournment now takes place from 2.30 to 3.00 p.m. instead of from 4.00 to 4.30 p.m.

38 If debate on the preceding items on the order paper finishes before 10.00 p.m., then there is more than half an hour available; in practice, this rarely happens.

39 See Valentine Herman, 'Adjournment Debates in the House of Commons', in Leonard and Herman, p. 119, and Chapter 8, Table 8.2, below.

40 It is, as Dr Borthwick has noted, a 'guaranteed half-hour' (Borthwick, 'The Floor of the House', p. 58), but this means that there is automatically half an hour from the time that the adjournment motion is moved. It is not unknown for some Members to raise points of order arising from previous business, and the time taken up in this way eats into the half-hour.

41 See Herman, 'Adjournment Debates in the House of Commons', pp. 121–4.

42 *First Report from the Select Committee on Procedure, 1977–8* (HC 588), p. cxv.

43 The wording was introduced in 1967; the previous wording had been considered too restrictive.

44   Standing order 9 (4).

45   *House of Commons Debates*, 962, c. 970. The matter was raised on another occasion as well. See *ibid*, 963, c. 909—10.

46   *ibid*., 972, c. 1385—8. On a free vote, voting was 196 to 110.

47   Figure based on the table in Borthwick, 'The Floor of the House', p. 53.

48   Justice, *The Citizen and the Administration: The Redress of Grievances* (Stevens, 1961), p. 41. The background to the report — and the subsequent 1967 Act — is fully recounted in Frank Stacey, *The British Ombudsman* (Oxford University Press, 1971).

49   As, for example, the Sachsenhausen prisoner-of-war compensation case in 1967, the television licence case in 1975, and the Court Line case also in 1975.

50   Geoffrey Marshall, 'Parliament and the Redress of Grievances: The Parliamentary Commissioner in the 1970s', in Walkland and Ryle, p. 223.

51   In his evidence to the Procedure Committee, Sir Idwal Pugh described the Select Committee as an 'effective sanction in the rare cases where the Departments have not been prepared to implement a remedy I recommend'. *First Report from the Procedure Committee*, p. lviii.

52   Marshall, 'Parliament and the Redress of Government', p. 237.

53   *ibid*., p. 232.

54   *First Report*, pp. lviii—lix.

55   *House of Commons Debates*, 969, c. 41.

56   The Commons enjoys certain privileges, and the Committee of Privileges exists to investigate alleged breaches of privilege; the Committee of Selection selects members of Standing Committees and now of the new Select Committees (as well as exercising certain functions in relation to private business); the Services Committee advises the Speaker on certain aspects of accommodation and services within the Palace; the Committee on the Register of Members' Interests exists to supervise the Register; the Broadcasting Committee oversees the sound broadcasting of the House and its committees; and a Procedure Committee is usually appointed, either to conduct a general inquiry or one on a specific matter of procedure. The general administration of the House now comes under the auspices of the House of Commons Commission. This comprises Mr Speaker, the Leader of the House, a member of the Shadow Cabinet, the Liberal Chief Whip, a senior Labour backbencher (Arthur Bottomley, who answers questions addressed to the Commission in the House), and a senior Conservative backbencher.

57   Although described by the Exchequer and Audit Departments Acts of 1866 and 1921 as acting 'on behalf of the House of Commons', the Comptroller and Auditor General is nevertheless required under the Acts to undertake certain activities on the instructions of the Treasury. Also, his staff are appointed and paid subject to the approval of the Civil Service Department. The Procedure Committee described this as 'clearly unsatisfactory'. *First Report*, p. ciii.

58   See Anne Robinson, 'The House of Commons and Public Expenditure', in Walkland and Ryle, pp. 143—4.

59   *First Report*, pp. lvi—lviii and xcvii—civ.

60   An example would be its report, cited in Barker and Rush, p. 148n., on prisons and borstals in 1967. Its recommendation for conjugal visits for certain prisoners had little to do with cost-efficiency but fell more in the category of policy.

61   Nevil Johnson, 'Select Committees and Administration', in Walkland, p. 452.

For a fuller account of the committee in post-war years, see Nevil Johnson, *Parliament and Administration* (Allen & Unwin, 1966).

62   See below, Chapter 8.

63   Bernard Crick saw in the committee's reluctance to have permanent specialist advisers a 'certain uncertainty in the minds of the Committee about their task: no one who knows what he wants is dominated by his expert assistants or specialised advisers'. *The Reform of Parliament*, 2nd revised ed. (Weidenfeld & Nicolson, 1970), p. 98. However, though some observers, such as W.T. Thornhill and Professor Hanson, argued that the committee should be serviced by a quasi-independent agency of specialists, David Coombes took the view that 'it is not important, or even necessary, for specialist committees to have expert staff.' *The Member of Parliament and the Administration* (Allen & Unwin, 1966), p. 210.

64   Ian Mikardo, MP, 'The Select Committee on Nationalised Industries', in A. Morris (ed.), *The Growth of Parliamentary Scrutiny by Committee* (Pergamon Press, 1970), p. 70.

65   For example, the Government appointed a special advisory group under Sir Ivan Stedeford to investigate the railways at the same time as they were under study by the committee.

66   Donald R. Shell, 'Specialist Select Committees', *Parliamentary Affairs*, 23 (4), Autumn 1970, p. 380.

67   *First Report*, p. xlix.

68   See John P. Mackintosh, 'The Failure of a Reform', *New Society*, 28 November 1968.

69   Quoted in Shell, 'Specialist Select Committees', p. 400.

70   See Arthur Palmer, 'The Select Committee on Science and Technology', in Morris, pp. 15–31.

71   Shell, 'Specialist Select Committees', p. 403.

72   Bernard Crick in conversation with Ronald Butt, 'Reform of Parliament', *Sussex Tape P1*, 1971 (Educational Productions, 1975).

73   It was appointed 'to consider any papers on public expenditure presented to this House and such of the estimates as may seem fit to the committee and in particular to consider how, if at all, the policies implied in the figures of expenditure and in the estimates may be carried out more economically, and to examine the form of the papers and of the estimates presented to this House'.

74   See the comments of Paul Isaacson, 'Reforming Parliament: A Footnote to a Saga', *Public Administration Bulletin*, 30, August 1979, p. 62.

75   Nevil Johnson, 'Select Committees as Tools of Parliamentary Reform: Some Further Reflections', in Walkland and Ryle, p. 188.

76   Nevil Johnson, 'Select Committees and Administration', in Walkland, p. 466.

77   Frank Stacey, *British Government: Years of Reform 1966–75* (Oxford University Press, 1975), p. 25.

78   S.A. Walkland, 'The Politics of Parliamentary Reform', *Parliamentary Affairs*, 29 (2), Spring 1976, p. 196.

79   Johnson, 'Select Committees as a Tool of Parliamentary Reform', p. 199.

80   *First Report*, p. lii.

81   *First Report*, p. liv. For a summary of its recommendations, see pp. cxxv–cxxix.

82   The committee comprises twelve members from each House, and is appointed

each session to consider Consolidation Bills. Its work is both unspectacular and uncontentious.

83 Though not altogether original. The *Eleventh Report from the Expenditure Committee* in 1977 (HC 535) had recommended department-related Select Committees.

84 *The Times*, 4 August 1978.

85 *House of Commons Debates*, 969, c. 247–50.

86 Standing order 86A.

87 The committee had proposed an Industry and Employment Committee and a Trade and Consumer Affairs Committee. In the event, Employment was separated to form an individual-subject Committee, and Industry and Trade were combined.

88 *House of Commons Debates*, 977, c. 1687–1718.

89 Its members include Edward du Cann (former PAC and Expenditure Committee chairman), Robert Sheldon (former Financial Secretary to the Treasury), Kenneth Baker (former Minister in the Civil Service Department), Terence Higgins (a former Minister of State and Financial Secretary to the Treasury), and Michael English (former chairman of the Expenditure Committee general subcommittee that produced the report on the Civil Service); Messrs du Cann and Baker are regarded as especially influential parliamentarians. The Committee also appears well served by its specialist advisers.

90 According to one source, the Government whips were worried that a number of independently minded Members may be elected chairmen, and so encouraged a number of senior (and reliable) Conservative backbenchers to seek membership of certain committees, knowing that their seniority might result in their being elected to the chairmanships. (In the event, this appears to have happened in the case of at least three committees.) Confidential source to author.

91 The only Conservative Member of the Committee interested in its work is Christopher Brocklebank-Fowler, regarded by other Conservatives as being on this issue 'almost a Labour Member'.

92 S.A. Walkland, 'Whither the Commons?', in Walkland and Ryle, p. 246.

93 Chester, 'Questions in the House', p. 160. In the 1979–80 session, Labour Member Austin Mitchell tabled multiple written questions designed to elicit from Ministers their definition of monetarism.

94 As, for example, by a number of MPs to the author. See also the comments of Bryan Gould, 'The MP and Constituency Cases', in John Mackintosh (ed.), *People and Parliament* (Saxon House, 1978), pp. 87–8. See generally Philip Norton, 'The Influence of the Backbench Member', *The Parliamentarian*, 58 (3), July 1977, pp. 164–71.

95 Labour MP to author.

96 See especially *The Times*, 30 December 1968. The case concerned the delay of the Ministry in reaching a decision on whether or not to deal in isolation with part of the Essex County Development Plan relating to the designation of Hockley in Essex. It was an unusual case in that Sir Bernard referred it to the PCA *twice*.

97 See Sir Donald Kaberry, MP, 'On Long Speeches', *The Parliamentarian*, 56 (1), April, 1975, pp. 91–5, and *Daily Telegraph*, 23 August 1974.

98 See Philip Norton, *Conservative Dissidents* (Temple Smith, 1978), pp. 130–4, 289–90 (fn. 81) and 299 (fn. 39).

99   Norton, 'Intra-party Dissent in the House of Commons: A Case Study', pp. 404–20.
100 *House of Commons Debates*, 967, c. 1266–77, 1339–42. Sir Bernard Braine, MP, to author.

7

The Commons and decision makers: Ministers, civil servants, and the European Communities

The House of Commons is no longer a major part of the decision-making process in this country. As a result of the developments of the nineteenth century, the effective decision-making capacity has been acquired by the Government. However, to speak of the 'Government' as the main decision-making body is rather imprecise, for what is encompassed by the term in practice is not only the collectivity of Ministers appointed on a party basis by the Prime Minister, but also the much larger and permanent body of civil servants who man the Ministries. The purpose of this chapter is to consider the relationship between the Commons and (1) the collectivity of Ministers forming the political apex of Government, (2) the Civil Service, and (3) that other decision-making body with which Britain now has a formal and significant relationship, the European Communities. Although there is an interrelationship between all three, and a specially close relationship between Ministers and civil servants, it is important to distinguish between them when considering the House of Commons and its function of scrutiny and influence. The relationship of the Commons with the first of the three (the collectivity of Ministers) is direct; with the latter two (the Civil Service and the EC) it is indirect.

Ministers

Following a general election, the sovereign summons the leader of the party with the largest number of seats in the new House of Commons (other than in certain exceptional circumstances)[1] and invites him or her to form a Government. The leader 'kisses hands' (to use the formal term) upon becoming Prime Minister, and proceeds to select senior Ministers, the top twenty or so being included in the Cabinet, and junior Ministers. The collectivity of Ministers so appointed[2] constitute formally Her Majesty's Government, though, as we have noted, the decision-making capacity of Government is shared with the Ministers' permanent officials, the so-called Whitehall mandarins. By convention, as we have seen, Ministers are drawn normally from either the Commons or the Lords, predominantly (again by convention) the former. Selected from Parliament, Ministers also remain within it (as MPs or peers), and are dependent upon it for consent to supply and the passage of legislation. They are also responsible to Parliament for the exercise of their powers. (In the United States, there is a formal separation of both powers and personnel between the legislature and the executive.) Ministers are responsible to the House both individually and collectively, and the relationship between Government and the Commons is determined largely by the twin conventions of ministerial and collective responsibility. In terms of definition and application, neither convention is precise, and the two are not necessarily harmonious with one another. They are central, though, to British government.

Ministerial responsibility

The convention of ministerial responsibility is best described as a weak one. There is no agreed definition of it, and, in so far as the convention is understood to involve culpability for actions of officials within a Department, tends to be more honoured in its breach than in its practice. The most common definition, rather a general and near tautological one, is 'that each departmental Minister is responsible to Parliament for the work of his Department. That includes the way its money is spent, and all aspects of its performance.'[3] The problem lies in trying to translate this convention into practice. What is meant by 'responsibility'? As Marshall and Moodie have noted, the word itself has a range of nuances.[4] It may attribute action to the author, indicate a relationship or division of function, or designate blame or praise. To substitute 'accountability' or 'answerability' does not really take us much further. The same problem arises.

Under the convention, a Minister is clearly expected to 'answer' to Parliament for the work of his Department. That is, he regularly appears in the House to answer Members' questions about his Department and matters that fall within its jurisdiction. In any debate on the policy of a particular Department, the Ministers from that Department are the ones who are expected to open and wind up the debate by explaining, justifying and defending that policy. In a debate on the economy, for example, the convention dictates that the relevant Ministers participate, usually the Chancellor of the Exchequer and the Chief Secretary to the Treasury (sometimes the Prime Minister as First Lord of the Treasury on important occasions), and *not,* say, the Under-Secretary of State for the Royal Air Force (though that is technically possible), or a backbencher designated to speak for the Government, or the Permanent Secretary to the Treasury (an official and not a Member), or, for that matter, nobody at all. Similarly, when a Department sponsors legislation, the Minister is the one who brings in the Bill and both explains and defends its provisions during the various legislative stages. In this way, Ministers may be said to be 'answerable' or 'responsible' to Parliament.

The convention becomes more complex when one considers responsibility in the sense of the attribution of action to the author and the allocation of blame or praise. Not only is a Minister expected to appear to answer questions about his Department, but he is deemed also to be responsible — the person to 'carry the can', as S.A. de Smith put it — for his own actions and those of his officials. If he or his officials make errors of judgement, engage in unbecoming conduct or maladministration, then the Minister is expected to shoulder the blame. The convention is interpreted as making the Minister culpable. In practice, it is not as simple as it may sound. The meaning of responsibility, as Professor de Smith aptly noted, will vary according to context.[5] The least unambiguous instance of culpability occurs in cases where a Minister himself is at fault, having engaged in behaviour which is accepted generally, on a non-partisan basis, to be scandalous or contrary to accepted norms of procedure. In such cases, the Minister would normally be expected to resign. In 1935, J.H. Thomas resigned after revealing Budget secrets to persons in a position to profit from such information; in 1947, Hugh Dalton resigned after giving Budget details to a journalist before his Budget speech in the House; in 1962, John Profumo resigned after admitting lying to the House about his relationship with Miss Christine Keeler; and in 1973 Lord Lambton and Lord Jellicoe resigned because of their admitted associations with prostitutes. (Profumo and Lambton, who held a courtesy title, also resigned from the Commons.) Even this category is not without its complications, given that the dividing line between behaviour which is considered scandalous and that which is not is not always clear and changes over time.[6]

Greater difficulties arise over what may be termed policy culpability. If a Minister initiates and is personally identified with a particular policy, and that policy fails or is unacceptable to the Government or the House, then he is deemed to be culpable and is expected to resign. In practice, if the policy fails and/or is unpopular, but the Prime Minister and Cabinet are prepared to stand by it, the convention of collective responsibility provides the Minister with a shield. Only in the unusual circumstances of his colleagues' failure to stand behind him will a Minister feel compelled to resign, and even then that may not be necessary if he is prepared to accept the new policy substituted for his own. The convention as it applies to policy culpability is thus essentially a weak one, undermined by the principle of collective responsibility and the conditions which support it; few resignations in recent years can be attributed to this category. The resignation of Sir Samuel Hoare in 1935 in consequence of the Government's abandoning of the Hoare—Laval Pact is often cited as falling under this heading, but the Minister could have remained had he accepted the Cabinet's new policy; he refused and hence fell foul of the doctrine of collective responsibility.[7] In 1967 James Callaghan resigned as Chancellor of the Exchequer when the pound was devalued, something which he had previously opposed, but he accepted the new policy and remained in the Government as Home Secretary; indeed, as one source noted, 'he probably welcomed the change of office.'[8]

As a convention that requires Ministers to shoulder the blame for mistakes made by their civil servants it creates as many or rather more problems. The Minister heads his Department; he formally determines departmental policy; he answers for the Department in the House. But Departments are now large decision-making structures. Every day a great many decisions, of which a Minister can have little or no knowledge, are made. If a civil servant makes a serious mistake, can the Minister be expected to resign because of it? In practice, there is no clear answer. Some attempts have been made to distinguish between, on the one hand, acts carried out in accordance with a Minister's wishes, or which the Minister could reasonably have been expected to have some know-ledge, and those which might be attributable to defective supervision on the part of the Minister, and, on the other, actions which may have been dishonest, carried out against the Minister's instructions, or indulged in for reasons of perversity or stupidity, or which were at such a level that the Minister could not possibly have known of them. In the former case, the Minister would be expected to resign. In the latter case, the Minister would probably be expected to answer questions in the House, explain what had happened, and announce the taking of corrective action. It would be extremely rare for a Minister to resign in such cases. Sir Thomas Dugdale did resign in 1954 in the celebrated case of Crichel Down, primarily because he appears not to have recognised the foregoing distinction. His resignation was very much the exception to the rule. Ministers tend to blur the distinction, as Dugdale did, but take the opposite action, sometimes summed up in the paradox 'the Minister accepts responsibility, and then takes action against those who are responsible'; if attempts are made by the House or more usually elements within it, primarily the Opposition, to force the Minister's resignation, the doctrine of collective responsibility again serves as a protective shield. As a result, apart from Dugdale, no Minister in recent years has resigned on grounds of being culpable for the errors of his officials.[9]

In the sense of attributing action and allocating blame or praise, requiring resignation in the event of serious blame, the convention of ministerial responsibility can be seen to be rather a weak one. It has been weakened by the inability of the House of Commons to maintain it through the formal powers of impeachment and requiring a Minister to resign. The former power is now considered obsolete, and the latter is considered to be near impossible to achieve for political reasons. The rise of party Government and parliamentary party cohesion, and the development of the convention of collective responsibility, have provided a Minister with colleagues and a party prepared usually, if sometimes reluctantly, to stand behind him. Scandalous behaviour is not covered by such loyalty (the Minister in question would be considered a political liability), nor for that matter is being a poor Minister (failing to answer questions or participate in debate effectively, regardless of one's policy stance), but in cases in which to admit error would provide the Government's opponents with political ammunition, the tendency is to rally round the Minister. If a Minister is forced to resign for policy culpability, it is likely to be as a result of pressure from elements within the House (the parliamentary party on the Government side of the House being especially important), and the Minister's departure is generally cloaked in some excuse such as old age or a desire to return to private life; in some cases, the Minister may be retained in Government, but transferred to another less sensitive post. The chances of the House itself censuring a Minister by formal vote are negligible. If the Minister has the support of his own party (if in a majority) he is safe; if he does not, he may quietly be edged out of office.

The weakness of the convention of ministerial responsibility may thus be seen as being to the advantage of Ministers but to the disadvantage of the Commons as a whole. The convention itself is useful to the Government (as it ensures that the Ministers are the heads of the Departments, and that civil servants are deprived of an alternative power source to which to appeal and to pit against their political masters — as is possible in the USA, given the formal separation of powers),[10] and, in so far as it remains extant, has certain benefits for the Commons. It does provide the House with one or more of its own number to answer questions for each Department and to do so in plenary session (Ministers in the United States are questioned only before committees of Congress, Congress itself being a body to which they are outsiders), and it provides a coherent structure through which the work of Departments and officials can be explained; it is easier for Members to ask a Minister for information on disparate points than to track down the various individual officials responsible and ask them for the information.[11] It would have more benefits if it were a strong convention, as it was in the middle of the last century,[12] but for political reasons, as we have seen, it is far from strong. Party provides a Minister with a protective cloak.

Collective responsibility

The convention of collective responsibility 'implies that all Cabinet Ministers assume responsibility for Cabinet decisions and action taken to implement those decisions'.[13] Once a decision is reached, the Cabinet stands united before the House and the country. The convention is the product of the need for accountability, not only to the House but also to the country. As party developed in the nineteenth century as a means of aggregating the wishes of voters, so Cabinet unity developed in order to provide some cohesion for Government and in response to the attacks of the opponent party. The convention has two well-known consequences: a Minister who refuses to accept a decision of the Cabinet must resign; and the Cabinet must resign or seek a dissolution if defeated on a vote of confidence in the House of Commons. Both are adhered to, the latter more stringently than the former.

A Minister is bound by the convention to accept the decisions of the Cabinet and to defend them publicly. A failure to accept publicly a decision requires the resignation of the Minister. If he refuses to resign, the Prime Minister is expected to require his resignation. Although the convention applies formally to the Cabinet,[14] it has been extended in practice to incorporate all Ministers. Junior Ministers are required, on pain of dismissal, to support Cabinet decisions, and to a limited extent some Prime Ministers have even sought to extend the doctrine to encompass the unpaid Parliamentary Private Secretaries (the PPSs) who, strictly speaking, are not members of the Government. (Prime Ministers Wilson and Callaghan on occasion instructed Ministers to dismiss their PPSs for voting against the Government in the division lobbies.) Although this extension of the convention would appear to suggest its strenthening, it has in some respects been weakened in recent years. The convention requires public adherence to Cabinet decisions, but private disagreement (even when leaked) has been tolerated. More recently, semi-public disagreement has been tolerated as well. The best-known examples are probably those of the opposition of the Home Secretary, James Callaghan, to the Labour Government's proposals to reform industrial relations in 1969, and Tony Benn's opposition to the economic and other policies of the 1974–9 Labour Government; in 1976, a Cabinet member, Reg Prentice, actually absented himself from the Second Reading vote on the Scotland and Wales Bill without encountering prime ministerial retribution.[15] There are various other examples of such disagreements.[16] In addition, the convention has been suspended on three occasions to allow Ministers to express their conflicting views in public. The first occasion was in 1932, when Liberal members of the Cabinet were permitted to dissent on the issue of tariff protection. The remaining two occasions were during the 1974–9 Parliament: in the 1975 EC referendum Ministers were allowed to speak against the recommendation of the majority of the Cabinet that Britain should remain a member of the European Communities on the terms then renegotiated,[17] and in 1977 Ministers were permitted to vote against the Second Reading of the Government's European Assembly Elections Bill.[18] The convention, though strong (and reinforced by the Prime Minister's power of dismissal), can be described as somewhat blurred at the edges, and capable of being dispensed with on occasion at the discretion of the Prime Minister. Problems may arise, however, when the convention is considered in conjunction with that of ministerial responsibility. Though Ministers can hide behind the cloak of collective responsibility, there is a tendency to distinguish between the Minister who has promulgated a particular policy and his colleagues who have supported it publicly; if the policy fails, it looks bad for the Government — it is Government policy — but the Minister concerned takes the brunt of the blame.[19] Nevertheless, in its effect on the House of Commons, the convention is a strong one: it ensures Government solidarity in the face of attack or criticism from wherever in the House it may come, and it ensures a unity of voting behaviour on the part of Ministers, the so-called payroll vote. It now has a similar impact on the Opposition side of the House, where the Leader of the Opposition tends to apply the convention to the Shadow Cabinet (though with some degree of latitude)[20] and on occasion even to junior spokesmen.[21]

This unity on the part of Ministers in the lobbies extends beyond their own ranks in confidence votes. As we observed in Chapter 4, one of the functions of the House is to sustain the Government in office. This sustenance is provided by a majority of the House affirming its confidence in the Government in the division lobbies. Should the Government lose a vote of confidence, the convention requires that the Government either resign or request a dissolution. This part of the convention is a very strong one, and has been adhered to ever since the precedent was set in 1841. There are essentially three types of confidence votes in the Commons: those which are explicit votes of confidence ('That this House has confidence in Her Majesty's Government'); those which are made votes of confidence by the declaration of the Government (usually on items at the heart of Government policy, as, for example, the Second Reading of the European Communities Bill in 1972); and those which are implicit votes of confidence (implicit by virtue of the importance of the matter being divided upon, such as the Budget), though this latter category has fallen into desuetude.[22] If the Government survives a confidence vote, it is constitutionally free to continue in office regardless of how other votes (not ones of confidence) are decided. Should it lose a confidence vote, and seek to continue in office, it is presumed that the House would deny it Supply, the traditional method of removing a Government; in practice, a constitutional crisis would be precipitated immediately, and political conditions would probably be such that the Government would have difficulty in continuing in office anyway. Given the pull of party loyalty, and the wish of Government supporters to maintain their party in office (even if in disagreement with some of its policies) — and, conversely, the desire of Opposition MPs for their party to be in office — confidence votes normally maximise party cohesion in the lobbies. Only in exceptional circumstances will MPs vote against their own side in a confidence vote (fifteen Conservatives voted against the European Communities Bill in 1972),[23] and a Government with an overall majority is normally guaranteed that majority in such votes. The only occasions in the twentieth century in which a Government has lost a confidence vote — twice in 1924, once in 1979 — have been in Parliaments in which the Government was a minority one; on the first occasion the Government resigned, and on the latter two occasions it went to the country.

In the post-war years, from 1945 to 1970 especially (though the view, as we recorded in Chapter 4, was held well before this time),[24] a number of observers were of the opinion that this confidence doctrine extended to votes other than those explicitly of confidence. Some expressed the view that it extended to important votes (a three-line whip constituted a 'formality which warns supporters of an administration that the Government will resign if the vote in question goes against them', according to Sir Philip de Zulueta in 1971),[25] while others believed it extended to *all* whipped votes; as late as 1977 Lisanne Radice was asserting that, even in committee, 'the fiction is maintained that every vote is a vote of confidence.'[26] This belief was harboured by many MPs themselves, and hence had an effect upon parliamentary behaviour; cohesion in the lobbies was a notable feature of the years from 1945 to 1970. However, it was a belief based upon no authoritative source, nor upon any consistent practice of behaviour, and was largely dispelled by the experience of the 1970s: the Government suffered numerous defeats, responding to each in a manner in line with precedent, and not until defeated on an explicit vote of confidence in May 1979 did it seek a dissolution. The realisation that a Government can be defeated in votes which are not declared confidence votes and can continue in office has been seen as a beneficial one to both Government and backbenchers: Members can combine to defeat the Government without jeopardising necessarily its future (hence enjoying greater freedom in their own voting behaviour), while the Government can govern without the uncertainty which previously surrounded defeats on important issues. It is required to resign or request a dissolution only if defeated on an explicit vote of confidence, and not otherwise.[27]

So, to summarise, the Government is derived from the House of

Commons (and, in part, the House of Lords), and the Ministers of the Government remain as Members of Parliament; they face the House, answering for their Departments individually, and accepting responsibility for Government policy collectively. This relationship is governed by the conventions of ministerial and collective responsibility, though the two can be conflicting rather than complementary in determining a Minister's responsibility to the House. The growth of party government has ensured that no Minister is likely to be censured formally by the House, nor a Government with an overall majority turned out on a vote of no confidence; the elective function, as we detailed in Chapter 2, now for all intents and purposes rests elsewhere. Nevertheless, a Government is restricted in the extent to which it can indulge in irresponsibility: it has to face the House directly; Ministers have to appear to answer questions; they are subject to the confidence of their own supporters; and political constraints operate to reinforce the formal constitutional requirements. The various elements of the House have tended to supersede the House as a collective entity in ensuring that Ministers are responsive: the public scrutiny by the Opposition and the private, and sometimes not so private, scrutiny by their own back-bench supporters provide important political constraints. If Ministers are unresponsive to such scrutiny, then there is always the danger, one realised in the 1970s, that Government backbenchers might combine with Opposition MPs to defeat the Government in the division lobbies.

The Civil Service

Whereas the relationship of the Commons with that part of it which forms the Government is direct, its relationship with the Civil Service is *indirect*, both formally and, with a few exceptions, in practice. Under the convention of ministerial responsibility, the officials within a Department are accountable to the Minister (or rather to the Permanent Secretary, and through him to the Minister), and only through the Minister can the House question what is going on within his Department. Formally, this helps create a well-defined line of accountability: civil servants to Ministers, Ministers to Parliament. This can be represented diagrammatically, modifying Figure 1.3 (see Figure 7.1). The advantages of this relationship we have touched upon already: it deprives civil servants of separate masters whom they could play off against one another; it provides an identifiable line of accountability. In practice, what actually happens does not quite match the formal position. The problems associated with the Minister—House relationship we have considered already. In addition, in certain limited cases the relationship between the House and civil servants is not as indirect as the formality implies, and the relationship between Ministers and civil servants not quite what the convention of ministerial responsibility requires.

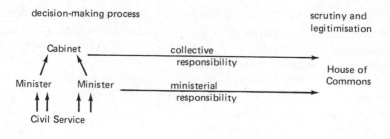

Figure 7.1 Civil Service, Government and Commons: the line of accountability

Civil servants are not totally immune to direct contact with or investigation by the House of Commons or its agents as the formality implies, though it is possible to argue that the point is a marginal one. Spending by Departments is audited by the Comptroller and Auditor General and his staff, and he reports to the Public Accounts Committee. The Permanent Secretary in each Department is normally the accounting officer for his Department, and he is responsible for the way in which its money is spent. The relationship with the House as such is still largely indirect, though in this instance bypassing the Minister.[28] Similarly, investigation of cases of alleged maladministration are carried out by an agent of the House, the Parliamentary Commissioner for Administration, who, as we saw in Chapter 6, reports to the Select Committee on the PCA, and who investigates only cases channelled to him through MPs. Again, the relationship is basically indirect, as far as the House as a whole is concerned, and the Minister bypassed, at least until the PCA issues his report. However, direct contact between civil servants and the House, or rather some of its official subunits, does take place when Select Committees summon officials to testify before them. This is an important feature of investigations by committees, though its importance is limited. Although civil servants may present themselves physically before committees, the opportunity for them to present their own views is severely circumscribed. They appear on behalf of their Department, which means, formally, on behalf of the Minister.[29] A Government *Memorandum of Guidance for Officials appearing before Select Committees,* drawn up in 1976 (and revised in 1980), declared that 'officials appearing before Select Committees do so on behalf of their Ministers' and that, accordingly, it was Government policy for Ministers to decide which officials should give evidence to committees on their behalf. 'Official evidence to Select Committees is normally given, with ministerial agreement, only by permanent Heads of Departments or by officials nominated by them for this purpose.'[30] Though the questioning of officials can prove extemely valuable for the purpose of exploring departmental policy and the reasoning behind it, there are clear limitations to penetrating what actually goes on *within* Departments; the convention of ministerial responsibility provides officials on this occasion with a protective cloak. There are other occasions on which MPs individually may have contact with civil servants — they may meet at some social occasion; a Member may write to a local official in pursuing a constituency case[31] — but essentially the relationship between the House of Commons (bar that part of it which forms the Government) and the Civil Service remains an indirect one. The House deals with the Civil Service, and vice versa, through Ministers.

The formal position requires much greater qualification when one considers the line of accountability between officials and Ministers. Officials, as we have seen, are deemed to be responsible to Ministers. Ministers determine policy; their officials advise them and ensure that their decisions are carried out. The convention of ministerial responsibility supposedly gives Ministers political mastery of their Departments. 'The civil servant's duty is to serve his Minister and nobody else.'[32] In practice, it is not as simple as that. Though few people question the dedication of civil servants, there is serious disagreement among observers as to whether it is the Ministers that enjoy mastery of their Departments and policy-making or their officials. If it is the latter, then the possibility of the Commons' effective scrutiny of the work of Departments is much undermined.

There are approximately three-quarters of a million civil servants in Britain (those of Principal level and above forming the important hierachy in the Whitehall Departments), compared with fewer than a hundred Ministers. Officials enjoy security of tenure; Ministers come and go at a rate that some would describe as rapid. The amount of time that an individual Minister can devote to departmental policy-making is limited; his knowledge of the subject covered by his Department may be slight. A Minister relies upon his officials for expert advice and advice on policy options;[33] the Permanent Secretary is his chief policy adviser within the Ministry, and, in some cases, his sole adviser. Officials engage in much interdepartmental co-ordination, and committees of civil servants exist in parallel to ministerial committees. In view of their opportunities for the selection of material, their presentation (or non-presentation) of facts to Ministers, their knowledge of the subject and its administrative implications gained through experience, it is not difficult to appreciate how officials might be seen as being in a position to manipulate Ministers. Also, they can seek to circumvent ministerial wishes by leaking criticisms to the press, or by contacting officials in other Ministries and enlisting their help (in persuading their Ministers to take the opposite line), or by diverting the matter to an interdepartmental committee for further discussion, or, according to Mr Benn, by channelling their alternative views through the Central Policy Review Staff.[34] Where officials do enjoy undue influence over a Minister, the convention of ministerial responsibility helps to protect them from outside scrutiny. The convention provides them with anonymity — decisions are taken in the name of the Minister — and leaves the Minister to answer for them if questioned in the House. Few Ministers would be prepared to concede that they are not in charge in their own Departments (Carson's announcement, on his arrival at the Admiralty, that he was 'very much at sea' and would carry out the policy of the Department[35] would appear to be very much the exception), hence a tendency to support, defend and if necessary cover up departmental decisions. The Commons is hampered in investigating the work of Departments by having to work through Ministers, by the secrecy of decision-making which is hidden behind the twin conventions of ministerial and collective responsibility, and by the House's own limited resources.

The view that civil servants wield too much power in the decision-making process, that ministerial control and, through it, parliamentary scrutiny is effectively a sham, has been advanced by various writers. Criticism of the Civil Service that developed in the later 1950s and in the 1960s[36] led to the establishment of the Fulton Committee on the Civil Service, which reported in 1968. It has been expressed more recently by Richard Crossman in *The Diaries of a Cabinet Minister*; by other former Ministers, such as Michael Meacher, Lord Crowther-Hunt, Tony Benn, and Alex Lyon; by Brian Sedgemore in his alternative first chapter to the Eleventh Report from the Expenditure Committee in 1977[37] (and in his subsequent book *The Secret Constitution,* published in 1980); by Joe Haines in his book *The Politics of Power*;[38] and even to some extent by Chapman Pincher in his book *Inside Story,*[39] in which he emphasised the extent to which the security services could be described almost as a law unto themselves, a view reinforced in 1979 by the controversy over the treatment of confessed spy Anthony Blunt. Although all the writers named, with the exception of Mr Pincher, are on the left of the political spectrum, this criticism is not confined to those within the Labour Party. Ian Gilmour (now a Cabinet Minister), while not subscribing to the thesis of departmental conspiracies, expressed in *The Body Politic* the opinion that 'only about one Minister in three runs his department,'[40] and in 1980 the Prime Minister, Mrs Thatcher, was reported to be so highly critical of the influence wielded by officials over both Ministers and the choice of where expenditure cuts were to fall that the *Economist* went so far as to refer to her 'bitter disaffection from the Whitehall ethos'.[41]

To counter some of these criticisms, a number of observes have drawn attention to the loyalty of officials to their political masters, and the amount of time spent by civil servants on parliamentary matters. The task of officials is not to force their views on Ministers but to tender advice and to ensure that they are aware of the options available. In preparing legislation, according to Peter Walker (a member of Mr Heath's and now Mrs Thatcher's Cabinet), Ministers are in command: 'For example, the major legislation I was responsible for on the environment [1970–4] was very much legislation that I decided on in Opposition and . . . I went to the Department and told the Department I wanted legislation achieving the following objectives.'[42] In particular, civil servants feel bound to try to find ways of helping Ministers to carry out promises made in their election manifesto,[43] and look for Ministers who are capable of reaching decisions; once a Minister has 'taken a view', they can carry it out.[44] Also, through their Ministers, officials are very sensitive to the concerns and criticisms of the Commons. Officials, as Bruce Headey noted, look for Ministers who can defend their Departments against parliamentary criticism; while this may suggest a desire for pliant Ministers, it does at least reveal some sensitivity to what goes on in the House.

Civil servants in the Whitehall Departments spend much of their time on parliamentary business. Preparing answers for parliamentary questions is 'almost invariably given top priority';[45] answers go through a 'long process of checking and scrutiny' before being put before the Minister.[46] Much time is spent on briefing Ministers for debates, and doing homework ready for appearances before Select Committees. Indeed, the Fulton Committee found that senior civil servants spent up to a quarter of their working time on parliamentary matters. Responding to parliamentary questions and questioning before a Select Committee is sometimes seen as a valuable means of keeping officials on their toes. 'Because so much of their work can at any time be the subject of a Parliamentary Question, civil servants trying to decide on a line of action tend to ask themselves consciously or unconsciously, "Is it reasonable?" This is no bad criterion for public servants to use in deciding what to do.'[47]

These points are valuable in helping to provide some balance to the criticisms levelled against the Civil Service. The argument is not a one-sided one. Nevertheless, despite the claims made in defence of ministerial control and parliamentary scrutiny, there does appear to be a strong case for more effective scrutiny of Departments and their officials. However loyal officials may be, however strong a Minister may be, a great many decisions (of necessity) are made by civil servants. Even though they may be made in line with the presumed wishes of the Minister, or with what is perceived to be Government policy, such decisions need to be subject to scrutiny, and their makers accountable to political authority. One way suggested to achieve more effective scrutiny and accountability is to strengthen Ministers: to give them greater control over the hiring and firing of officials within the Departments, for example, or to increase the average length of tenure of a Minister in one office. Another is to make the Commons more effective.

Two means of achieving this, complementary to one another, have been posited, and, indeed, to a limited extent, witnessed: the strengthening of Select Committees, and greater assertiveness by Members in the division lobbies. The Expenditure Committee, in its report on the Civil Service in 1977,[48] recognised the need for committees to exercise more effective scrutiny of Departments, and foreshadowed the Procedure Committee's report of 1978 recommending the setting up of Department-related Select Committees. In its subsequent report, it declared: 'We believe that the power of the Executive, particularly the Civil Service, has outgrown the power of Parliament and the balance should be redressed.'[49] Although committees, as we have observed, have difficulty in getting behind the public face of Departments, their investigations nevertheless can help to focus attention on particular aspects of departmental policy and to flesh out more information from officials than would otherwise be possible. Hence the potential value of the new Department-related Select Committees set up in 1979. Their effectiveness may be enhanced by the willingness of Members to assert themselves in the division lobbies, and this brings the two points together. Part of the explanation of the presumed strength of civil servants is that once they have persuaded the Minister (or the Cabinet) of the need for a particular course of action it is normally approved by the House through the Government's majority. The Opposition may question it, but numerical inferiority and lack of information may limit its ability to do anything. However, with the realisation that the Government may have superior resources through the Civil Service (though there are instances where this is questionable) but not necessarily a monopoly of wisdom, Members have proved willing to pit their own views against those of the Government and its officials. The greater the willingness of Government backbenchers to challenge the action of particular Departments, the greater the potential to act as a check on the Civil Service, and, surprising as it may seem, to strengthen Ministers in relation to their officials. If the House says 'no' to a Government proposal, the Minister has to go back to his officials and tell them 'The House won't have this,' and in some instances this may be to the advantage of the Minister.[50] The importance of this for Select Committees is that if Ministers and officials believe that a committee's report or recommendations may be brought before the House on a substantive motion, with the possibility of dissent and even defeat in the division lobbies, they are much more likely to be open and responsive to the committee's investigation. As Kenneth Baker observed in the debate on the motion to set up the new Select Committees in 1979, if committee reports are to be effective, 'the circle must be completed, and they must come back and be debated on the Floor of the House.'[51] A combination of strong Select Committees and assertive Members on the floor of the House could help to ensure more effective scrutiny of the Civil Service, albeit formally and to a large extent in practice still channelled indirectly via the convention of ministerial responsibility.

To summarise: the relationship of the House of Commons with the Civil Service is indirect (governed by the convention of ministerial responsibility), with serious limitations on the ability of the House to keep the actions of Departments under effective scrutiny. The Commons' role of scrutiny could be, and to some limited extent is being, strengthened, though it is unlikely that the House or its committees will ever have sufficient resources or stamina to achieve anything approaching comprehensive scrutiny of the official bureaucracy. It can, though, make a few steps in the right direction.

The European Communities

Before 1973, the Government and the Civil Service formed the regular decision-making apparatus, formulating policy and taking decisions which were designed to have general applicability and enforcibility in this country, subject usually to the normally given approval or prior consent of Parliament. However, the position changed on 1 January 1973. From that date, as a result of British accession to the European Communities, legislation emanating from the EC has had general applicability and enforcibility in this country. Membership of the Communities has added an extra decision-making body, the EC itself, as represented by the Council of Ministers and the Commission.[52]

Membership of the EC has created problems for the House of Commons. Its relationship with the Council of Ministers (and with the Commission), and its scrutiny of legislation emanating from that body, is *indirect*, and indeed, in the opinion of some, tenuous. The House is called upon to give its assent to treaties or treaty amendments (primary legislation) which, under the EC treaty, require ratification by member states in accordance with their respective constitutional requirements. Under the 1972 European Communities Act, such ratification is provided under the statutory instrument procedure, the relevant treaty being embodied in an order-in-council and subject to affirmative resolution. The House may also play a role requiring assent in those cases in which it is left to each of the member states to determine how a Community directive is to be carried into effect. Other than that, though, the House of Commons has no formal power to determine or withhold consent to any measure agreed upon by the Council of Ministers or the Commission. All it can do is attempt to scrutinise draft legislation proposed to the Council by the Commission, and then influence the British Government, and the relevant Minister, prior to the Council meeting at which the Commission's proposals are considered. The procedure of the House has been modified, albeit not altogether successfully, in order to facilitate this limited role. Though the House now exercises some scrutiny and influence over European secondary legislation, problems remain.

The procedure employed by the House for its role of scrutiny and influence of EC legislation can be briefly outlined. After the Government has received draft Community legislation and other documents published by the Commission for submission to the Council, it submits this material to the Select Committee on European Legislation. (The Committee was established in 1974 consequent on the report in the 1972–3 session of the Select Committee on European Community Secondary Legislation, the so-called Foster Committee.)[53] It then submits an explanatory memorandum to the Committee, giving factual information about the Commission's proposals, detailing their legal and policy implications for the United Kingdom, and indicating when they are likely or are expected to be considered by the Council. Each memorandum is signed by a Minister, and is submitted usually within a fortnight of the proposal's deposition. The Committee may seek further information, either orally or in writing, from Government Departments, outside bodies or individuals. In practice, it tends to rely heavily upon evidence from Departments. It considers the documents, and has the task of informing the House about whether or not they raise questions of legal or political importance, and what matters of principle or policy may be affected by them. It has the duty of recommending whether any documents to which it has drawn attention as raising questions of legal or political importance should be further considered by the House. The Government has committed itself, save in exceptional circumstances, to provide time for such consideration on the floor of the House prior to the proposals being discussed by the Council of Ministers, a commitment which Governments have sought to honour, though one, as we shall see, that has not been altogether trouble-free. In order to alleviate some of the pressure on the floor of the House, it has been possible since 1975 for documents to be referred for debate in Standing Committee, though few have been so referred.[54] Until 1980, the debates (unless commencing before 10.00 p.m. on the floor of the House) were limited to one and a half hours and were also held usually on neutral motions.

This procedure is clearly an improvement on reliance upon the traditional devices of Question Time and general debates. Nevertheless, a number of problems can be identified, some the products of the Community's method of decision-making, others the products of the Select Committee's (and the House's) procedure. An example of the former is the pace at which EC decisions are made: 'Some proposals are extremely fast moving and are adopted within a few days; others may take years.'[55] The Select Committee finds it difficult to adapt itself to this variable pace, and it is not unknown for some EC legislation to have been adopted by the Council of Ministers before the Committee has had an opportunity to report on it. (The annual Budget and Farm Price Review, for example, have timetables that make it difficult for the House to consider the published proposals before they are considered in Council.) Another EC-related problem is that important changes may be made to proposals after the Commission's initial submission of them to the Council. Despite Government undertakings to keep it informed of such changes, the Select Committee has some difficulty in keeping abreast of them and in performing what is known as 'second-stage' scrutiny. A procedural difficulty is finding time for debate on the floor of the House of a document recommended for further consideration. By the time it is arranged, the time between its occurrence and the meeting of the Council of Ministers can be very short indeed.

The Select Committee also operates under certain constraints, some imposed by its terms of reference, others more self-imposed. Unlike its equivalent Committee in the Lords (the Select Committee on the European Communities), it does not have the power to pronounce on the merits of documents. Though it has two subcommittees, it does not make extensive use of them, certainly not to the extent that the Lords Committee makes use of its seven subcommittees; nor does it make use of specialist advisers and outside witnesses to the same extent. (In the Upper House, peers who are not members of the Select Committee may attend subcommittee hearings, thus providing additional experience and knowledge in certain cases.)[56] The approaches of the Commons and Lords Committees differ — the former concentrating on the political implications of documents, the latter on the wider legal and administrative implications[57] — but the success of the Lords Committee does suggest that the Select Committee on European Legislation could be modified further, largely through the willingness of its own members, in order to further its effectiveness.

Some of the problems associated with scrutinising EC legislation have been variously commented upon, and, following consideration by Procedure Committees in two separate sessions, further changes took place in 1980. In its 1978 Report, the Procedure Committee (following the recommendations of its namesake of the 1974–5 session) proposed that Standing Committees be permitted to debate documents on substantive motions and be empowered to hold up to three two-and-a-half hour meetings to consider a particular document.[58] It wanted debates on documents on the floor of the House to be on substantive motions as well, and asked that the Government commit itself by a declaratory motion not to approve any EC legislation in the Council until it had been debated by the House in those instances where the Committee on European Legislation had recommended such debate. The recommendations for debates, both in Standing Committee and on the floor of the House, to be on substantive motions was accepted by the Leader of the House, Mr St John-Stevas, in 1980, as was the proposal for the Committees to be able to spend longer considering a document. The Procedure Committee recommended also that the proposed new Select Committees should be permitted to debate the merits of EC documents in their respective areas, the task of technical scrutiny remaining with the Select Committee on European Legislation. Though the Select Committees are now in operation, they have not had, nor — given their other interests and wide ambit of investigation -- are they likely to have, much time to devote to this task. As T. St John Bates has observed, the new committee structure may help to increase the scrutiny of Commission policy and legislative proposals; 'however, it is unlikely to have a dramatic effect on such scrutiny.'[59]

The various recent changes, in 1980 and before, are in themselves useful, though all they can do is improve the rather limited scrutiny by the House and its committees of proposed EC secondary legislation. There is no way in which the House can exert anything other than limited and indirect influence over such legislation. By expressing disapproval of draft legislation, in debate and on a substantive motion, the House may influence the Government. No Government will willingly incur the public displeasure of the House, that is, the Opposition and some of the Government's own supporters. The Select Committee on European Legislation (and that in the Lords), through its scrutiny and informal contact between its clerks and liaison officers in Departments, may serve also as an early warning system for politically contentious documents.[60] Nevertheless, whatever the House does, it cannot bind the Government. As David Coombes has remarked, 'Where Community business is concerned, Parliament has to accept certain special limitations.'[61] Not only can it not bind the Government, it cannot always keep track of what Ministers are doing in EC negotiations. Such negotiations take place in a forum which is legally separate from Parliament, and are conducted on a multilaterial basis. The Minister representing Britain is but one of nine. Decisions may be made which deviate from the declared view of the Commons, and in some instances may be decisions of which the House had no prior knowledge. The House itself cannot complain: under the terms of the treaty, national Parliaments have no legal right to be consulted. A further limitation may also be (indeed, is) emerging: the now directly elected European Parliament. Prior to direct elections in 1979, members of the European Parliament were drawn from national Parliaments. With the members (MEPs) now being elected by so-called Euro-constituencies, this link between the two Houses and the Community forum has been lost (only five British MPs were elected as MEPs in 1979); no official forum exists in which MPs and British MEPs can meet.[62] And as the elected European Parliament begins to flex its own limited political muscles (in December 1979 it rejected the draft Community Budget for 1980), so the position of national Parliaments will be overshadowed. The European Parliament has the power to reject the Community Budget and to force the resignation *en bloc* of the Commission: a national Parliament does not. The focus of attention can already be seen to be shifting.

When Britain acceded to the European Communities, the effect was that Parliament effectively handed over its decision-making capacity, formal or otherwise, in a number of areas. Parliament retains the ultimate power to repeal the 1972 European Communities Act, but as long as the Act remains on the statute book (or until it is amended),[63] all that the House of Commons can do is seek to exercise a very limited and indirect scrutiny of proposed EC legislation. This scrutiny is now more effective than was previously the case, though problems remain. The House exercises greater influence — indeed a formal decision-making capacity — over primary legislation and over directives which are implemented in a manner determined by the 'national authorities'. The House can and does make use as well of its traditional expedients of Question Time and general debates to influence Government.[64] Some observers take the view that the potential for parliamentary influence is enhanced by the fact that most EC documents do not touch upon the Government's policy or general programme, and hence Ministers can afford to listen more carefully to the views of the House.[65] Nevertheless, the relationship of the House to the decision makers of the EC remains indirect and the most tenuous of the relationships identified in this chapter. That this should be so is inescapable. The House is seeking to deal with a body which, as David Coombes has written, 'has a momentum of its own and has its own constitutional legitimacy',[66] one that exists on an supranational, and not a national, basis.

Conclusion

The House of Commons does not constitute part of the regular decision-making apparatus in Britain. Though it has the power, rarely exercised, to negate or amend decisions taken elsewhere, it does not itself play an initiating or formulating role in the process of decision and policy-making. Instead, it seeks to scrutinise and, if necessary, influence the decisions reached by those bodies vested with the authority to make decisions designed to have general applicability in the United Kingdom, decisions which require legitimisation by the House.

The relationship of the House to Ministers, individually and collectively, is direct, and governed by the twin conventions of ministerial and collective responsibility. Ministers are drawn from, remain within, and answer to the House for their official actions. Under the convention of ministerial responsibility, Ministers answer for their Departments. As a result, the relationship of the House to civil servants is formally and, to a great extent in practice, indirect; the House has to deal with officials through that part of it which forms the Government. These relationships, as we have seen, are not trouble-free: the extent to which the House can exercise effective scrutiny and influence is limited by both political and structural factors. Nevertheless, attempts have been made, and are being made, to make the House more effective in overseeing both Ministers and their officials.

More difficulties are faced in the relationship of the House to the European Communities. The relationship is indirect and somewhat tenuous. The legitimisation required of the House has, for most purposes, been given already through the 1972 European Communities Act. What scrutiny and influence of EC secondary legislation it can exercise it does through the Government (though the treaties governing membership of the Communities provide the House with no formal role), the Government itself constituting but one of nine in the Communities. Parliament itself, of course, constitutes but one of nine national Parliaments in the EC, the EC now having a separate, directly elected Parliament which is developing a scrutinising role of its own. Though the House of Commons has evolved new procedures for the oversight of EC legislation and Commission documents, its role of scrutiny and influence is clearly limited.

NOTES

1 The monarch summons the person deemed most likely to command a majority in the House; on occasion, this might apply to the leader of a minority party if it enjoys the support of another party.
2 The maximum number of holders of paid ministerial office in the Commons is provided for by statute. For the size of Cabinets and Governments in this century, see D. Butler and A. Sloman, *British Political Facts 1900–79* (Macmillan, 1980), p. 78.
3 Charles Morris, Minister for the Civil Service, in a debate on the Civil Service. *House of Commons Debates,* 960, c. 1356.
4 G. Marshall and G. Moodie, *Some Problems of the Constitution,* 4th revised ed. (Hutchinson, 1967), p. 58.
5 S.A. de Smith, *Constitutional and Administrative Law* (Penguin, 1971), p. 171.
6 At the time of Lord Lambton's resignation, for example, there were those who felt that private indiscretions by Ministers should not be grounds for resignation as long as they were not illegal, were not threats to security, or did not interfere with

the ability to perform ministerial duties. (Unfortunately for Lord Lambton, he still fell foul of the first two of these qualifications. Lord Jellicoe, for whom there was much sympathy in political circles, did not.)

7   See Marshall and Moodie, pp. 70–1. Though see K. Middlemas and J. Barnes, *Baldwin* (Weidenfeld & Nicolson, 1969), ch. 31, for the assertion that the Cabinet forced him to resign.

8   Peter Bromhead, *Britain's Developing Constitution* (Allen & Unwin, 1974), p. 69.

9   In 1960, Alan Lennox-Boyd refused to resign as Colonial Secretary on the issue of the Hola death camps, and Julian Amery refused to resign as Aviation Minister in 1964 when a mistake by his Department led to the Ferranti company making excessive profits on an aviation contract.

10   In the USA, each Government Department and agency is dependent for its funding on Congress, a body with a decision-making capacity independent of the executive; see Chapter 1, above. In practice, it is possible for officials to play off their political masters against the relevant congressional committees and in consequence achieve some measure of independence. (They may seek also to pit one of their 'attentive publics' off against their political masters.) See, for example, Francis Rourke, *Bureaucracy, Politics and Public Policy* (Little, Brown, 1969).

11   This is borne out by the experience of the Department of Health and Social Security. Many letters from MPs to Ministers cover matters pertinent to Area Health Authorities or local offices of the Department of Health and Social Security, and the Ministers' officials have to contact them in order to reply to the Members' letters.

12   See the comments of John Mackintosh, *The British Cabinet,* 3rd ed. (Stevens, 1977), pp. 529–30.

13   de Smith, p. 176.

14   Because it applies formally only to Cabinet Ministers, MPs are permitted to table questions to the Prime Minister asking if a speech of a Cabinet Minister constitutes Government policy, whereas a similar question about a speech by a junior Minister would be rejected by the Table Office.

15   Philip Norton, 'The Guillotine Motion and the Government Defeat: 22 February 1977', *British Politics Group Newsletter* (USA), No. 8, Spring 1977, p. 12.

16   See Mackintosh, p. 532.

17   See Sir Harold Wilson, *The Governance of Britain* (Sphere Books, 1977), pp. 235–9. (However, Ministers were not allowed to speak against the Government recommendation in the House, and Eric Heffer was dismissed for so doing.)

18   Philip Norton, *Dissension in the House of Commons 1974–79* (Oxford University Press, 1980), pp. 263–5.

19   See Marshall and Moodie, p. 61.

20   For example, in 1968 Iain Macleod, a member of the Shadow Cabinet, was allowed to vote against the Second Reading of the Commonwealth Immigration Bill; however, in 1976 Alick Buchanan-Smith was required to resign as Shadow Scottish Secretary because of his support for the Scotland and Wales Bill.

21   As, for example, in the 1978 vote on the Rhodesian sanctions order; for defying the leader's instructions by voting against the order, two junior spokesmen, Winston Churchill and John Biggs-Davison, were required to return to the back benches, though this was considered something of an exceptional case.

22   Philip Norton, 'Government Defeats in the House of Commons: Myth and Reality', *Public Law*, Winter 1978, pp. 362—5.

23   See Philip Norton, *Dissension in the House of Commons 1945—74* (Macmillan, 1975), pp. 404—6, and, by the same author, *Conservative Dissidents* (Temple Smith, 1978), pp. 73—4.

24   Norton, 'Government Defeats in the House of Commons', p. 360, and above, Chapter 4.

25   Sir Philip de Zulueta, letter, *The Times*, 13 July 1971.

26   Lisanne Radice, *Reforming the House of Commons*, Fabian Tract 448 (Fabian Society, 1977), p. 4.

27   Norton, 'Government Defeats in the House of Commons', pp. 376—8.

28   As accounting officers, Permanent Secretaries regularly appear before the PAC. Ministers are not involved.

29   The exception is when Permanent Secretaries appear before the PAC as accounting officers — they do so on their own behalf and not that of Ministers.

30   The *Memorandum* is reproduced in the *First Report from the Procedure Committee, 1977—8* (HC 588), pp. 38—50.

31   Contact with local officials is quite common, and is something Departments do not discourage. In addition, the Leader of the Opposition or other Shadow spokesmen may, on the instructions of the Prime Minister or relevant Minister, be briefed on a sensitive issue by senior officials.

32   Maurice Wright, 'Ministers and Civil Servants: Relations and Responsibilities', *Parliamentary Affairs*, 30 (3), Summer 1977, p. 296.

33   See Bruce Headey, 'Cabinet Ministers and Senior Civil Servants: Mutual Requirements and Expectations', in V. Herman and J. Alt (eds), *Cabinet Studies: A Reader* (Macmillan, 1975), pp. 122—31.

34   Interviewed on Granada TV programme 'World in Action', 7 January 1980.

35   Quoted in Ian Gilmour, *The Body Politic*, revised ed. (Hutchinson, 1971), p. 201.

36   For example, Dr (now Lord) Balogh, in his essay in *The Establishment* (1959), Professor Brian Chapman in *British Government Observed* (1963), Peter Shore in *Entitled to Know* (1966), and Max Nicholson in *The System* (1967).

37   An ex-civil servant himself, Mr Sedgemore claimed that officials relegated Ministers to the second division through various devices, including delay, interpreting minutes in ways not wholly intended, slanting statistics, giving Ministers insufficient time to make decisions, taking advantage of Cabinet splits, and even going behind Ministers' backs.

38   Coronet, revised edition, 1977.

39   Sidgwick & Jackson, 1978.

40   Gilmour, p. 201.

41   *Economist*, 9 February 1980, p. 13. See also Hugh Stephenson, *Mrs Thatcher's First Year* (Jill Norman, 1980), ch. 2.

42   Speaking in the BBC Radio 3 programme 'The Parliamentary Process: Politicans and Bureaucrats', broadcast 26 February 1976.

43   Note the comments in J. Mackintosh, B. Lapping, and N. Percy, *Inside British Politics* (Granada and Political Broadcasting 8, Granada TV, 1977), pp. 20—1.

44   See Headey, 'Cabinet Ministers and Senior Civil Servants', pp. 131—5, and, by the same author, *British Cabinet Ministers* (Allen and Unwin, 1974), pp. 143—4.

45 John Cockroft MP, speaking on his experiences as a civil servant. *House of Commons Debates*, 960, c. 1424.

46 Enid Russell-Smith, *Modern Bureaucracy: The Home Civil Service* (Longman, 1974), p. 54.

47 Russell-Smith, p. 55.

48 *The Civil Service: Eleventh Report from the Expenditure Committee* (HC 535—1).

49 *Twelfth Report from the Expenditure Committee* (HC 576), para. 18.

50 See Norton, *Dissension in the House of Commons 1974—1979*, p. 462. The defeat on the Crown Agents affair in 1977 has been cited as a possible example.

51 *House of Commons Debates*, 969, c. 116.

52 The Council of Ministers comprises representative Ministers of each of the nine members states. (The Ministers are normally those relevant to the subject being discussed.) It has power to issue secondary legislation made in pursuance of primary treaties. Its decisions can bind member countries. It can only act on proposals submitted by the Commission. The Commission is a collegiate body, and fulfills an executive role in the EC. It is responsible only to the European Parliament, which has the power to dismiss it *en bloc*.

53 Select Committee on European Secondary Legislation, 1972—3, *First Report* (HC 143), *Second Report* (HC 463—1). The Committee had been established after a promise made by the Chancellor of the Duchy of Lancaster, Geoffrey Rippon, during the Second Reading debate on the 1972 EC Bill, that special arrangements would be made under which the House 'would be apprised of draft regulations and directives before they go to the Council of Ministers for decision'. *House of Commons Debates*, 831, c. 278.

54 In the 1975—6 session, fifteen documents were referred to Standing Committee, and only five in the following session.

55 T. St John Bates, 'British Government and the EEC', *Most*, No. 21, October 1979, p. 26.

56 On the Lords Committee, see Caroline Moore, 'The Role of the House of Lords in the Scrutiny of EEC Legislation', third-year undergraduate dissertation, Hull University Politics Department, April 1979, and *The House of Lords and the European Communities*, House of Lords Factsheet No. 2, 3rd ed. (House of Lords Information Office, 1979).

57 Hansard Society, *The British People: their voice in Europe* (Saxon House, 1977), p. 40.

58 *First Report from the Select Committee on Procedure, 1977—8*, p. xiv.

59 T. St John Bates, 'British Government and the EEC', p. 27.

60 See Harris N. Miller, 'The Influence of British Parliamentary Committees on European Communities Legislation', *Legislative Studies Quarterly*, 2 (1), February 1977, pp. 66—8.

61 David Coombes, 'Parliament and the European Communities', in S.A. Walkland and M. Ryle (eds), *The Commons in the Seventies* (Fontana, 1977), p. 214.

62 There are, though, one or two unofficial forums. The Europe Standing Committee of the Bow Group, for example, provides a forum in which Conservative MPs and MEPs can meet.

63 The 1979 Labour manifesto included the promise to legislate 'to ensure that British Ministers are accountable to the House of Commons before making any

commitment in the Council of Ministers'. Enlargement of the EC would provide the opportunity for seeking changes in the Treaty of Rome, 'which would enable the House of Commons to strengthen its powers to amend or repeal EEC legislation'. That would involve consequential amendments to the 1972 Act. *The Labour Party Manifesto 1979*, p. 34. The reference to 'seeking changes' should perhaps be emphasised.

64   For example, in January 1978, an Opposition amendment calling for the European Green Pound to be devalued by 7½ per cent instead of the 5 per cent recommended by the Government was carried by 291 votes to 280; *House of Commons Debates*, 942, c. 1097–1106. Though not binding, the Government accepted the decision of the House. *ibid.*, 942, c. 1107–8.

65   See Coombes, 'Parliament and the European Community', p. 220.

66   *ibid.*, p. 214.

8

The Commons and Departments: a sectoral analysis

There are various means by which the House of Commons can seek to scrutinise and influence that part of it which constitutes the Government, and, through the Government, the Civil Service and the Council of Ministers of the European Communities. The means available to the House, and the relationship of the House to these decision-making bodies, we have considered in the preceding chapters. However, the extent to which the means available to scrutinise and influence legislation and executive actions can be and are employed, and the relationship between the House and Government, varies from policy sector to policy sector, and (in so far as these sectors are allocated to specified Departments) from Department to Department. Though the creation of Select Committees covering all Government Departments ensures a greater coherence of scrutiny than before, a number of structural and other factors cause the means employed for scrutiny, and the effectiveness of that scrutiny, to differ from sector to sector: the way in which the House considers Government economic policy, for example, is not the same as that in which it considers foreign affairs. The purpose of this chapter is to illustrate this sometimes overlooked point[1] by considering the extent and the effectiveness of the Commons' scrutiny and influence in a number of sectors. Of necessity, our coverage will be selective rather than exhaustive.

That scrutiny by the House of Commons will differ from sector to sector, from Government Department to Government Department, should not be considered surprising. Some policy sectors are inherently more contentious than others; Governments are prone to legislate in some areas more than others; some Departments, because of the sectors they encompass, come more into contact with citizens than other Departments; some MPs, because of their backgrounds or interests, are more likely to scrutinise one area of Government responsibility than another. Thus, the degree of parliamentary time and interest accorded to a particular sector will vary considerably. An analysis of how much parliamentary time is taken up by matters falling within the responsibility of different Departments illustrates this point, as does an analysis of the means employed for scrutiny on the floor of the House. Departments that cover important policy areas, particularly those of salient interest, will attract attention through general debates; they will tend also to sponsor a significant amount of legislation. Those Departments with responsibilities that bring them into close contact with members of the public, or have responsibilities that affect local communities, will tend to be accorded attention through questions and half-hour adjournment debates.

These points are borne out to some extent by Tables 8.1 and 8.2. As the former table reveals, the politically contentious sectors of economic and social affairs generate a substantial number of Bills; for reasons that will be discussed later, the sector of foreign and defence affairs does not. The table also shows that measures in the economic sector, be they introduced by a Conservative Government (1970–4) or by a Labour one (1974–9), are more likely to be divided against by the Opposition than are measures in other sectors. In the field of foreign and defence affairs, not only are few Bills introduced, but those that are are passed usually without official opposition. Table 8.2 reveals that Departments which have to reply most often to adjournment debates are those, most notably the Department of Health and Social Security (DHSS), which impinge most directly upon the daily existence of the citizen. Through its local offices and the National Health Service, most members of the

TABLE 8.1

BILLS INTRODUCED, 1970–9

Sector	Parliament	
	1970–4	1974–9
Foreign and defence	12 (1)	11 (0)
Home affairs	35 (4)	49 (4)
Scotland and Wales	18 (2)	30 (8)
Social policies	60 (15)	71 (15)
Economic policies	52 (14)	86 (29)
Total	177 (36)	247 (56)

Notes: All Government Bills, except perennial and consolidation legislation, reaching Second Reading in the Commons included. Each measure classified according to the Minister introducing it. The number of Bills divided against on Second Reading by the official Opposition given in parenthesis.

The sector of economic affairs includes agriculture, employment, trade and industry, as well as the Treasury. Home affairs includes the Home Office and legal and parliamentary measures. Social affairs encompasses health and social security, education, and environment.

Source: Richard Rose, *Do Parties Make a Difference?* (Macmillan, 1980).

TABLE 8.2

ADJOURNMENT DEBATES, 1976—7 AND 1978—9

Department replying	Adjournment Debates[a]	
	Session 1976—7	Session 1978—9
Health and Social Security (DHSS)	43	23
Environment	21	16
Transport	22	12
Home Office	19	10
Education	16	4
Industry	9	10
Scottish Office	12	7
Employment	12	4
Defence	8	4
Treasury	8	3
Foreign and Commonwealth Office	7	4
Trade	6	3
Agriculture	2	5
Price and Consumer Protection	4	1
Energy	2	2
Northern Ireland	3	1
Law Officers	1	3
Overseas Development	2	0
Welsh Office	2	0
Civil Service Department	1	0
Lord President of the Council	0	1

[a] Comprising half-hour adjournment debates, Consolidated Fund Bill debates, and recess adjournment debates.

Departments listed in order on basis of aggregate number of adjournment debates for the two sessions.

public at some stage have some dealings with the DHSS; those having any dealings with the Foreign Office or the Civil Service Department are few and far between. (The table reinforces the similar findings of Valentine Herman in his study of adjournment debates in the 1966—7 session).[2] A rough analysis of written and oral questions reveals a similar pattern, with the Departments that generate the most casework for MPs (notably the DHSS and the Department of the Environment) attracting the most questions.[3] As can be gleaned from the foregoing, certain Departments — especially those that cover fields which are inherently politically contentious *and* affect directly the lives of citizens — attract a great deal of parliamentary attention; for one reason or another, a number of others (such as the Welsh Office) do not.

Not only does the amount of time and attention afforded Departments differ; so does the effectiveness of the House in fulfilling its functions of scrutiny and influence of them. The more time and attention given a Department, the greater one might think the scrutiny and influence to be. However, a number of important variables help to ensure that the correlation is far from complete. Some matters which formally occupy a significant amount of the time of the House are those over which the House cannot be said to exert much effective scrutiny: this is especially so in the case of public expenditure, to take perhaps the best-known example. Some sectors may not occupy more time than others, but they may attract more intense or more knowledgeable scrutiny; it would appear that agriculture may fall into this category.[4] The nature of the subject, Members' specialisations, the relevance to constituency interests, procedural rules, and the Constitution are all factors that can influence the ability of the House to scrutinise and influence certain sectors, regardless of the amount of time afforded them relative to other sectors.

The time and attention afforded by the House of Commons, and the scrutiny and influence undertaken, thus clearly varies from sector to sector. In the remainder of this chapter we propose to demonstrate this point by an analysis of selected sectors, represented as appropriate (except for one case) by Government Departments. We have chosen for study economic and financial affairs, foreign affairs, home affairs, health and social security (each so far as represented by the relevant Department), and a sector that is not the responsibility of any one Department, constitutional affairs. We shall consider each in turn.

Economic and financial affairs

The granting of supply, as we have seen, is central to the Commons' historical role in the political process. In order to raise and to spend money, the executive must obtain the assent of Parliament. Given the importance of this role, it is perhaps not surprising that by comparison with a number of other subjects, economic and financial affairs enjoy, formally at least, a substantial amount of the time and attention of the House. There is the annual debate on the Budget and the consideration of the resulting Finance Bill, the committee stage of which differs from that of other Bills (part of it being considered in Standing Committee, and the remainder in Committee of the Whole House); there are the annual Consolidated Fund and Appropriation Bills, and the Estimates which precede them; and there are the debates on the Government's Expenditure White Papers. In addition, for more detailed scrutiny, there are the Public Accounts Committee and, since 1979, the Treasury and Civil Service Committee, successor to the Estimates and the Expenditure Committees. Over and above this, of course, the subject is one which receives attention through Question Time and general debates.[5]

In practice, the granting of supply constitutes one of the formal rather than the real functions of the House (see Chapter 4). The developments of the nineteenth century have ensured that no Government with an overall majority is likely to be denied supply as such. Specific Estimates are unlikely to be defeated (though the eventuality is not unknown) because of the belief that a Government would treat any defeat on supply as a 'resigning matter'; though this view may be regarded as constitutionally unsound, it has been sufficient to influence parliamentary behaviour. The developments of the nineteenth century and of this one have also helped to ensure that, even if the Commons as a collective body wanted to subject the Government's raising and spending of money to detailed and rigorous scrutiny, it would find it extremely difficult so to do. Even with party political considerations cast aside, the ability of the House to scrutinise Government policy in this sector is both limited and fragmentary.

The House of Commons lacks the resources and the information available to Government. Though a Select Committee may seek the advice of respected economists, the House has no facility to match the resources of the Treasury. In an advanced industrialised economy, in which Government has played an increasingly central role in the economic life of the nation (public spending accounted for over half the Gross Domestic Product in 1976), the Commons has become increasingly dependent on Government itself for information. When measures are brought before the Commons, they are the products usually of complex and important negotiations – be they negotiations within Government, between Departments, or between Government and other bodies, as, for example, the TUC or the International Monetary Fund – and are presented as packages, which the House has neither the political will nor the technical knowledge to alter, let alone reject.

The growth of Government itself, and of Government expenditure, coupled with the adoption of a form of economic planning by Government since 1961, has further resulted in a diminution of the Commons' role of scrutiny. It has not developed effective oversight machinery commensurate with these developments. Recognition of the Commons' inability to scrutinise specific Estimates in detail has existed for some time, and has found expression in the fact that individual Estimates are no longer debated (Supply Days now constituting days at the disposal of the Opposition for general debates), and that the Second Reading of the Consolidated Fund Bill is used not to debate financial matters but instead topics raised by private Members. The failure of the Commons to keep pace with the Government's systematic methods of financial planning (such as the Public Expenditure Survey exercise)[6] is reflected in the fact that debate of expenditure remains generally divorced from consideration of taxation. Furthermore, consideration of legislative measures is divorced from that of expenditure planning. The parliamentary year also does not coincide with the financial year; the latter begins in April, in the midst of the parliamentary session. A combination of unco-ordinated calendars and the timing of the presentation of Estimates means that at times the House is considering, albeit formally, Estimates for the previous, current and next year. The result is a House of Commons which considers economic and financial matters on a very limited and unco-ordinated basis, and one that is not well-informed.

However, though the function of granting supply is essentially a formal one, the Commons has not abandoned its function of scrutiny and influence in this area. In addition to the traditional means of scrutiny employed, there have been a number of piecemeal improvements in recent years; the changes have been both structural and behavioural. The 1960s witnessed a simplifying of financial procedures in the House, experimentation with committing the Finance Bill to a Standing Committee, the creation of functional subcommittees for the Estimates Committee, and the establishment of new Select Committees, commencing with the Select Committees on Agriculture and on Science and Technology. The changes of the 1970s were more substantial. The Expenditure Committee began life in 1971. Debates of annual Government Expenditure White Papers were instituted. The Treasury and Civil Service Committee, and the other Department-based select committees were created in 1979. The same year, the Treasury began producing the Estimates on the same price base as cash limits, a practice that produced more realistic figures for the money that was needed, and reduced the need for Supplementary Estimates. The following year, the Government for the first time published its Expenditure White Paper at the same time as the Budget, and the Chancellor presented his financial and monetary strategy for the medium term. The result was to enhance the potential for more effective scrutiny of Government policy, which also began to be realised as a result of behavioural changes.

Estimates cannot be amended by the Commons: they have to be accepted or rejected. The same does not apply to the Finance Bill; this has to go through the normal legislative process, though with certain limitations (the Commons can reduce but not increase the taxation requested by Her Majesty's Ministers). Perhaps surprisingly, it is one measure in the passage of which Members sometimes play an important role. The Budget is drawn up in a cloak of secrecy. Not until the Chancellor's Budget speech are the House and the country aware of its contents. Hence, the response of affected interests is greater after its announcement than in usually the case with other measures. Attempts to influence the consequent legislation, the Finance Bill, are often channelled through MPs, the Members expressing views that, on other measures, the groups or interests concerned would have expressed earlier and directly to officials in the initiation and formulation stages. Hence, the Chancellor and other Treasury Ministers may be somewhat more responsive to Members' representations during the passage of the Bill, knowing that they may speak for important interests outside the House. In addition, the 1970s witnessed a greater willingness on the part of Members, regardless of outside influences, to exert pressure on the Government to amend Finance Bills that they found objectionable, pressure that on occasion led to Government defeats. Indeed, as a result of Opposition parties combining against a minority Government or a number of Government backbenchers voting with the Opposition, successive Governments suffered defeats which affected their economic policies. In 1973, the Conservative Government suffered an embarrassing defeat in Standing Committee, when an amendment to limit the initial period of the Part II statutory policy of the Counter-Inflation Bill to one year was carried by a combination of Opposition and Conservative votes (reversed largely, though not wholly, at report stage);[7] a combination of Opposition parties resulted in the minority Labour Government's suffering seven defeats during Standing Committee stage of the 1974 Finance Bill; a combination of Opposition parties succeeded in carrying Opposition amendments to the 1978 Finance Bill to reduce the basic rate of income tax and to raise the level at which higher rates would apply; dissent by Government backbenchers resulted in various defeats in Standing Committee, most notably on the so-called Rooker/ Wise amendments to the 1977 Finance Bill.[8] In addition, dissent by Tribune Group MPs resulted in the Government's defeat on its Expenditure White Paper in March 1976,[9] and a combination of Opposition parties was sufficient to carry a motion disapproving the Government's policy of sanctions against firms breaking its 5 per cent pay limit in December 1978, a defeat which the Government reluctantly accepted. As a result, parliamentary behaviour affected Government economic policy; it was not sufficient to influence the Government to change direction, but it did affect significantly the policy it was pursuing. Thus, though unable to influence to any great extent the spending of public money (the 1976 defeat was on a declaratory motion, which failed to deflect the Government from its course), the House has had a sporadic influence on the raising of public funds.

Though the Commons' consideration of economic and financial matters remains limited, the structural and behavioural changes of the 1970s may point the way to greater scrutiny and influence in the 1980s. The return of a Government with an overall majority in 1979 removed the possibility of the amendment or defeat of the Government's economic policy or its financial measures by a combination of Opposition parties. The Government's overall majority was such as to suggest that the chances of defeat because some of its own supporters might enter the Opposition lobby were small. Nevertheless, the changed behaviour of the 1970s created an important precedent. Government backbenchers were prepared to be more assertive, and this change has been carried over into the new Parliament. Mrs Thatcher's Government ran into opposition from Conservative MPs when, as part of its policy of reducing public expenditure, it sought to cut the BBC's external services (it back-tracked when it seemed likely to suffer a defeat on the issue); again when it sought to permit local authorities to charge fares for busing children to school from rural areas (the Government abandoned the measure after it ran into trouble in the House and was then defeated in the Lords);[10] when it sought to introduce charges for eye examinations (the measure was withdrawn in the face of likely defeat); it also faced dissent from a number of its own supporters when the Chancellor in 1980 announced only a small increase in child benefit allowance. More generally, the Government has faced acknowledged disquiet among Conservative Members (not confined to the back benches) because of its adherence to a strict policy of monetarism. Though it is unlikely that Government backbenchers would ever be prepared to defeat a Government on the central tenet of its economic policy (at least not on a binding vote), mainly because economic policy is at the heart of a Government's programme, it is for this very reason that a Government needs to be responsive to back-bench criticism. Dissent creates embarrassing publicity, and it undermines the Government's confidence and credibility. The need to be responsive is now enhanced by the fact that, if things are felt to be going 'badly awry', the Government knows that it cannot rely upon the unthinking loyalty of backbenchers to see it through.[11] Hence, as one of the influences that it must take into account in considering economic policy, the Government is now likely to pay more attention to the House of Commons, especially elements within it, than was previously the case. Nevertheless, scrutiny of Government policy on the floor of the House tends to be sporadic rather than continuous. For detailed scrutiny, Members' hopes now rest with the Treasury and Civil Service Committee in particular, and the other Select Committees in general. Though it is too early to comment authoritatively upon the committees' impact, they do offer some hope. They are clearly great improvements on what went before. The Treasury and Civil Service Committee is of particular importance, and has the advantage, unlike some committees, of having a strong membership. A significant number of its members have competence in economic and financial matters.[12] If it makes full use of its powers (including the power to appoint specialist advisers, something which the Expenditure Committee did with some limited success), as it appears to be doing, it has the potential to develop an important oversight role. Whether that potential will be fully realised remains to be seen.

To summarise, the Commons has the potential to develop, and it could be argued that it is developing, a more effective role of scrutiny and influence of Government economic and financial policies. Nevertheless, this role is likely to remain a limited and reactive one. The Government alone retains the resources, and the political and constitutional capacity, to determine economic policy, which it formulates after having taken into account the views and representations of a great many interests, foreign as well as domestic. World economic conditions, as well as pressure from such bodies as the IMF, the TUC or the CBI, are generally accepted to constitute influences that carry considerably more weight with the Government than does the House of Commons. Indeed, the Labour Government of 1974–9 was busy seeking to limit public spending in order to meet the conditions of an IMF loan while maintaining a level of spending that was acceptable to the TUC. One critic asserted in 1979:

> the shape of incomes policy in the last few years has owed far more to the TUC than to Parliament, as have the levels and incidence of public expenditure. It is also small exaggeration to say that the last three Labour Budgets have been substantially written by the TUC Economic Committee.[13]

Though the TUC now carries considerably less weight with the Conservative Government of Mrs Thatcher, such interests remain very important indeed; the CBI, for instance, carries much greater political influence than previously. As one informed observer has noted, 'All that the House of Commons can hope for is to be one influence among the many impinging on the process of determining public spending.'[14] Though some critics would deny it, the Commons would appear to have the ability to be that, a limited but not insignificant influence on Government in the shaping of economic and financial policies. And, as Michael Shanks has noted, it is important that it should be so.[15]

Foreign affairs

One sector in which the ability of the Commons to exercise scrutiny and influence is unusually limited, both formally and actually, is that of foreign affairs. As David Vital has written, Parliament's influence in the making of foreign policy is slight: 'Above all, Parliament is in no sense a regular participant in the process, either by right or custom.'[16] There are a number of reasons, peculiar to foreign affairs, which explain the Commons' limited role.

First, the conduct of foreign affairs is largely a Crown prerogative, exercised now on behalf of the Crown by the Government. The making of war and peace, and the negotiation of treaties, are tasks carried out under the prerogative power. Only if legislation or money is required is the House of Commons required to give its assent. In foreign affairs, little of either is usually needed. 'There is little legislation involved, and, with the notable exception of defence, expenditure is small.'[17] (See also Table 8.1.) In consequence, though the Commons may debate and ask questions about the Government's foreign policy, it is rarely called upon to provide formal, definitive assent to it. Motions approving or expressing opinions on foreign policy are declaratory only. (The position of the Government is further strengthened in that a declaratory motion involves usually only one division, and in that general debates on foreign affairs tend to be held on adjournment motions.) The result is that the Government has a much freer hand, formally and to some extent in practice, in the conduct of foreign affairs than it has in areas in which legislation or definitive authorisation by the Commons is required.

Second, the two front benches tend to adopt a bipartisan approach on foreign policy. It is in the interests of both the Government and the Opposition to seek some common ground. As the alternative Government, the official Opposition is reluctant to undermine the Government's position, partly because of the perceived need not to threaten national interests and partly because it could create problems for itself if later returned to office;[18] as a party seeking office, it also wishes to avoid the electorally damaging opprobrium that could result if it seemed to undermine the efforts of Her Majesty's Government abroad.[19] For the Government's part, it recognises the value of a united front in speaking on Britain's behalf in international negotiations. A consequence of this is that the Prime Minister and the Foreign Secretary occasionally take Opposition leaders into their confidence, and brief them privately. This helps to encourage the support, or at least the silence, of Opposition leaders, who either accept what they are told or, if not, are not free under the terms of the briefing to reveal it anyway.

A result of this bipartisanship is that if there is some serious questioning of Government policy, it tends not to come from the House as a whole or from the official Opposition, but rather from disparate elements within the House, or even individual Members. For example, the Labour Government's Vietnam policy in the 1960s came under fire from Labour left-wingers; its Biafra policy was opposed by a number of backbenchers on both sides of the House.[20] The decision of successive Governments to renew Rhodesian sanctions was regularly opposed by a small number of right-wing Conservatives, at least until 1978, when it attracted the opposition of a significant cross-section of Conservative Members.[21] As William Wallace commented in his thorough study of the foreign policy process:

what seems to the front benches to be a responsible attitude to their
country's international position often looks to these [dissident] groups
a sordid compromise of party principles; and the vigour with which
they criticize their leaders make reasoned debate between the two front
benches more difficult.[22]

There are two important consequences: the most vigorous debate on
foreign policy often takes place within party forums (both parties have
well-established foreign affairs committees), and the Government is
usually guaranteed a majority in the division lobbies on issues on which
there is bipartisan agreement, the votes of dissident Government backbenchers being offset by Opposition support.

Third, a related limitation is that this sector is one in which the
Government can, if it wishes, fall back on a claim of secrecy; it may
assert that to reveal too much would be detrimental to the national
interest.

This is only partly a matter of the Officials Secrets Act, for Winston
Churchill showed in the 1930s that this need not prevent effective
criticism of defence policy. Much more important than this is the
existence of a tradition of secrecy and discretion which the leading
members of both main parties generally respect.[23]

Backbenchers seeking to penetrate the Government's policy on a contentious matter of foreign policy may thus find themselves rebuffed on
grounds on secrecy; the rebuff may be supported or acquiesced in by
the Opposition front bench, and may occur not only in debate but also
at Question Time. Ministers may decline to answer questions on grounds
of public policy, 'and the Foreign Secretary is on this account allowed
great latitude.'[24] Though it has proved possible in recent years to elicit
more information from the Foreign Office than was previously the case,
a long-standing defensiveness on its part has encouraged a 'tendency in
drafting answers to withhold information'.[25]

Fourth, though a number of Members have a particular interest in the
subject (and many travel abroad, in either a parliamentary or a private
capacity),[26] foreign affairs do not impinge greatly on the public consciousness, certainly not by comparison with domestic affairs. Opinion
polls have confirmed the low salience of international issues compared
with the staple issues of the cost of living, housing, taxation, and the
domestic economy.[27] Except on rare occasions when a constituent may
be detained or lost abroad, an MP rarely makes representations to the
Foreign Office in pursuit of constituency interests. In the constituency-
orientated half-hour adjournment debates, for example, it is exceptional
for a topic to be raised that requires a response from a Foreign Office

Minister. The position was perhaps most aptly illustrated in a variously quoted comment by one MP, George Jeger, several years ago:

> When I was in my constituency last weekend I asked my constituents who are concerned with this matter which they would rather I did — endeavour to catch Mr Speaker's eye in the grand foreign affairs debate tomorrow or raise the question of their bus shelter, which is only a local problem. They told me that any fool can speak on foreign affairs, and no doubt several would, but that if I did not speak about their local bus shelter, then nobody else would.[28]

There are few votes in foreign policy issues — elections are not usually fought on them — and dissent by Members will tend to strike fewer chords within their parties than is the case in the domestic sphere.[29]

Fifth, and last, there was until recently no specific Commons forum for the consideration of foreign affairs. Though both main parliamentary parties have their own foreign affairs committees (the Conservative one dating back to at least 1924, the Labour one to 1945), the House as such had to rely until 1979 on Question Time and occasional debates. Debates, as a number of commentators have observed, do not take place often enough.[30] There are usually two general debates each session (one during the debate on the Address, the other on an adjournment motion), and debates on specific issues (as, for example, the Middle East or Zimbabwe), as occasion demands. Not only are such debates few, but they tend also to be unsatisfactory in content. Lacking structure, speeches tend to bear little relationship to one another.[31] Recognition of the sporadic and unsatisfactory attention given to foreign affairs resulted in various calls for the establishment of a Select Committee on the subject. Such calls were made over a period of time and emanated from various sources.[32] The Foreign Office itself was clearly not keen on Select Committees; it resisted attempts by the Estimates Committee to investigate it in the 1950s, and took umbrage at the intentions of the new Agriculture Committee in 1967;[33] as Foreign Secretary, George Brown was reputedly keen on setting up a Select Committee, but reversed his opinion when he realised it would investigate the merits of policy.[34] Nevertheless, the Select Committee on Overseas Development was set up, and continued (though not without interruptions) in its tenure until 1979,[35] and one of the Expenditure Committee's sub-committees covered Defence and External Affairs; a Select Committee was also set up in 1975 to consider British policy during the 1974 Cyprus crisis. Not until the committee reorganisation of 1979, though, did the House get a committee devoted primarily, indeed exclusively, to foreign affairs as such.

A combination of these variables has meant that the ability of the House to engage in the scrutiny and influence of foreign policy has been severely limited. It is one of the few sectors in which its limited role is both formal and real. However, though the influence of the House in this field has been, is, and may remain limited, it is important to record that at times, according to Wallace, it can act 'as a powerful constraint, a negative if not a positive force of considerable strength'.[36] Though not requiring formal assent to certain policy decisions, Foreign Office Ministers will consider it prudent to inform the House of them. Given the need for unity abroad, a negative reaction in the House, even if coming from only a small number of Members, can create embarrassment for the Government; indeed, on rare occasions, the result of a Commons vote may be watched with more interest abroad than at home. In exceptional circumstances, the Government may even modify its policy in response to feelings within the House. For example, the Foreign Secretary altered his position on the sale of arms to South Africa in the 1970–1 session when it became clear that he lacked the support of a number of Conservative Members as well as that of the Opposition;[37] pressure from both sides of the House may have been responsible for the Government's decision to offer substantial aid to Bangladesh in 1971;[38] the Government's Lancaster House negotiations on the future of Rhodesia in the summer of 1979 were clearly influenced by the Government's fear that it could not ensure that a majority of Conservative Members would support the Rhodesian sanctions order when it came up for renewal in the autumn (though it was assured a majority, given Opposition support); and in 1980 the Government decided not to introduce retrospective economic sanctions against Iran when it looked as if it might be defeated in an emergency debate on the issue.[39] Nevertheless, such cases remain rare (albeit not as rare as hitherto), for the reasons we have given; indeed, the factors we have identified contribute to a Commons often more supportive on foreign affairs than on domestic affairs, resulting sometimes in majorities for the Government that are much higher than their normal overall majority would suggest; examples would include Vietnam and Biafra in 1969 (a bipartisan approach), Rhodesian sanctions orders 1969–78 (a bipartisan approach), the Middle East in 1973,[40] Government support for a boycott of the Moscow Olympic Games in 1980,[41] and initially the Iran (Temporary Powers) Bill in the same year.[42] And, as we have seen, little legislation is introduced in this field; when it is, it is exceptional for the Opposition to divide against it (see Table 8.1, p. 171). An increased willingness on the part of the House to demand information from the Government and to be more assertive in the division lobbies, coupled with the more structured scrutiny undertaken by the Foreign Affairs Committee, may increase the ability of the House to exert influence in this sector, but because of the limitations we have detailed (which, in combination, are peculiar to foreign affairs) it is unlikely to be as effective as Members may wish.

Home affairs

The sector of home affairs, inasmuch as it constitutes a coherent policy sector at all, is covered by the Home Department. Though, with the Treasury and the Foreign Office, the Home Office (as the Department is commonly known) is considered to be one of the three main Departments of State, it is nevertheless very different from all other Departments. The difference stems from the range and content of responsibilities that fall within the Department's very broad ambit.

The Home Office deals mainly with the domestic functions in England and Wales not assigned to other Departments; the Home Secretary, according to one source, operates as a kind of 'residual legatee'.[43] The responsibilities of the Department cover, *inter alia*, the administration of justice, the prison service, immigration and nationality, fire and civil defence services, parliamentary and local election law, general questions of broadcasting policy, public safety, community relations, the treatment of offenders, the control of gambling, the supervision of the control of explosives, firearms and dangerous drugs, requests for the extradition of criminals, certain responsibilities for the police force and the internal security services (MI5). The Home Office also advises the sovereign on the exercise of the prerogative power of pardon, and until the abolition of the death penalty for murder, the Home Secretary was responsible also for advising the sovereign on the exercise of mercy in such cases. These may be described as the main responsibilities of the Department.[44] There are a host of other somewhat formal or less important matters that fall within its jurisdiction. For example, it has to prepare patents of nobility for peers; it grants licences for scientific experiments on animals, and has responsibility for the exhumation and removal of bodies; and the Home Secretary is the channel of communication between the Government of the United Kingdom and the Governments of the Channel Islands and the Isle of Man. So many and varied are the matters falling within the competence of the Department that it is not unknown for a Home Secretary to leave office without having known just how many powers and responsibilities actually fell within the remit of his office.[45]

Both the range and the content of the responsibilities have produced a number of features distinctive to the Department. The range of responsibilities and their disparateness has meant, in the words of one former Minister, that 'it is difficult to achieve an integrated organisation of the sort familiar in the rest of Whitehall.'[46] (Until recently, this disparateness was exacerbated by the fact that the Home Office was housed in over twenty separate buildings throughout London, though it has now been brought together in one large, modern building in Queen Anne's Gate, close to New Scotland Yard.)[47] Coupled with the nature of the responsibilities, most of which are peculiar to the Home Office, requiring little interdepartmental or interministerial contact, this has meant that the Department is 'surprisingly detached from the rest of Whitehall'.[48] In the past, this detachment was reinforced by a tendency for officials to spend most of their careers in this one Department,[49] though apparently this is not so much the case nowadays. This detachment, and the emphasis in some sections on casework, on practical problems (and presumably precedent) rather than broad policy considerations, may have contributed to the Department's somewhat conservative (or, in the words of one close observer, 'fuddy-duddy') reputation.

The matters falling within the Department's jurisdiction are also unusual in that many cannot be described as being within the ambit of its direct administration. Much of the Home Office's responsibility for various matters is essentially indirect — for example, the police outside the metropolis. Furthermore, by their nature, many matters within the Department's jurisdiction lend themselves to third-party consideration. When issues of criminal law or procedure come up, it is not unknown for the Home Secretary to refer them to the Criminal Law Revision Commission or the Royal Commission on Criminal Procedure; matters of electoral law are usually referred for consideration by a Speaker's Conference. Though such reference to authoritative bodies is a legitimate and important practice, there is the danger, through regular usage, that it may be exploited to excess; MPs sometimes view it as unnecessary when they believe the point of principle at issue is clear-cut.

The range and content of Home Office responsibilities, be they direct or indirect, produce other features of particular importance to the House of Commons. The *range* of responsibilities ensures that the Home Office receives considerable parliamentary attention. This attention is all the greater given the *nature* of the responsibilities. A number of Home Office concerns, especially immigration and matters of 'law and order', are controversial. They generate much discussion both within and outside the House. Other areas entail a great deal of casework. Immigration, again, falls in this category; so too do matters covering the treatment of prisoners and those detained in police custody. The result is a fairly heavy burden of work for Home Office Ministers. They have to deal with representations made to them personally by Members,[50] as well as a not inconsiderable correspondence. In July 1979, the Minister of State responsible for immigration (Tim Raison) received no fewer than 1243 letters from MPs and peers.[51] (Indeed, in the mid-1970s the Home Office was a popular recipient of letters from the public as well, receiving some 1.6 million pieces of correspondence a year, excluding simple acknowledgements.)[52] Given this and, more important, the need to obtain and study material in specific cases, it is perhaps not surprising that the Department is rather slow in answering Members' letters; in

1973 and 1974 it took on average between three and four weeks to reply to a Member's letter.[53] Over and above receiving personal and written respresentations from MPs, the Ministers have, of course, to deal with matters raised on the floor of the House. In the 1976–7 and 1978–9 sessions, the Home Office ranked fourth (after the DHSS, Environment and Transport) in the number of half-hour adjournment debates that fell within its jurisdiction (see Table 8.2). Analysed in terms of individual Departments, it would appear to sponsor more Bills, and certainly more contentious Bills *vis-à-vis* other Departments, than is suggested in Table 8.1 – of Bills introduced in the two sessions of 1976–7 and 1978–9 that were debated and divided upon at Second Reading, only Environment sponsored more than the Home Office[54] – and a rough estimate suggests that the Home Office ranks about second or third among Departments in the number of parliamentary questions it answers.[55] Given the nature of its responsibilities, the Home Office also attracts a number of general debates; in the 1974–9 Parliament, the Opposition was keen to discuss the theme of 'law and order' and related topics.[56] In terms of parliamentary demands made of Departments, it would appear that only the DHSS and the Environment Department can make claims to be more in demand than the Home Office; of these three, the Home Office has the fewest Ministers.

The nature of the matters covered by the Home Office also facilitates sudden parliamentary controversy. The escape of a dangerous murderer from prison, police behaviour in a particular case, arbitrary action by immigration officials – such cases can arise suddenly, attract publicity, and necessitate at short notice the attention of the Home Secretary. This aspect of a Home Secretary's work has been noted by various occupants of the office. Roy Jenkins summed it up by describing the climate of the Home Office as 'one of tropical storms that blow up with speed and violence out of a blue sky, dominate the political landscape for a short time, and then disappear as suddenly as they arrived. When they are over it is difficult to recall what the fuss was all about.'[57] Other Departments are generally less prone to such sudden political squalls (certainly on such a scale); Mr Jenkins observed that at the Treasury he was more concerned with the general 'ebb and flow' of events.[58] How Home Secretaries respond to such sudden political controversies, or seek to anticipate them, varies from Home Secretary to Home Secretary. Henry Brooke, for example, was generally poor in both anticipating and reacting to sensitive and controversial issues; his handling of the Enahoro case in 1963 was judged generally to have been maladroit, not to say disastrous. His predecessor, R.A. Butler, was more successful, having learned from the experience of a telephone-tapping controversy (which led to the establishment of the Birkett Committee) shortly after taking up the office. The incident, he said, taught him a useful lesson; thereafter he spent most evenings in the Commons' Smoking Room in order to detect signs of incipient trouble that might blow up on the floor of the House.[59] The current occupant of the office, Mr Whitelaw, has also institutionalised procedures designed to keep him abreast of parliamentary opinion. He has a ministerial meeting each morning, which is attended not only by his junior Ministers, the Permanent Secretary, private secretary, and the Department's information director, but also by the Ministers' Parliamentary Private Secretaries, the PPSs being present to help provide a 'parliamentary input'.[60] In addition, Mr Whitelaw and his Ministers maintain close contact with the officers of the party's Home Affairs Committee, seeing them regularly after each Monday's meeting of the Committee.[61]

Although it is possible to generalise about the amount of time and attention accorded Home Office matters by the Commons, it is less easy to quantify the effectiveness of such attention. The scrutiny of executive actions may be limited by a number of factors we have considered already. On matters for which Home Office responsibility is indirect, few questions may be asked; the Isle of Man, for example, rarely features in the questions asked by Members. Other matters, for which responsibility is more direct and which are politically contentious, may attract considerable parliamentary attention; parliamentary questions on prisons and immigration are common, and the Home Affairs Committee of the House has a subcommittee to cover race relations. Responsiblity for certain sensitive areas, such as the internal security services (MI5) and the deportation of undesirable aliens, sometimes limits the information which the Home Office is willing to release. Refusal to disclose information in such cases may cause a parliamentary storm (as with the refusal to reveal the reasons for the deportation of two American citizens in 1977), and such refusal, coupled with the generally conservative image of the Department, has led to much criticism of the Home Office by a number of Labour Members. They view it as unnecessarily secretive, immune to parliamentary scrutiny; in giving his reasons for quitting the House in 1979, Paul Rose singled out the Home Office as one of the two Departments with the thickest 'armour plating' in Whitehall.[62]

However, such generalisations can be misleading. For one thing, a Home Secretary is usually sensitive to his powers in respect of individuals. Advising the monarch about whether or not to reprieve a condemned man was not an easy task; nor is that of deciding whether or not to deport an alien. When the power is exercised, it usually attracts a parliamentary outcry; if handled badly, it can do irreparable damage to a Minister's reputation. The experience of such cases acts as a reminder to future Home Secretaries of what is in store for them if they take similar action. (Roy Jenkins was clearly conscious of this when he observed that 'deportation cases, as Lord Brooke's experience showed, need particularly careful watching.')[63] And the refusal to supply information in such cases on grounds of national security (as in 1977) can be as much to the Minister's disadvantage as it is a demonstration of his power; a Minister who cannot provide reasons for his decisions appears to be in a weak position. For another thing, though the Department may have a somewhat insular and conservative reputation, its secretiveness and unresponsiveness in certain areas does not necessarily extend to other areas. Outside the realms of national security, one Opposition spokesman has conceded that the Home Office is not very different from other Departments in its willingness (or unwillingness) to answer questions; and that its response to Members' letters, apart from those requiring time to call in and study information on specific cases, differs little from that of other Departments as well.[64] Certainly, officials in the Department attach considerable importance to parliamentary questions, and much time is devoted to them; one Minister has contended that parliamentary business is very much at the centre of Home Office discussions.[65] An inside observer has also noted that officials are 'terrified, absolutely terrified' when called to appear before the Home Affairs Committee of the House.[66] It is worth noting as well that in one particular area of Home Office responsibility, MPs carry great weight. If immigration officials seek to deny a foreign national entry to Britain, or to return a foreign national who is in the country to his or her country of origin, the intervention of an MP can considerably delay the process. Whereas the person would normally be put on the next flight, an MP's telephone call to Home Office officials can help to keep the person in the country for several weeks. Indeed, so effective are MPs in this area that the Government is contemplating how to deal with the problems such intervention causes. (Members' interests in such cases are often encouraged by constituency concerns; Members in constituencies with large immigrant populations often receive a great deal of case-related correspondence.)[67] In short, Members' effectiveness in scrutinising Home Office actions may vary considerably.

Similarly, it is difficult to generalise about the effectiveness of Members in scrutinising and influencing legislation (primary or delegated) that emanates from the Home Office. Given the range of Home Office responsibilities, such legislation takes different forms. Bills arising from its limited or less important responsibilities may attract little attention. Those arising from its responsibilities for immigration and race relations may dominate the parliamentary stage. Immigration is an obvious area of controversy. Not only does it arouse serious disagreement between both sides of the House, but also often attracts much intra-party disagreement. The Conservative Government's 1971 Immigration Bill attracted some criticism from Conservative Members as well as from the Opposition, and a new provision was inserted against the Government's wishes;[68] the following year, the Government suffered its most embarrassing defeat when its immigration rules were rejected.[69] The Labour Government's 1977 immigration rules attracted the opposition of some sixty-six Labour Members,[70] and the Conservative immigration rules introduced in the 1979–80 session ran into serious criticism from both sides of the House, that from the Government back benches motivating some modification of them. Any measure dealing with criminal law will also attract the interested scrutiny of Members on both sides of the House. This is in part because of the disproportionate number of lawyers in the House, and also because several Members have a special interest in civil liberties (a number, primarily though not exclusively on the Labour side, are members of the National Council for Civil Liberties); interest may also be stimulated by concern at the incidence of criminal acts, an issue which may be particularly salient in certain constituencies, or because of specific constituency-related cases. Among measures modified in recent years in deference to the wishes of Members have been the 1972 Criminal Justice Bill, the 1976 Bail Bill, and the 1977 Criminal Law Bill. Measures dealing with gambling also attract considerable interest, both from nonconformist Members opposed to it and from Members with personal knowledge of the subject (one MP, Brian Walden, was well-known as the paid consultant of bookmakers); measures dealing with horserace betting in particular appear to attract special attention.[71] Measures of electoral law will also attract the interest of Members, who after all have a knowledge of, and vested interest in, the subject. Indeed, these areas illustrate a difference between many Home Office matters and those covered by other Departments: Members may know as much about the subject as the Ministry; even if they do not, Ministers do not have the same opportunity as those in economic or technical Departments to hide behind claims of detailed knowledge and complex data. Members, as one Minister conceded, are 'not afraid to have a go'.[72] (When statistics are involved, the Home Office's credibility has been undermined by a number of mistakes, as in its calculation of figures for immigration and emigration.) This does not necessarily mean that measures introduced by the Home Office will be subject to rigorous and effective scrutiny. However, Home Office measures would appear to attract somewhat more attention, and often more intra-party disagreement, than measures emanating from most other, though not all, Departments.

To summarise, the range and content of Home Office responsibilities are varied, as is the ability of the House to scrutinise and influence the actions and the measures of the Department. In some areas, Home Office responsibility is limited and/or indirect; in many such cases, though not all, parliamentary interest is similarly limited. In others, a combination of direct responsibility and domestic controversy produce a high level of parliamentary interest. Overall, the range of Home Office responsibilities, and the nature of those responsibilities ensure that the Department spends more time on parliamentary business than the other great Departments of State. As Roy Jenkins observed, 'The ministerial job of administering the Home Office was heavier than that of administering the Treasury. There were far more individual decisions to be made. There was also more Parliamentary work.'[73] ('Even for unadventurous spirits,' as Lord Butler put it, 'the Home Office can never provide a rest cure.')[74] With the introduction of the Select Committe on Home Affairs, which covers important topics that were outwith the purview of its predecessor subcommittee of the Expenditure Committee, even more parliamentary work is now involved.

Health and social security

The Department of Health and Social Security, presided over by the Secretary of State for the Social Services, occasionally comes to the fore in parliamentary interest because of Government policy; issues such as pay beds in the National Health Service (NHS), expenditure on the NHS, NHS reorganisation (as in 1973), or, in the current Parliament, Health and Social Security Bills are politically contentious and often the subject of bitter partisan debate. More important, though, the Department is one which attracts attention from Members in all parts of the House, and on a more regular basis, because of constituency or more general non-party interests. While constituents may complain generally about the level of taxation or about the Government's economic policy, and have no great interest in foreign affairs, their concern for health and social security matters is often personal and parochial. Services provided under the NHS, the operation of a local hospital, the benefits to which one is entitled, are matters of personal interest to the individual; the DHSS, through the services for which it is responsible, is the Government Department with which more citizens come into direct contact than any other. Whereas an MP will receive few letters or visits from constituents raising individual problems that are the concern, say, of the Foreign Office, or the Departments of Energy, Industry, or Trade, he will receive a great many that are the concern of the DHSS. Dealing with such problems forms an essential part of the Member's 'social welfare' role. In that role, he will pursue such cases through the use of private correspondence with Ministers (an analysis of Tony Benn's constituency correspondence for 1972–3 revealed that he wrote more than four times as many letters to the DHSS as to any other Department),[75] through questions (both oral and written), and through half-hour adjournment debates. As we have seen (Table 8.2, p. 172), it is the Department which has to reply to more adjournment debates than any

other Department. In practice, most cases are resolved through correspondence. In the current Parliament, Ministers at the DHSS receive
over two thousand letters a month from Ministers, and as a rule no fewer
than five hundred a week.[76] (This represents an increase over recent
years, and Ministers are encouraging Members to write direct to their
local DHSS offices or Area Health Authorities where relevant, as a
means of speeding up replies.) Given that most cases can be dealt with
by letter and occasional informal encounters with Ministers in the
House, formal deputations by Members to the Department are rare.
Where cases are taken as far as adjournment debates, they tend to cover
services provided locally or even, in some instances, the problems of a
named individual; in the 1978—9 session, for example, Ronald Bell raised
the issue of maternity services in South Buckinghamshire and East
Berkshire, whereas Andrew Bowden raised the matter of mobility help
for a named constituent, Mrs Maureen Tower. In pursuing such cases
on behalf of constituents, Members are rarely acting in their capacities
as Conservative, Labour or Liberal Members of Parliament; they are
acting as Members of Parliament. As Roy Hattersley noted, 'it is part of
the job' (see above, p 57). Similarly, party considerations are usually not
pertinent to a Minister in replying to the cases on behalf of the DHSS.

The DHSS is thus a Department which attracts much attention from
Members, especially in their capacity as representatives of constituents
or constituency interests. It is also one which attracts attention from
Members as representatives of general social interests; several Members,
for example, take a special interest in the problems of the elderly and
the disabled in the country generally and not just in their own constituencies. There is an All-Party Disablement Group which has not been
without influence in keeping the Department aware of the problems
and needs of disabled people; on one occasion, according to Jack Ashley,
it influenced significantly the level of mobility allowances.[77] Though
Members thus play a very important role, and in cases of clear injustice,
as Brian Walden noted, 'can be very relentless indeed' in forcing them
on the Government's attention,[78] there are problems. The role of most
Members would appear to be a reactive one (they wait for complaints),
and once complaints have been made, lack the resources to investigate
many of them adequately. The position has been eased somewhat by the
appointment of a Health Service Commissioner under the 1973 National
Health Service Reorganisation Act, but though this has provided an
alternative to the DHSS itself for the investigation of complaints of maladministration,[79] it has removed the constituent—MP link; complaints
may be made directly to the Commissioner. Complaints not within the
Commissioner's jurisdiction will continue to find their way to Members,
who will pursue them through the traditional means already identified.
The 1979 Select Committee reorganisation resulted in the creation of a

Social Services Committee (Social Services and Employment being covered previously by one of the Expenditure Committee's subcommittees), but it is not a body through which individual cases can be pursued (except perhaps, for the occasional *cause célèbre*); as a body to keep the DHSS on its toes, though, especially in the provision of certain services, it is a useful addition.

In terms of the scrutiny of legislation emanating from the Department – and, indeed, of general scrutiny of the Department's functioning – a number of problems can be identified. As we have noted, the more important items of legislation brought forward tend to be the cause of conflict between the two main parties. The Conservative Government of Mr Heath introduced the NHS Reorganisation Bill (albeit not with the wholehearted support of all Conservative MPs): the Labour Opposition flatly opposed it. The Labour Government of Mr Callaghan wanted to phase out pay beds in NHS hospitals (some Labour MPs wanting to go faster than the Government's timetable allowed): the Conservative Opposition was all in favour of retaining them. The result has often been that the party battle has tended to dominate, to the detriment of detached or detailed scrutiny of the provisions of such measures. This was the finding of a recent study of the years from 1970 to 1975; it found that scrutiny of the NHS Reorganisation Bill in particular was inadequate.[80] In terms of overseeing the DHSS generally, there is the problem of the size of the Department; an additional problem has been the multi-tiered structure of the health service brought about by the 1973 Act: a recent study found that Area Health Authorities (now due for removal under proposals announced by the Government in 1980) had achieved near semi-autonomous status.[81] The disparateness of the NHS has meant that adequate supervision of its activities and spending has been difficult enough for the Government, let alone the more distant House of Commons. Nevertheless, there have been some minor improvements in recent years. Members have proved more willing on occasion to combine and influence the Government on matters of detail during the passage of DHSS legislation,[82] and the creation of the Social Services Committee provides at least the opportunity for a more structured look at the activities of the Department. They constitute perhaps marginal but nonetheless welcome improvements, and the experience of the Social Services Committee to date has been promising.

Constitutional affairs

In 1976, when the Labour Government's proposals for devolution came on to the political agenda, the Conservative parliamentary party added a Constitutional Committee to its existing party committee structure. (The committee still exists.) The House itself lacked, and still lacks, a forum for the specific discussion of constitutional affairs, of proposals and measures affecting the basic structure and details of the government of the United Kingdom. There is no Minister with specific responsibility for constitutional affairs; it is a subject not covered by any Select Committee. It is, however, an area in which the House has exerted a significant influence in recent years. A number of important measures have been brought before the House, measures which have attracted the critical attention or opposition of Government as well as Opposition backbenchers; procedural factors, coupled with more recent changes in behaviour, have made it possible for Members to exert considerable influence over the content and passage of some of them.

Though not covered by any Department or Select Committee, important constitutional measures do have one common feature: in the legislative process, they will normally have their Committee stage taken in Committee of the Whole House and not in Standing Committee (see Chapter 5). This is important, not only because it formally provides all Members with the opportunity to engage in committee proceedings, but also because it enhances in practice the likely effectiveness of back-bench influence, especially if Government backbenchers are not fully dedicated to the measures in question. Such Bills, if contentious (which, by their nature, they often are), attract publicity, and the Opposition can exploit the floor of the House to expose any perceived weak points; while occupying the floor of the House, there is little other competing parliamentary news. If a Bill is a substantial and contested one, the Government may feel constrained to move a guillotine motion; this, though, is something it would prefer not to do given the political capital that the Opposition would make out of it and that opponents of the measures on the Government back-benches may view it as an opportunity to defeat the Bill on a procedural rather than a substantive point. Taken on the floor of the House, the Government needs to keep a House, that is, a majority in order to carry the many divisions that may be forced; even if there are few amendments (which would be unusual in the case of a contested measure), opponents have the opportunity to divide the House on the 'stand part' motion for each clause. In addition, if a guillotine is not in operation, the Government will need to keep at least one hundred Members present throughout late-night sittings in order to carry contested closure motions. These procedural points take on special significance, of course, if dissident Government backbenchers as well as Opposition Members are prepared to exploit them; in recent years they have been prepared so to do.

The importance of the foregoing is borne out by the experience of the past ten to fifteen years. Since 1968, three Bills of great constitutional significance have been introduced, each brought in by a different Government: the 1969 Parliament (No. 2) Bill to reform the House of

Lords; the 1972 European Communities Bill to facilitate Britain's entry into the European Communities; and the 1976 Scotland and Wales Bill (succeeded by separate Scotland and Wales Bills) to devolve certain powers to elected Assemblies in the two countries. The second of these Bills was enacted; but if each of the other two had been passed in the form intended by the Government of the day, Britain would now have a completely reformed Second Chamber, and elected national Assemblies with devolved powers operating in Edinburgh and Cardiff.

The first of the three Bills, the Parliament (No. 2) Bill, was withdrawn despite the support of both front benches. It came under criticism from both sides of the House, criticism which clearly influenced a number of Members who had previously been prepared to support it, so that in the event they either opposed it or abstained from voting. The more the provisions of the Bill were debated in Committee, the less support there was for it. The Government was unsure of its ability to carry a guillotine motion, and so backbenchers on both sides were able to pursue their critical examination of each of its clauses. A number of late-night sittings were held, but the Government was not always able to maintain sufficient support to carry closure motions. As a result, discussion of the Bill's provisions was prolonged, and — being taken on the floor of the House — was eating into the parliamentary timetable; a bottleneck was being created in the Government's legislative programme. Realising that the measure did not have the widespread parliamentary support that it would have wished for (though at no time was there a defeat in the division lobbies), and was causing severe timetabling problems (an Industrial Relations Bill was waiting in the pipeline, although it too was subsequently abandoned), the Government decided not to proceed with the Bill. After having been moved on Second Reading by the Prime Minister, who described it as a 'desirable, necessary, step in the long overdue modernisation of the institutions of our democracy', and after two months in Committee of the Whole House, the Bill faded into oblivion. Although both main parties have experienced pressure more recently for reform or abolition of the Lords, the experience of 1969 would appear to have cooled the ardour of successive Governments in pursuing such a course.

The Second Bill, the European Communities Bill, was carried, and indeed went through Committee stage unamended (thus obviating the need for a Report stage), but even though it enjoyed the support of a majority of Members its passage was not a smooth one. Despite its being the most important measure introduced by Mr Heath's Government, the Second Reading was secured by a majority of only eight votes on a vote of confidence; the Government's overall majority at the time should have produced a majority at least three times higher than that. (In the wake of the vote, one distinguished commentator actually queried whether the Bill would be proceeded with.)[83] A guillotine motion helped to ensure that the Bill passed the Commons by the summer recess, but even without a Report stage it still occupied three months of parliamentary time. And even though passed, and enjoying the support of a majority of the House, the manner in which it was passed had certain repercussions: the Opposition made political capital out of it (membership of the EC being deemed electorally unpopular); dissident Conservative Members resented it and later took opportunities to vent their anger; and loyal Government backbenchers were apparently none too happy at having to go through the lobbies in support of the measure on over a hundred occasions.[84] The Government carried its most important measure, but its passage was not quite as smooth as Ministers might have hoped, and certainly not as smooth as some critics of the House of Commons would have expected.

The third Bill, the Scotland and Wales Bill, was introduced in December 1976 and was expected to dominate the session. It was not given the opportunity to do so. It got bogged down in Committee early in the new year, and the Government decided that a guillotine motion would be necessary to see it through. Opponents of the measure on the Government back benches saw this as an opportunity to defeat the measure on a procedural rather than a substantive point, and so entered the Opposition lobby: the motion was lost by 312 votes to 283.[85] As a result, the Government decided not to proceed with the Bill as it stood. Instead, it introduced separate Bills for Scotland and Wales. It subsequently obtained guillotine motions for both Bills, but certain provisions of each did not meet with the approval of a majority of the House. The Government suffered ten defeats in the lobbies during the passage of the Scotland Bill, and four during the passage of the Wales Bill. The most significant change effected was the provision of a 40 per cent 'yes' vote in the proposed referendums. Because of parliamentary pressure, and fearing defeat were it not to agree the provision, the Government agreed reluctantly to hold referendums in Scotland and in Wales on its devolution proposals. Amendments carried against it in Committee stage of both Bills wrote in the requirement that if less than 40 per cent of eligible voters did not vote 'yes', then orders would be laid for the repeal of the measure(s). Attempts by the Government to reverse these provisions were thwarted. The ground was thus laid for the failure of the Government's devolution proposals. In referendums on 1 March 1979, the 40 per cent requirement was not realised, and as a result the relevant orders were laid. Because of parliamentary actions, and the procedure that made those actions possible, Britain does not now have a devolved form of Government in Scotland and Wales.

It could be argued, quite justifiably, that such cases are exceptional. Effectively to prevent the Government from obtaining important con-

stitutional changes in two out of three cases is remarkable. If such a
record were achieved in other sectors, the Government would be severely
constrained. The point is that it is not. The House of Commons is not
often called upon to consider Bills of constitutional significance. When
it is, such Bills are dealt with differently from most Bills. In recent
years, such Bills have been remarkable for their failure to command
unanimous support on the Goverment side of the House. In short, the
Commons' scrutiny and influence in this sector has been atypical.

Conclusion

The House of Commons has various means available by which it may
scrutinise the measures and actions of Government. The extent to which
such means are employed, and their effectiveness, varies from sector to
sector. Half-hour adjournment debates are frequently used to raise
matters of concern in the health, transport and education sectors; a
Member rarely seeks such a debate on a Foreign Office matter. The
House has greater formal opportunity to discuss economic affairs (and
other related subjects) than it does foreign affairs. Members will engage
in a considerable amount of correspondence with certain Departments
in representing the interests of constituents, most notably the DHSS,
but very little with others. The House is more often called upon to give
assent to requests for supply than it is to pass Bills of constitutional
significance; yet procedural and political variables would appear to give
Members greater opportunity to scrutinise and influence the latter than
the former. The creation of Select Committees based on Departments
has provided the opportunity for more comprehensive scrutiny, but the
work of these committees can and does vary, depending in part on the
interests of the Members, the resources of which a committee avails
itself, and the nature of the Department being covered. Certain subjects,
not the designated responsibility of individual Departments, lack committees devoted exclusively to them; the Conservative parliamentary
party, as we have noted, has a Constitutional Committee, the House
does not. The extent to which the means employed for scrutiny, and
their effectiveness, varies from sector to sector is a subject worthy of
comprehensive study. The purpose of this chapter has not been to
provide such a study, but merely to illustrate the basic point that the
different responsibilities and policy sectors covered by Government do
not receive uniform attention by the House of Commons.

NOTES

1   A small number of studies have analysed the Commons and its scrutiny of

specific sectors – as, for example, Peter Richards's *Parliament and Foreign Affairs* (Allen & Unwin, 1967), and Ann Robinson's *Parliament and Public Spending* (Heinemann, 1978) – but hardly any have undertaken a comparative study of several sectors. An exhaustive analysis would require a volume of considerable length; hence the limitations of this chapter.

2   Valentine Herman, 'Adjournment Debates in the House of Commons', in D. Leonard and V. Herman (eds), *The Backbencher and Parliament* (Macmillan, 1972), pp. 108–25; see especially table 3, p. 119.

3   This rough estimate is based not on a count of questions but on the space occupied by Departments in the *Hansard* sessional indexes. The amount of space taken up gives a rough but useful guide to the demands made of a Department, *vis-à-vis* other Departments, by written and oral questions. (Most entries under departmental headings are those of oral or written questions. Bills are listed separately, and references to general debates occupy very few lines.)

4   A sectoral investigation by the Study of Parliament Group revealed that 'interest in agricultural policy is notable.' See the comments of S.A. Walkland, 'Parliament and the Economy in Britain: Some Reflections', *Parliamentary Affairs*, 32 (1), Winter 1979, p. 12.

5   For a summary of the House's consideration of financial and economic matters (to the late 1970s), see Eric Taylor, *The House of Commons at Work*, 9th ed. (Macmillan, 1979), ch. 6, and Robinson, ch. 2. For a detailed study, see Michael Ryle, 'Supply and other Financial Procedures', in S.A. Walkland (ed.), *The House of Commons in the Twentieth Century* (Oxford University Press, 1979), ch. 7.

6   See H. Heclo and A. Wildavsky, *The Private Government of Public Money* (Macmillan, 1974) for details. For a succinct summary of the Government's annual financial calendar, see the schools brief, 'Power of the Purse', *Economist*, 8 December 1979, pp. 22–3.

7   See Philip Norton, 'Dissent in Committee: Intra-Party Dissent in Commons' Standing Committees 1959–74', *The Parliamentarian*, 57 (1), January 1976, pp. 18–19.

8   Named after the two Labour MPs responsible for the amendments being carried, namely, Jeffrey Rooker and Mrs Audrey Wise. The amendments raised the levels of income tax allowances and partially indexed them against inflation.

9   See Philip Norton, 'The Government Defeat: 10 March 1976', *The Parliamentarian*, 57 (3), 1976, pp. 174–5.

10   Had the Government sought to reinstate the provision in the Commons, it may well have faced defeat, opposition to the proposed charges having further hardened on the back benches, especially as a result of pressure from constituencies.

11   Geoffrey Smith, 'The Younger Men that Mrs Thatcher must Convince of her Strategy', *The Times*, 21 March 1980.

12   See above, Chapter 6, f. 89.

13   S.A. Walkland, 'Parliament and the Economy in Britain: Some Reflections', p. 11.

14   Robinson, p. 160.

15   Michael Shanks, *Planning and Politics* (PEP, 1977), p. 92.

16   David Vital, *The Making of British Foreign Policy* (Allen & Unwin, 1968), p. 48.

17   James Barber, *Who Makes British Foreign Policy?* (Open University Press, 1976), p. 25.

18   For example, Conservative MPs were advised not to divide against the annual Rhodesian sanctions order when in Opposition, in order not to tie the hands of a future Conservative Government. See also Vital, p. 75.

19   The Conservative Opposition's disunity on the issue of Rhodesia in 1965, for example, appeared to damage its electoral appeal. Mr Heath was perceived as failing to give the Government unequivocal support at a time of international crisis.

20   See Philip Norton, *Dissension in the House of Commons 1945–74* (Macmillan, 1975), pp. 266–7, 336–8, 369–72, 374–6.

21   See Norton, pp. 362–3, 380–1, 521–2, 597–8, and, by the same author, *Dissension in the House of Commons 1974–1979* (Oxford University Press, 1980), pp. 21–2, 122–3, 192, 273–4, and 377–9.

22   William Wallace, *The Foreign Policy Process in Britain* (Royal Institute of International Affairs/Allen & Unwin, 1977 ed.), p. 93.

23   A.H. Birch, *Representative and Responsible Government* (Allen & Unwin, 1964), p. 152.

24   O. Hood Phillips, *Constitutional and Administrative Law*, 5th ed. (Sweet and Maxwell, 1973), p. 170.

25   Sir Ivone Kirkpatrick, quoted in Wallace, p. 94. Kirkpatrick was writing in 1949, but as Wallace points out, his comments 'would not be too unkind today'.

26   See Wallace, p. 91.

27   Wallace, p. 113.

28   *House of Commons Debates*, 580, c. 710. Quoted in both Wallace, p. 95, and Barber, p. 27.

29   Though overstating the case, Vital makes a similar point, at p. 77.

30   As, for example, former Foreign Secretary Selwyn Lloyd in *Mr Speaker, Sir* (Jonathan Cape, 1976), p. 168. He lists other topics not debated often enough, but foreign affairs heads the list.

31   Richards, p. 113. Wallace, pp. 92–3, also comments upon their unsatisfactory nature.

32   See, for example, Harold Laski, *Reflections on the Constitution* (Manchester University Press, 1951), p. 88, and the comments of Wallace, p. 95, and Richards, ch. 8.

33   See James Johnson, 'The Select Committee on Agriculture', in Alfred Morris (ed.), *The Growth of Parliamentary Scrutiny by Committee* (Pergamon Press, 1970), pp. 36–7.

34   See Wallace, p. 293, fn. 21. For reasons given for Government resistance to the idea, see Roy E. Jones, *The Changing Structure of British Foreign Policy* (Longmans, 1974), p. 172.

35   On the work of the committee, see Sir George Sinclair, 'The Select Committee on Overseas Aid', in Morris, pp. 43–53, and the evidence of Sir Bernard Braine, MP, to the Procedure Committee, *First Report from the Select Committee on Procedure, 1977–8*, Vol. II (HC 588–2), pp. 224–36.

36   Wallace, p. 98.

37   Philip Norton, *Conservative Dissidents* (Temple Smith, 1978), pp. 40–5.

38   Wallace, p. 98.

39   *House of Commons Debates*, 985, c. 30–48, 254–63; *The Times*, 20 May 1980. For other examples, see Wallace, pp. 98–9.

40   Norton, *Conservative Dissidents*, pp. 139–41.

41   *House of Commons Debates*, 981, c. 163–7.

42   *ibid.*, 984, c. 1007–12. Voting was 230 to 85 on Second Reading.

43   As quoted in the Earl of Kilmuir, *Political Adventure* (Weidenfeld & Nicolson, 1964), p. 198.

44   Until the creation of the Northern Ireland Office in 1972, the Home Secretary also had responsibility for the province, and until the creation of the Welsh Office in 1964 he was also Minister for Wales.

45   It is possible to contend that one Home Secretary, Mr Maudling in 1972, actually resigned because of a misunderstanding of his powers; he appeared to believe that his responsibility for the police force was greater than it was.

46   Lord Windlesham, *Politics in Practice* (Jonathan Cape, 1975), p. 19.

47   With one or two important and necessary exceptions: the immigration section, for example, is housed separately.

48   Roy Jenkins, 'On Being a Minister', in V. Herman and J. Alt (eds), *Cabinet Studies* (Macmillan, 1975), p. 210.

49   See Jenkins, 'On Being a Minister', pp. 210–11.

50   Leon Brittan, MP, to author.

51   Written answer, Lord Belstead to Lord Avebury, House of Lords, 7 November 1979. *House of Lords Debates*, 402, c. 978. Also commented upon by the Home Secretary, Mr Whitelaw, in *Sunday Times Magazine*, 27 April 1980, p. 72.

52   Windlesham, p. 19.

53   Windlesham, p. 179, fn. 8.

54   Of six Bills introduced by the Home Office that were debated in the House on Second Reading, five were divided against. (Environment introduced ten Bills, six of which were divided against.)

55   See fn. 2 above.

56   For example, in the 1976–7 session, the Opposition actually used its Supply time to debate the topic of crime prevention twice. (In the same session, Conservative backbenchers sponsored Private Members' motions on prisons, and police pay and conditions.) In the 1977–8 session, the Opposition used its time to debate crime and, on another occasion, law and order.

57   Jenkins, 'On Being a Minister', pp. 215–6. See also the comments of Lord Butler, *The Art of the Possible* (Penguin, 1973), pp. 199–200.

58   Jenkins, 'On Being a Minister'.

59   Butler, p. 200.

60   Leon Brittan, MP, to author. See also William Whitelaw, *Sunday Times Magazine*, 27 April 1980. Other people may be asked to attend these meetings as appropriate.

61   Leon Brittan, MP, to author; Alan Clark, MP, to author.

62   Paul Rose, MP, 'I'm Sick of the Whitehall Secret Brigade', *Daily Express*, 7 March 1979.

63   Jenkins, 'On Being a Minister', p. 219. The reference is clearly to the Enahoro case.

64   George Cunningham, MP, to author.

65   Leon Brittan, MP, to author.

66   Confidential source.

67   Labour MP to author.

68   *Parliamentary Debates: Standing Committee B*, 6 April 1971, c. 275–6; *House of Commons Debates*, 819, c. 445–50; *Economist*, 10 April 1971, p. 26.

69   Philip Norton, 'Intra-Party Dissent in the House of Commons: A Case Study. The Immigration Rules 1972', *Parliamentary Affairs*, 29 (4), Autumn 1976, pp. 404–20.

70   Norton, *Dissenssion in the House of Commons 1974–1979*, pp. 257–8.

71   The Labour Government's 1969 Horserace Betting Levy Bill ran into trouble, especially in Committee, and the Conservative Government's Horserace Totalisator and Betting Levy Boards Bill, introduced in the 1971–2 session, encountered so much criticism from Conservative MPs (both in the party Home Affairs Committee and on Second Reading) that the Home Secretary agreed to amend it at Committee stage.

72   Leon Brittan, MP, to author.

73   Jenkins, 'On Being a Minister', p. 217.

74   Butler, p. 199.

75   Frances Morrell, *From the Electors of Bristol*, Spokesman Pamphlet No. 57 (Spokesman, n.d.), p. 19.

76   The number of letters received by the Ministers' offices in three sample four-week periods were as follows: 3–29 June 1979, 2360 letters; 1–26 October 1979, 2196 letters; 3–28 March 1980, 2699 letters. In no one week did the number fall below 489, and in all weeks bar this one the number exceeded 500. (A small number of these letters were not from MPs but from large organisations or Ministers' own constituents.) Casework material normally dominates, though in the 1979–80 session, because of Government legislation, there were about as many letters covering policy being received as those covering particular cases. Mrs Lynda Chalker, MP, Under Secretary of State for Health and Social Security, to author.

77   G. Morgan, 'All Party Committees in the House of Commons', *Parliamentary Affairs*, 32 (1), Winter 1979, p. 63.

78   Brian Walden, interviewed in BBC Radio 3 programme, 'The Parliamentary Process', broadcast 25 January 1976.

79   The NHS Commissioner also has wider terms of reference than the PCA. See Frank Stacey, *British Government 1966–75* (Oxford University Press, 1975), pp. 190–7.

80   S.J. Ingle and Philip Tether, *Parliament and Health Policy* (Saxon House, 1980).

81   H.J. Elcock and S. Hayward, *The Buck Stops Where? Accountability and Control in the National Health Service* (University of Hull Institute for Health Studies, 1980).

82   The most notable example was as early as 1975, when the Government was defeated on the issue of the earnings rule for pensioners; having been defeated in Committee, it was defeated again on Report stage when it tried to reverse the Committee defeat, on clause 1 of the Social Security Benefits Bill. Norton, *Dissension in the House of Commons 1974–1979*, pp. 41–2.

83   David Wood, *The Times*, 18 February 1972.

84   Norton, *Conservative Dissidents*, especially chs 3 and 9.

85   *House of Commons Debates*, 926, c. 1361–6.

9
Diagnosis and prescription: approaches to reform

In nineteenth-century Britain, the political demands and expectations of a growing electorate, and the demands made of Government by groups in a developing industrial economy, were to result in the House of Commons ceasing to form a regular element of the political decision-making process. Though legislatures in other Western industrialised economies were at some stage to experience a diminution of their effectiveness, especially in the initiation and formulation of measures, this changed role was especially marked in Britain, with its system of parliamentary and unitary Government. As we have seen (Chapter 2), the decision-making power accrued largely to a party Government, one derived from and supported by a majority in the House of Commons. Lacking not only a formal separation of powers and personnel, but also a separation of constituencies and fixed-term elections, the Government's continuance in office was grounded on the support of a majority of the House, a support which its Members had been elected to provide. The result was a growing cohesion in the Commons' division lobbies. By the turn of the century, according to Samuel Beer, 'party whips, although used more sparingly when the party was in Opposition than at present, could produce results comparable to the monolithic unity of recent times'.[1] By the middle of the twentieth century, party cohesion was so close to 100 per cent, wrote Beer, that there was no longer any point in measuring it.[2] Increasingly, the House of Commons was viewed as a body that provided unquestioning assent for the decisions of Government.

With the growing, though not immediate, realisation that the House had lost the functions of election and legislation previously ascribed to it by Bagehot, the former going to the electorate and the latter to the Cabinet, there developed some doubts about the role of the House of Commons in the new political environment. The initiation and formulation of legislation was something now largely, if not almost exclusively, undertaken by Government. A party majority in the House of Commons then assented to that legislation. Even if the function of the House was deemed to be one now of scrutiny and influence — Members scrutinising the measures and actions of Government in their capacities as representatives of disparate interests (Chapter 4) — how was that function to be fulfilled given the information and resources at the disposal of Government, and the knowledge that at the end of the day the Government controlled not only the parliamentary timetable but also the outcome of votes? Was the Government not free to ignore MPs if it wished to, knowing that it would get its way? This century has witnessed a growing belief on the part of many observers that the developments of the nineteenth as well as those of this century tipped the balance in the relationship between Parliament and that part of it which forms the Government not merely in favour of the Government but too far in favour of the Government, the House of Commons being deprived of the ability both to act effectively as a scrutiniser of Government measures and actions, and to provide the broad parameters within which it could govern. The result has been that, throughout this century, though at certain times more than others, parliamentarians and political scientists have drawn attention to the perceived lowly and inadequate role played by the Commons in the political process, and various proposals for reform have been advanced in an attempt to make effective its function of scrutiny and influence. The aim has been not to restore the House to a full partnership with Government — the events of the nineteenth and twentieth centuries have largely removed that possibility — but rather to give it the status of an effective overseer, a body that Government has to submit its proposals to, listen to, be influenced by, and, in certain circumstances, accept the judgement of. However, even if this aim is accepted by those who wish to restore to the House of Commons an effective role in the political process, the means by which it is to be achieved are not.

Recognition of the Commons' limited role in the political process, of its inability to provide the effective parameters for Government, is not new. Though not immediately apparent in the wake of the widened franchise in the latter decades of the nineteenth century, it has been variously noted throughout the twentieth, most notably in the late 1920s and the 1930s, and in more recent post-war years. The fact that attention should be called to Parliament's inadequate role in periods of economic crisis, and that the calls for its reform are more strident then, is probably no coincidence. At such times there is a tendency to look critically at national institutions, and Parliament has been found wanting. Appearing before the Select Committee on Procedure in 1931, Lloyd George declared:

> My . . . criticism would be that the control of the Executive by the House of Commons is confined to rather perfunctory discussions, which do not excite any real interest, apart from an element of censure which is conducive to excitement, but does not achieve the real purpose of establishing control over the Executive . . . The fact of the matter is

that the House of Commons has no real effective and continuous
control over the actions of the Executive.[3]

Professor Ramsay Muir, in his book *How Britain is Governed*, was equally
severe in his conclusions. The Cabinet, he said, was too omnipotent; by
subjecting Parliament to its power, it had 'atrophied' control on behalf
of the nation by the latter's elected representatives.[4] In his evidence to
the Procedure Committee, he expressed the opinion that there was no
country in north-western Europe 'in which the control exercised by
Parliament over the Government — over legislation, taxation, and
administration — is more shadowy or unreal than it is in Britain'.

Proposals for reform were many and varied. Professor Muir favoured
a series of committees based on each large Government Department.
Lloyd George, Ivor Jennings, and former Labour Minister Fred Jowett
(a long-standing advocate of reform), among others, also favoured a
new committee structure; the proposal to make more extensive and
effective use of committees, as the authors of *Parliamentary Reform
1933—60* noted, 'was much in the air in the 1920s and 1930s'.[5] Muir
also advocated electoral reform and the removal of the Prime Minister's
power of dissolution. Winston Churchill favoured the creation of an
Economic Sub-Parliament, comprising forty MPs, twenty peers, and
sixty others — businessmen, trade union representatives, and economic
experts (a form of functional representation); Beatrice Webb in 1931
restated her call for a social Parliament to coexist with a political one.
The Procedure Committee itself was notably less adventurous, recommending an enlargement of the Estimates Committee (otherwise its
main conclusion was that the procedure of Parliament was 'sufficiently
flexible to meet all the demands made upon it', a conclusion described
by Jennings at the time as 'ludicrous').[6] Various other reforms, including
disparate procedural ones, were advocated.[7] Few, though, were implemented. A Government Bill to introduce the alternative vote for British
elections was introduced by the minority Labour Government in January
1931 (to fulfil a promise to the Liberals), but it was defeated in the
Lords. Other important reforms failed to find much favour with Government (Prime Ministers MacDonald and Baldwin were clearly not much
interested), and more pressing matters came to dominate the political
agenda in the 1930s. In the latter half of the decade, literature on
reform was not much in evidence. Then came the exceptional circumstances of war.

The House of Commons emerged from the experience of the Second
World War with its reputation enhanced. During the war, the Government
had been given greater powers than ever before, but had depended for
its support upon a House of Commons in which party ties were less
relevant than before; the House was united in its war aim, but the

Government had to strive hard to maintain that unity.[8] Recognising the importance of the changed circumstances, Members were vigorous in representing constituents' grievances, keeping under surveillance the Government in the exercise of its new powers, and overseeing war expenditure (1939 witnessing the creation of the Select Committee on National Expenditure); various ginger groups, notably the 'Active Back-benchers Committee', took on the role of 'loyal Oppositions' to keep the Government on its toes. In the unusual circumstances, the Commons performed well. 'In 1945', declared two later critics of the House, 'the reputation of the British Parliament stood as high as ever before in its long history.'[9] It was a view echoed by others, including a Procedure Committee. The Committee concluded in its 1946 Report that there was not, at that time, 'any strong or widespread desire for changes in the essential character of the institution'.[10]

However, with the reversion to peacetime and partisan parliamentary behaviour, the position began to change. As early as 1949 Christopher Hollis's *Can Parliament Survive?* was published; in 1950, Lord Cecil of Chelwood called attention in a Lords debate to the growing power of the Cabinet,[11] and in 1952 Lord Campion in a similar vein noted the increasing subordination of the Commons to the executive.[12] Analyses of parliamentary decline, and prescriptions as to how that decline might be arrested or reversed, became more prevalent in the late 1950s and throughout the 1960s. In 1959 came the publication of Bernard Crick's influential Fabian tract *Reform of the Commons*; five years later came his book, *The Reform of Parliament*, which made six separate appear-ances in as many years.[13] An article by Professors Hanson and Wiseman, calling for committee reform, also appeared in 1959,[14] as did Michael Foot's *Parliament in Danger!*[15] and Paul Einzig's *The Control of the Purse*,[16] followed in 1960 by *Has Parliament a Future?*, written by the long-standing critic, Christopher Hollis.[17] Subsequent important contri-butions to the reform literature included the pamphlet *Change or Decay* by a group of Conservative MPs (1963),[18] an article in *The Times* by Michael Ryle on 17 April 1963, the pseudonymous Hill and Whichelow's *What's Wrong with Parliament?* (1964), and the Study of Parliament Group's submission to the 1964–5 Procedure Committee, subsequently published in October 1965 as a monograph, *Reforming the Commons*.[19]

While the Government and the civil service were expanding in size and developing new techniques for expenditure planning, the House of Commons was viewed as a large, amateurish body, incapable of scruti-nising effectively the increasingly complex work of Government. The reforms proposed for making effective the Commons' role of scrutiny were varied, though most writers appeared to favour the greater use of Select Committees – or some form of committees (the authors of *Change or Decay*, for example, advocated the creation of 'standing economic committees') — to scrutinise executive actions and, in some instances, Bills, the committees to cover specified areas or Departments; a number of writers, such as Einzig, emphasised the need for some form of Expenditure Committee. Other proposals put forward included better pay and facilties for Members, the creation of a Swedish-style Ombudsman,[20] the televising of proceedings,[21] revised hours of sitting, and the reform of various procedures within the House.[22] This growing pressure for reform elicited no significant response from the Macmillan Government. Though one or two Ministers were sympathetic to reform, the Government as a whole was not; according to one informed source, the pamphlet *Change or Decay* was not popular with the party leadership.[23] However, with the return in 1964 of a new Parliament and a new Government, attitudes towards reform began to change. The era of parliamentary reform was about to begin.

The 1964 election brought into the House a number of new, reform-minded Labour Members, with leaders who had previously given voice to the need for investigatory Select Committees. Within the PLP, a Labour Reform Group was formed. Though deflected somewhat by various contentious issues on the political agenda,[24] members of the Group lobbied Ministers and exploited Members' frustrations with existing procedure. The PLP responded with a working party on reform, though this achieved little and soon adjourned. More effective as a vehicle for reform suggestions was the Procedure Committee set up at the beginning of the Parliament. Though not going all the way with the proposals of the Study of Parliament Group that a series of separate specialist Select Committees be established, it did recommend in its Fourth Report in 1965 that the Estimates Committee be enlarged, and that it should have a series of specialist subcommittees to examine Estimates and to inquire into the activities of Departments. (The Committee also produced other reports with a number of useful proposals.) Though rejecting the idea that they should be permitted to examine policy, the Leader of the House, Herbert Bowden, did agree to the subcommittees being allowed to cover specific sectors of Government responsibility, and this reform was implemented in December 1965. However, given the short life of the Parliament and the fact that Mr Bowden himself was known not to be too keen on reform, little else was achieved. The prospects for reform brightened in the 1966 Parliament. The 1966 Labour manifesto expressed support for 'modernising Parliament' ('Changes must improve procedure and the work of committees, and reform facilitates for research and information');[25] the election resulted in the return of more Labour Members favouring reform; and in the first session a reform-minded Leader of the House, Richard Crossman, was appointed. The result was to be the 'Crossman reforms' of the 1960s.

Responding to the various calls for reform, and prompted by his own sympathetic approach (an approach, though, not based on any previously well-thought-out ideas on the subject), Mr Crossman introduced a collection of measures (not an especially well-balanced one) designed on the one hand to make more efficient the House's dispatch of business and, on the other, to make more effective its scrutiny of Government. The most important reform was the creation of new specialist Select Committees, starting with the Science and Technology Committee and the Agriculture Committee. Though the life of the latter was to be brought to an early end, other committees followed: Education and Science, Race Relations and Immigration, Scottish Affairs, and Overseas Aid, all appointed in the lifetime of the 1966–70 Parliament.[26] (In addition, the Committee on the Parliamentary Commissioner for Administration was set up.) We have already commented briefly on these committees in Chapter 6. The new committees constituted but the best-known of the reforms that were introduced. The Leader of the House also introduced morning sittings of the House on two days a week (Monday and Wednesday), and later obtained the approval of the House, albeit largely on party lines, to send the Finance Bill 'upstairs' to Standing Committee instead of having its Committee stage taken on the floor of the House. Changes were made to the terms under which the Speaker could grant requests under standing order 9 for emergency debates (designed largely to free the chair of the shackles of precedent); the procedure under which a Bill could be considered by a Second Reading Committee was regularised in a standing order (see Chapter 5); and financial procedure was simplified with the abolition of the Committees of Supply and Ways and Means; the interruption of proceedings by Black Rod calling Members to the Lords to hear the Royal Assent to measures (an interruption especially unpopular with new Labour Members) was also brought to an end.[27] Though Mr Crossman took many of his proposals (somewhat selectively) from reports of the Procedure Committee, his name was popularly associated with them; they were viewed as 'his' reforms. Also associated with him was the proposed reform of the House of Lords, though the measure to give effect to this reform, the Parliament (No. 2) Bill, was not proceeded with when it ran into opposition from Members on both sides of the House.

Further reforms were to follow in the Parliaments of the 1970s. The Heath Government accepted the recommendation for the setting up of an Expenditure Committee. It met for the first time in 1971 (see Chapter 6). The European Legislation Committee was created as a response, albeit a somewhat slow response, to Britain's membership of the European Communities and the need to scrutinise proposed EC legislation (see Chapter 7). The Joint Committee on Statutory Instruments was set up. After having rejected the televising of Parliament on a free vote in

1972, the House in 1975 agreed to the radio broadcasting of proceedings on a trial basis, and subsequently agreed to it on a permanent basis. The provision of public funds to Opposition parties for the carrying out of their parliamentary duties was also agreed to.[28] The result was to be that in the decade or so following Crossman's first adventure in the field, many reforms of one description or another were carried through. In terms of structure and procedure, by the time of the 1974–9 Parliament the House of Commons differed somewhat from its predecessor of ten years before. Unfortunately, the difference was not as great as the reformers would have wished.

The reforms of the period from 1966 to 1976 were, as we have seen, several in number.[29] Unfortunately, their impact was restricted. A number failed to achieve their desired ends; others had only limited effect. Morning sittings proved unpopular, especially (though not exclusively) on the Conservative benches, and were soon brought to an end in 1967; the sending of the Finance Bill to Standing Committee similarly proved unpopular, particularly with the Conservative Members of the Committee, and a compromise (part of the Bill being taken in Standing Committee, the rest in Committee of the Whole House) was agreed upon; the reform of standing order 9 had little practical effect (successive Speakers and the Government have generally not been keen on the interruption of business caused by emergency debates); only a few uncontentious Bills were committed to Second Reading Committees; the live radio broadcast of Prime Minister's Question Time proved unpopular,[30] and was not continued after the summer recess in 1979; and the Parliamentary Commissioner for Administration, brought into being in 1967, adopted a cautious approach and, despite one or two publicised successes, had only a limited effect on Government. The impact of the new Select Committees was not substantial, and the Agriculture Committee was wound up following its altercation with the Agriculture Department and, more important, the Foreign Office; it achieved unpopularity with Ministers, including Mr Crossman. The reorganisation of the Estimates Committee was affected adversely by the creation of the other committees. The need for more effective scrutiny of expenditure was recognised in the creation of the Expenditure Committee, but this too failed to live up to expectations; as Ann Robinson was to conclude in 1978, 'It cannot claim to have had either much concrete impact upon Government decisions about public spending or more than a limited amount of influence on the policy making process.'[31] Abolition of the Committees of Supply and Ways and Means helped to simplify procedure, but 'whether any substantial improvement was achieved by this drastic step may be doubted';[32] it certainly did nothing to make more effective the House's function of scrutiny. One or two other reforms were useful, if limited, in their impact, such as the European Legislation Committee. Overall, the picture was not an impressive one from the point of view of those seeking to rectify the imbalance in the relationship between Parliament and the executive. As Bernard Crick observed of the Crossman reforms, 'while they may have gone a long way to "streamlining" the passage of legislation, they have gone only a short distance towards increasing the power of the House to scrutinise and call to account administration or to increase its critical effectiveness in debate.'[33] If the House was to achieve an effective oversight and influence of executive actions and measures, a longer step was needed.

The realisation that the House had failed to achieve the effective role of scrutiny sought for it by the reformers found expression throughout the 1970s. In 1976, for example, Edward du Cann (then chairman of the Public Accounts Committee, and founder chairman of the Expenditure Committee) called attention to the fact that the House still lacked 'adequate machinery for scrutinising expenditure plans before being called on to vote the money involved'; Government spending, he said, was hopelessly out of control, and the House needed an effective monitoring committee.[34] Tony Benn, while still in the Cabinet, drew attention to Parliament's failure to oversee technological developments.[35] In 1977, the *Economist* weighed in with a blistering attack on the 'undignified, inefficient, undemocratic and, above all, unparliamentary government that is Britain's lot today'.[36] The House of Commons, it contended, had no method of defending the citizen against the power of the executive sitting in its midst; and it did not exercise any detailed supervision of legislation or financial policies. The Government, it declared, had absolute control of the House. Similar points were made by Liberal MP Cyril Smith in his autobiography,[37] and by Labour MP Paul Rose early in 1979 in announcing his decision not to seek re-election.[38] Such criticisms were supported also by a number of academics (of whom more below), and pressure for further reform began to build up. It was pressure that in some cases was generated or reinforced by the indecisiveness of the 1974 general elections and the growth of minor parties, interpreted by some as a demonstration of dissatisfaction with the existing party and parliamentary system of Britain. Reform was again in the air.

The pressure for reform in the 1970s, which reached a peak in the 1974–9 Parliament, was different from that of the 1960s. In the 1960s the reforms advocated were largely procedural reforms that concentrated on the internal workings of the House. However, in the 1970s there was marked dissatisfaction with this limited, 'internal' approach to reform, and as a result the pressure for reform took different forms. Indeed, at least five separate approaches could be identified in the 1970s, not all of them new: those of (1) internal reform; (2) external reform through the introduction of a new electoral system; (3) external reform through the enactment of a Bill of Rights; (4) anti-reform (including what we shall term the 'irrelevancy' thesis); and (5) the approach of this author, the 'Norton view'. Let us consider each in turn.

Internal reform

The internal reformers are those who continue to press for reform *within* the House of Commons, as, for example, a reformed Select Committee system, changed hours of sitting, and more effective means of scrutinising legislation. With Bernard Crick, they favour scrutiny that will produce more information that can be used to influence and educate the public. The role of the Commons is seen as a communicative one, mediating between the public and the Government, and vice versa. 'The only meanings of Parliamentary control worth considering, and worth the House spending much of its time on', declared Professor Crick, 'are those which do *not* threaten the Parliamentary defeat of a Government, but which help to keep it responsive to the underlying currents and the more important drifts of public opinion. All others are purely antiquarian shufflings.'[39] Hence an emphasis on reforms to enable Members to engage in scrutiny, to keep the Government on its toes, through probing the Government, finding out what it is doing, and subjecting the knowledge so gained to public debate.

Despite, or rather because of, the failure of the reforms of the 1960s to live up to the expectations of those advocating them, internal reformers now press either for different internal reforms or for those that were tried to be developed further to strengthen the House as a scrutinising body. Representative of this school of thought are Lisanne Radice, with her Fabian pamphlet *Reforming the House of Commons* (1977); Sir Peter (now Lord) Rawlinson with his two articles published in *The Times* on 12 and 13 September 1977; and, of necessity, various reports from a number of Commons Select Committees. In her pamphlet, Dr Radice argued for departmental Select Committees, a pre-legislative scrutiny stage in the passage of Bills, Standing Committees with the power of Select Committees, more debates on 'issues of the day', the televising of proceedings, shorter speeches, revised hours of sitting, and better pay and facilities for Members,[40] all fairly standard fare for those favouring internal reform. Similarly, Sir Peter Rawlinson argued for departmental Select Committees, more debates on the administration of Departments (the precise motions to be chosen by the Leader of the Opposition) and on Private Members' motions, as well as reform of the legislative process (each clause in every Bill to be discussed), but he was a little more radical and original than Dr Radice in some of his other proposals. Like Ramsay Muir in the 1930s, he wanted to remove the

Prime Minister's power of dissolution; he wanted Government Bills in any one session to be limited to those announced in the Queen's Speech (except in certain specified circumstances); and he wanted the size of the Commons to be reduced, from 635 Members to 318. Such changes, he believed, would help the Commons fulfil its role as the 'principal national forum in which national issues should be debated and Ministers questioned', and as the scrutineer of legislation. A variety of reforms were also recommended in the reports of several Commons committees (necessarily limited by their terms of reference), ranging from the Committee on the Preparation of Legislation — the Renton Committee; appointed in 1973, it reported in 1975, and made 121 recommendations designed especially to ensure that measures introduced were clearly explained and as easy to understand as possible[41] — to the Eleventh Report from the Expenditure Committee in 1977 and the First Report of the Procedure Committee the following year, both of which recommended the appointment of Select Committees to cover the individual Government Departments.[42]

The new Parliament returned in 1979 has witnessed not only the implementation of certain of the reforms recommended by a number of Select Committees — notably the establishment of a comprehensive Select Committee structure based on Departments (of which more later) — but also pressure in support of proposals which the Government has either not acted upon or fully implemented. The 1979–80 session, for example, saw not only a serious altercation between the Government and backbenchers on both sides of the House on the issue of Members' pay, but also an attempt (through a ten-minute rule Bill) to generate support for the televising of proceedings.

Pressure for internal reform, be it minor procedural change or more radical structural alteration (as with the proposal for fewer Members), has been an important feature of the campaign for parliamentary reform in the twentieth century. It could be described as the dominant feature of the 1960s. Though less dominant in the 1970s and now in the 1980s — other approaches have come to the fore — it remained and remains important. We shall have cause to consider its drawbacks later.

External reform through a new electoral system

The decade of the 1970s, and especially the two or three years following the inconclusive 1974 general elections, witnessed the development and indeed the rapid growth of a new school of thought. It was one that took a much broader view, and advanced more radical proposals, than the internal reformers. Its interests were not focused either exclusively or primarily on the House of Commons: it sought a reform that would alter not only the behaviour and composition of the Commons, but also of the British system of government. The way in which it wished to achieve this was through a reform of the electoral system, with the introduction of a form of proportional representation.

In the view of these external reformers, the proposals advanced by the internal reformers of the 1960s and the 1970s constituted no more than mere procedural tinkering that was not going to effect significantly the ability of the House to scrutinise and influence Government. Indeed, such proposals were seen as largely irrelevant, both to the House of Commons and to Britain's wider political and economic problems. The external reformers sought to provide an answer to both. They diagnosed Britain's political malaise and its economic problems as being in part the result of a dysfunctional party and electoral system. The existing first-past-the-post electoral system, it was argued, favoured disproportionately the two largest parties, with the party winning a plurality of votes often, though not always, winning an absolute majority of seats. A small swing in votes at an election could and did produce a change of Government. The two main parties thus competed for the all-or-nothing spoils of a general election, with the successful party once in office governing with an eye to the next election. Furthermore, in office 'each party has to reach some compromise between its left and right wings, in order to preserve its unity in the face of the Opposition',[43] the compromise falling somewhere between the two extremes in each party. Hence, the consensus position in the Labour Party could be described as being on the centre-left of the political spectrum, and that in the Conservative Party as being on the centre-right; neither falls in the centre of the political spectrum, which would appear to be at some mid-point between the attitudes of the two parties.[44] The consequence of this is that one party is returned to office, and pursues policies which, in S.E. Finer's terminology, are 'off-centre' (and opposed by its adversary party in the House of Commons, Commons procedure being based on this adversary relationship), with the possibility that a small shift in votes at the next election could turn it out, bringing in the other party to reverse its policies and pursue off-centre policies from the other side of the political spectrum. Such shifts from one party in office to another, with consequent changes of policies, produce uncertainty in economic management and industrial policy that undermines the confidence of investors and makes it difficult for industrialists to plan ahead. The adversary relationship between the parties and the changes of power may make for 'exciting politics', according to one critic, but they produce 'low-credibility Government strategies, whichever party is in power'.[45] The position was exacerbated in the 1970s, when the reformers argued that the parties were becoming even more polarised than before and electorally less relevant; in October 1974 the Labour Party formed the Government with a bare overall majority and pursued vigorously an off-centre programme, despite having received less than 40 per cent of the votes cast in the general election. The Labour Government of 1974– 9 reversed various of the policies of the Heath Government of 1970—4. Similarly, when returned to office in 1979, Mrs Thatcher's Govenment proceeded to reverse or dismantle some of the programmes implemented by its Labour predecessor. Hence, in the reformers' eyes, a dysfunctional electoral and party system, one that had serious repercussions for British industry and the economy.

The answer to this problem, went the argument, was and is to be found in replacing the existing electoral system with one based on proportional representation. (Of the methods of proportional representation that exist, the single transferable vote method would appear to be preferred.)[46] Not only would this be a fairer system than the existing one (the traditional argument in favour of proportional representation, associated especially with the Liberal Party), producing seats for a party proportional to its electoral support, but it would help to ensure continuity in policy and would also produce a more effective House of Commons. This would result from the fact that, on current voting patterns, no party would obtain an overall majority of parliamentary seats — no party in post-war elections having obtained more than fifty per cent of the votes cast[47] — and hence a coalition would be necessary to form a Government commanding a majority in the Commons. Furthermore, as one of the main parties would 'have to co-operate with a party or parties taking a more central political stance' in order to arrive at such a coalition, 'there would be a greater moderation in policy.'[48] The result would be a centre-coalition Government, responsive to the centrist views of the electorate, and one able to ensure continuity in policy given that it would be less likely to be turned out of office at a general election; as Professor Finer has noted, a swing of 1 per cent under a system of proportional representation would result in the loss of only about six seats. So, a more stable and moderate Government would be Britain's lot. Furthermore, the undermining of the strong party hold of the electoral system would free candidates to some extent of strict party ties. Not only would they be returned to represent the more moderate views of the electorate, but they would also be in a stronger position to call the Government to account and to engage in more rational and meaningful debate on Britain's problems. Being elected by preference voting, Members would be less firmly tied to the wishes of their party leaders and whips; a system of proportional representation would benefit independently minded Members such as Dick Taverne and Reg Prentice rather than penalise them, as the present system does. Hence, a more active House of Commons, fulfilling a meaningful role and deriving greater moral authority by virtue of the fairer means by which it would be returned.

The argument for electoral reform on grounds of fairness, as we have mentioned, is not new. It has been advanced for many years by the Liberal Party, and also through pamphlets and other publications by the Electoral Reform Society under the vigorous leadership of Miss Enid Lakeman. However, the events of the 1970s led to this new approach, emphasising the wider political and economic implications, or potential implications, of electoral reform, including its implications for the role of the House of Commons in the political process. The most important literature of this school of thought has been Professor S.E. Finer's collection of essays *Adversary Politics and Electoral Reform*, published in 1975,[49] and various articles from the pen of S.A. Walkland.[50] It is an approach which has found some support in each of the two main parties.[51] In May 1974 the organisation Conservative Action for Electoral Reform was founded by Mr Anthony Wigram (who initiated and published privately the volume edited by Professor Finer), and in 1976 a Labour Study Group on Electoral Reform came into being. Of these, the former has been especially active. Though this new approach has attracted a fair amount of attention, pressure for electoral reform would appear to have peaked in the latter half of the 1970s. Nevertheless, it is an approach which retains a respectable and important following, will continue to be advocated throughout the 1980s, and is likely to gain strength in the event of another period of minority Government or one during which one of the two main parties are out of office for two or more successive Parliaments. It is an approach, though, which has a number of limitations, and these we shall consider later.

External reform through a Bill of Rights

Those who began to press for electoral reform as a response to the adversary politics produced by the British party and electoral system were not and are not the only ones to constitute 'external' reformers. Another school of thought favouring external reform developed and gained strength in the 1970s, but the reform advocated was of a different nature, and had a very different intent, from that of the electoral reformers. Like the electoral reformers, it recognised the weakness of the House of Commons in relation to the executive, but, unlike the advocates of proporational representation, it did not seek to reform the Commons in order to strengthen the institution, but aimed rather to bypass the House and introduce a separate restraint upon Government, a restraint that would act also upon the Commons. This was and is the approach of those who favour the introduction of a written and, if possible, entrenched Bill of Rights.

Advocacy of a written Bill of Rights for Britain began to gain some attention in the late 1960s, notably with the publication of Anthony

Lester's *Democracy and Individual Rights* in 1968, John MacDonald's *A Bill of Rights* and Quintin Hogg's *New Charter* the following year,[52] two ten-minute rule Bills in the Commons and a debate in the Lords,[53] but pressure for such a remarkable constitutional innovation was most marked in the 1970s.[54] It found expression in a variety of publications,[55] with support forthcoming from a number of Liberal, Conservative and Labour politicians. It gained prominence as an issue worthy of serious political debate as a result of lectures by two prominent jurists: Sir Leslie (now Lord) Scarman in his 1974 Hamlyn lectures,[56] and Lord Hailsham (with views slightly different from those he expressed in earlier years) in the 1976 Dimbleby lecture.[57] Though wishing to go further than a Bill of Rights and to introduce a written Constitution with entrenched provisions, Lord Hailsham's thesis, known as the 'elective dictatorship' thesis, provided the basis for much of the argument for the introduction of a Bill of Rights, and has been much quoted since. It is especially important for those interested in Parliament.

The argument, or at least the most important one,[58] for a Bill of Rights was and is that the executive has become too powerful, and is using its powers to encroach on what were assumed previously to be the basic rights of British citizens. The case was put most succinctly by Lord Hailsham. In Parliament, he said, there was one effective chamber, the Commons. That chamber was dominated increasingly by the Government, and the Government was controlled by the Cabinet, which itself was often dominated by only a few of its members. The Cabinet had at its disposal the Civil Service, providing it with resources and information that could not be matched by Parliament. The consequence was an all-powerful Cabinet, introducing measures which Parliament did not and could not challenge or consider effectively.

> So, the sovereignty of Parliament has increasingly become, in practice, the sovereignty of the Commons, and the sovereignty of the Commons has increasingly become the sovereignty of the government, which, in addition to its influence in Parliament, controls the party whips, the party machine, and the Civil Service. This means that what has always been an *elective dictatorship* in theory, but one in which the component parts operated in practice to control one another, has become a machine in which one of those parts has come to exercise a predominant influence over the rest.[59]

This line of thought, as readers of the foregoing pages will realise, was not new. However, the solution offered was markedly different from those of both the internal and the electoral reformers. The 'elective dictatorship' of Government could, and in the eyes of some did, misuse its power to infringe the rights of the individual, and the way to prevent or curb such a misuse of power was not to strengthen Parliament (to act as a curb upon executive excesses) but rather to introduce a new Bill of Rights, if possible with entrenched provisions, to put the basic rights of the citizen beyond the reach of Government. Lord Hailsham himself wanted to go even further. 'If, as I think, the powers of Parliament need restricting at all, the restrictions should by no means be limited to the protection of individual rights.'[60] He favoured a system of checks and balances, with two elected Houses and regional devolved assemblies, such a new constitutional structure to be embodied in a written Constitution with entrenched provisions. He considered such a structure to be necessary if a Bill of Rights were to be effective. 'Otherwise it will prove a pure exercise in public relations.' A number of other reformers have been more modest in their aspirations, arguing for the enactment of a Bill of Rights as an ordinary piece of legislation — that is, with no entrenched provisions, and not as part of a wider constitutional restructuring — with its provisions either geared to the specific domestic circumstances of Britain or else, as Michael Zander has proposed, incorporating the European Convention on Human Rights, to which Britain already is a party. Especially popular would appear to be the proposal to incorporate the European Convention, with a provision that any future Act that conflicted with it would be invalid unless the intention to amend or repeal the Bill of Rights were expressly stated, and possibly with the creation of a Constitutional Court to deal with cases arising under it.[61] Entrenchment of its provisions, according to this view, would not be necessary; it would derive its strength from having 'greater authority' than any other statute.[62]

Pressure for the introduction of a Bill of Rights, especially of the variety envisaged by Lord Hailsham, would appear (like electoral reform) to have reached something of a peak in the period from 1974 to 1979. During that time, the idea appeared an attractive one to a number of Conservative politicians who considered that the Labour Government was introducing a number of measures which impinged upon what they regarded as the rights of the individual. Lord Hailsham himself gave voice to this view. The Government, he wrote, 'is persistently proposing legislation under the guise of its doctrine of mandate which would almost certainly be caught by any Bill of Rights legislation however formulated. The most obvious example of this is their trade union legislation.'[63] Similar views were expressed by Sir Keith Joseph and Sir Geoffrey Howe, two of Lord Hailsham's Shadow Cabinet colleagues.[64] However, with the return of a Conservative Government in 1979, such advocates of a Bill of Rights were faced with more pressing responsibilities, and the need for such a measure, in their eyes, appeared to be less acute. In particular, the return to the Woolsack of Lord Hailsham helped to quieten the most forceful and the most radical of the reformers. Nevertheless, pressure for the introduction of a Bill of Rights remains.

It has the support of various academics, jurists (Lord Scarman renewed his call for such a measure in April 1980),[65] and politicians (Liberal politicians tend to favour both a Bill of Rights and electoral reform), and will continue to be an issue of debate in the 1980s. Though none too popular in the Commons (where the interest in enacting such a measure was described recently by the Prime Minister's PPS as at an all-time low),[66] it retains significant support in the House of Lords.[67] Also, on the basis of its 1979 manifesto, the Government is nominally committed to all-party talks on this and other constitutional issues.[68]

The introduction of a Bill of Rights as an ordinary piece of legislation would not impinge upon the powers of the House of Commons, at least not formally, but one with entrenched provisions (as advocated by Lord Hailsham) would. Hence, this approach to reform differs from those we have considered already. Like the other approaches, though, there are various criticisms that can and have been levelled at it, and these we shall consider later.

The anti-reform approach

The approaches we have considered so far have been approaches that have advocated reform because of the perceived weakness of the House of Commons in relation to that part of it which forms the Government. However, a number of observers have not advocated reform — indeed, a number have strongly opposed it, either because they do not accept that the House of Commons is unable to fulfil effectively its role of scrutiny and influence, or else because they accept that Parliament plays a subordinate or even irrelevant role in the political process but believe that it should stay that way. These two somewhat conflicting views, differing in their analysis of the contemporary position of the Commons but agreeing on the conclusion to be drawn from it, we have grouped together under the label of the anti-reform approach.

This approach is by no means a new one. The House of Commons has always had its defenders, those prepared to argue that it performs well the tasks demanded of it. As we have noted already in passing, the conclusion of the Procedure Committee in 1931 was that 'the procedure of Parliament is sufficiently flexible to meet all the demands made upon it'. The two most recent works representing this school of thought appeared in response to the pressure for reform in the 1960s. Ronald Butt's *The Power of Parliament*, representing the view that the Commons was not as ineffective as its critics made out, first appeared in 1967,[69] and Henry Fairlie's *The Life of Politics*, taking the view that the House played a very limited role and should continue to do so, appeared the following year.[70]

In his well-researched work, which Bernard Crick conceded was a 'scholarly and splendidly argued reply to the reformists',[71] Mr Butt argued that the Commons had not 'declined' from some golden age as critics contended. Parliament had never claimed to govern; it had, though, obtained the right to have a Government whose policies were generally acceptable to it. Party had indeed become important in the House, but it was through the parties that Members could be effective in influencing Government. Members on the Opposition side of the House could exercise influence through the Opposition. Government could be and was influenced by the Opposition, both by the arguments it put forward and by the need to obtain its support or acquiscence in the dispatch of business. The spirit of Commons procedure, not the formal rules, was important. On its own side of the House, the Government depended on the support of its backbenchers. If there was general disquiet within the parliamentary party on a particular issue, the Prime Minister and Cabinet would be informed and the issue would then probably not be proceeded with. Party, in short, provided the parameters of Government. If the Government went too far, its supporters would rouse themselves and make their views known. The role of the House is essentially a negative one (basically, designed to keep the Government in check), but it is the role for which Mr Butt believes the House is best suited. As he argues, the House has not only never governed, but it has never shared with Government the power to initiate measures of public policy.[72] It serves instead to let the Government know what is or (more important) what is not acceptable, and at the end of the day still retains the ultimate power to turn the Government out.

Henry Fairlie, by contrast, had a less elevated view of the House and its role. Political power, he contended, had passed via parties to the electorate, and it was the electorate that now provided the check on Government. At the end of a Parliament, if the electorate disapproved of what the Government had done, it could turn it out. In between elections, the Government was strong. It controlled the time and the business of the House. This, Fairlie believed, could not be avoided; indeed, it was something that he clearly appeared not to disapprove of. He viewed MPs largely as amateurs, there to play the 'game of politics'. Their important functions were those of supporting their party, of choosing party leaders, and of providing the personnel of Government. Members were not likely to step out of line. The Government ensured control of its parliamentary party through the threat of expulsion and the threat of dissolution. Unlike the reformers, who would find much in this analysis to agree with, Mr Fairlie appeared content to accept the status quo. There was an adequate check on Government, but it was one provided by the electorate, and it was the relationship between Government and the electors that was important. The House of Commons and the election of its Members served primarily to facilitate that relationship. 'Electors ask no more than that, between elections, the MP should be the servant of the Government, or alternative Government, which he was returned to the House of Commons to support.'[73] It was and is a view sometimes shared by Ministers (not to mention some backbenchers), and Mr Fairlie's advocacy of it serves at least a useful purpose in that it 'raises the fundamental question of whether we do, in fact, want a Parliament with effective powers of scrutiny and influence. It is an important question, one often overlooked by the reformers.'[74]

The works of Butt and Fairlie, though conflicting in their analyses, served as strong expressions of the anti-reform approach, giving voice to what a number of observers were thinking. Though no similar work appeared in the 1970s, there were those who were prepared to give voice to their opposition to reform, or at least to go a long way in justifying the existing role and effectiveness of MPs in the House in which they sat. Two parliamentarians in particular were associated with the view that, while some changes may be desirable, the House of Commons fulfilled an important role of debate and influence, a role most effectively carried out on the floor of the House rather than in committee. The two Members, Michael Foot and Enoch Powell, were and are well-known speakers, and they pursued their view with some vigour. (Though supporting different parties, they also found themselves in agreement in 1969 in their opposition to the Parliament (No. 2) Bill, albeit for different reasons, and in 1971–2 in their opposition to British entry into the EC – an act which they regarded as undermining parliamentary sovereignty.) While conceding that he wanted the chance for backbenchers to influence Government to be strengthened, Mr Foot said in 1976 in his evidence to the Procedure Committee:

> It has always been a fallacy that, in fact, the Cabinet dictates to the House of Commons. The Government have some power over it, and some power to indicate what they want, but the idea that the legislation is not greatly altered by debate in the House of Commons and by individual backbenchers and by backbenchers in other committees influencing the legislation is entirely incorrect. Of course, in matters other than legislation backbenchers have a much bigger part than the modern theory states . . . As it happens now they have very considerable effect on what Governments dare to propose and what Governments are capable of getting through.[75]

Their belief that Members could most effectively call Government to account on the floor of the House led both Mr Foot and Mr Powell to oppose the Procedure Committee's recommendations for the creation of a series of Select Committees based on Departments. To drain away the energies of Members in committee would, Mr Foot believed, 'destroy the distinctive qualities of the British House of Commons'; it would be 'cutting the main vein in which the whole thing operates'.[76] As Lord President of the Council and Leader of the House, he was obviously well-placed to try to prevent acceptance and implementation of the Committee's recommendations. However, he was forced to back down under pressure from the House, while Mr Powell, who had served on the Committee, reluctantly conceded that if new Select Committees were to be created, they should cover Departments and should be introduced at that time rather than later.

The anti-reform views of Messrs Butt, Foot and Powell were motivated by a belief in the strength of the Commons and a clear feeling of affection for it. Mr Fairlie's view, by contrast, was based on a somewhat negative evaluation of the House. Another view that should be mentioned, going much further along the negative path trodden by Mr Fairlie, is that which may be termed the 'irrelevancy' approach, one based on the view that in an increasingly complex world in which power to make important decisions rests increasingly with disparate bodies such as the International Monetary Fund, the World Bank, multi-national corporations, trade unions, national bureaucracies, technologists, and the military, institutions such as Parliaments are irrelevant and that to reform them would not affect the ever-growing power of such bodies. This view would appear to be gaining ground, though its expression is often implicit rather than explicit. In analyses of power, references to Parliament are often not to be found. Writing in 1977 on the question of whether or not Britain was worse governed than before, Peter Self ended with the comment: 'This article hardly mentions parliament. I suggest the reader asks himself why.'[77] The conclusion to be drawn from his article, according to Richardson and Jordan, is that 'the significance of Parliament . . . is its very insignificance'.[78] As they note, 'pessimism runs deep.' It is a pessimism which is to be found not only in academic works (by implication or otherwise), but also in the cynicism of a number of non-academic obervers and electors. Speaking to the Procedure Committee, a former Leader of the House, Edward Short, complained of a 'general cynicism about Parliament', a cynicism that dated from the 1960s as a consequence of satirical television programmes such as 'That was the Week That Was' ('a satire that went far beyond creating a healthy irreverence about Parliament') and existed in 1976 in a 'rather acute form';[79] in 1975, a former Member, C.M. Woodhouse, complained of an attitude toward the House that amounted to a 'fashionable contempt of incomprehension'.[80] The attitude of the public towards the House appears to be somewhat ambivalent,[81] though it would appear to be not unpopular in certain circles to adopt a destructive or disparaging attitude towards Parliament, an attitude not supplemented by any constructive ideas as to how the institution might be revitalised or made more effective. Given the absence of any constructive reform proposals by those who engage in disparagement, they can make a claim, albeit a tenuous one, to fall into this anti-reform category; though in fairness (not to them but to the anti-reformers mentioned earlier) they probably deserve a separate category of their own.

Finally, under this heading one may include a view related to, but not quite the same as, that which believes the significance of Parliament is 'its very insignificance', and that is the view advanced by Marxist writers such as Ralph Miliband. Though admitting that in advanced capitalist countries 'legislatures do retain a certain degree of influence', Professor Miliband contends that such legislatures are dominated by conservative parties of one denomination or another – their members drawn from the middle or upper classes, and taking a favourable view of capitalist activity – and that the legislature with other bodies (Government, military, judiciary, et al.) make up the state, with power being exercised through these bodies by their leaders, the state elite.[82] The importance of Parliament lies in the fact that it is a body *through* which power is exercised, and concomitantly in the fact that its giving of assent to measures is accepted as legitimate and binding. (In other words, it is significant in the context of the third dimension of power as delineated by Steven Lukes.)[83] Even here, though, it is under challenge: Bob Jessop has drawn attention to the challenge to parliamentarianism posed by corporatism, parliamentary institutions in Britain increasingly being displaced by corporatist institutions as the dominant state apparatus.[84] As an intrinsic part of the state, a part used with others by the capitalist elite, talk of reforming Parliament, be it through internal reform or within the wider context of a new electoral system or a written Bill of Rights, is viewed as being largely irrelevant, apart from its demonstration of tensions within capitalist society (corporatist and parliamentary institutions being seen by Dr Jessop as a 'contradictory unity')[85] and its reflection of attempts by capital to maintain its position. Parliament, in short, will remain the handmaiden of the state elite in capitalist society.

There thus exist a number of participants in and observers of the parliamentary scene in Britain, and some very much on the sidelines, who for very different reasons take the view that the reform of the House of Commons is unnecessary, irrelevant, or, in some cases, outside the scope of their interests. Though forming a somewhat unwieldy collection, they may be grouped (albeit in some cases by default rather than by design) under the broad anti-reform banner.

The 'Norton' view

The final approach to be considered is the one taken by this author. This approach, the 'Norton view' for want of a better term, takes issue with the other approaches so far identified. It emphasises instead the importance of attitudes within Parliament, and the potential and actual power available already to Members, as the basis on which the Commons might achieve an effective role of security and influence. In this emphasis it makes no claim to originality. Its importance lies in the extent to which it draws on the experience of parliamentary behaviour in the 1970s, and in the fact that of the approaches favouring reform, it is the only one which not only draws on empirical evidence to identify the problem but also bases its answer to the problem on hard, empirical, domestic data; it employs a recognition of what *is* as the basis for bringing about what *ought to be*. Unlike the approach adopted by the external reformers, it posits no radical structural changes brought about by external devices. Indeed, it now advocates no radical change in attitude. Rather, it seeks to encourage and promote parliamentary attitudes which have begun already to change.

Let us consider the disadvantages of the approaches identified already. Despite the disparagement (sometimes mindless) of Parliament that is expressed in some circles, the House of Commons can and does have a role to play in the British political process, albeit, if one takes a Marxist view (which this author does not), a somewhat unacceptable capitalist political process. It is, for better or worse, the only national political body elected directly (however crudely) by the adult population of the United Kingdom. It should, and to some extent does, provide a link between electors and Government; indeed, it is *the* link between the elector *qua* elector (rather than as a member of an organised group) and Government. (It may even be viewed by some as a potential balance or counterweight to the growth of corporatist demands.)[86] As we have seen, the House itself does not govern; it never has and it seems fair to say that it never will. Instead, its function traditionally has been to give assent to measures and requests for supply emanating from the Crown, and, prior to giving its assent, to seeking the redress of grievances. That function has evolved into one of giving assent to measures and requests for supply emanating from Her Majesty's Government, and engaging in the process of scrutiny and influence identified earlier prior to giving that assent; indeed, the process of obtaining the redress of grievances, of engaging in scrutiny and influence, has evolved so that in practice it is conducted in part through procedures with a separate existence, such as Question Time, not connected directly with giving assent to executive requests. (Technically, of course, the link exists, but is rarely exploited.)[87] As the only elected element in the political process, at least at the national level, it is important that the House fulfils such a function, albeit an admittedly limited one. The electorate is not in a position to fulfil it, and despite Mr Fairlie's claim to the contrary, electors expect more of MPs than that they should be servants of the Government or alternative Government between elections. Polls have shown consistently that respondents want Members capable of looking after constituency problems;[88] in the 1972 Granada survey, 'supporting his party in Parliament' ranked only fourth in the list of jobs that respondents considered most important for an MP to carry out.[89] Yet in looking after constituents' interests, in fulfilling the function of scrutiny and influence on behalf of those whom they seek to represent, Members face a number of limitations. These limitations are clear from the foregoing chapters. Be it in seeking to question or influence a Minister's actions, in probing the activities of his Department, in scrutinising a Government Bill on the floor of the House or in Standing Committee, in overseeing delegated legislation, or influencing proposed European legislation, Members of Parliament are not as effective as they could or should be. They do not, or at least did not, provide the parameters within which Government could operate. Hence the disagreement with Ronald Butt. In order to function effectively, to carry out the task of scrutiny and influence of Government, some reform or at least some change is necessary within the House itself.

The problem with the internal reform approach was that it was too cautious and too limited in its conception. The reformers adhered to the 'strong', single-party model of Government, and sought in consequence to pursue two incompatible aims, 'strengthening the House of Commons without detracting from the power of government'.[90] Furthermore, their support in the Commons was both limited and partisan. 'The number of MPs firmly in favour of specialist commitees had probably never numbered more than a hundred, and the guiding forces in the movement could be counted on the fingers of one hand';[91] the Labour Reform Group turned away Conservative sympathisers, telling them to operate on their own side of the House.[92] Though some limited effort was made to influence other backbenchers, the most important mistake of the reformers was to place the onus for reform on the Government itself, and to leave too much to the Leader of the House. The reforms of the 1960s were the 'Crossman reforms'; when Crossman ceased to be Leader of the House, the drive for reform ended with the opposition of his successor, Fred Peart: 'He counts as much as I did.'[93] The Government was being left largely to determine what reforms it wanted introduced, reforms that were supposed to act as a means of scrutiny, of possible criticism, of its actions. As the Crossman *Diaries* helped to reveal, Ministers and their officials were and are not keen on the establishment of bodies that are likely to get in their way. As S.A. Walkland has observed, 'it seemed . . . inconceivable that any single-party Government, secure in its voting strength on the floor of the House, would allow any significant scope to powerful investigatory agencies of the type that were being proposed.'[94] Not surprisingly, the attempts to establish a series of effective select committees was undermined by Cabinet Ministers and their officials. No Minister was keen to have a committee covering his Department. Mr Crossman assuaged the Minister of Agriculture only by telling him he would be able to choose the topics the new Agriculture Committee studied. When the committee pursued its intention to visit Brussels, it aroused the ire of both Ministers and officials, and its 'experimental' tenure came to an end in 1969.[95] Despite their nominal commitment to reform, to improving 'procedure and the work of committees', in the words of their 1966 manifesto, Ministers from the Prime Minister down were not prepared to countenance investigative committees that would interfere with or question the policy of the Government or individual Departments. (For example, when Mr Crossman went to see the Prime Minister, Harold Wilson, on some procedural matter, he raised the possibility of having a Foreign Affairs Committee. 'I saw Burke [Sir Burke Trend, Cabinet Secretary] purse his lips and Harold open his mouth and I realise that it's extremely unlikely that this will ever happen.')[96] Hence, 'so long as it was left to the Government to determine the reforms, they were, for that very reason, likely to be ineffective.'[97] If they were to come about, it would have to be by another route. Yet, surprisingly, those who continued to press for internal reform failed to address themselves to this point. The remarkable feature of the pieces by Lisanne Radice and Sir Peter Rawlinson was not the reforms they suggested, but the fact that they failed to consider how such reforms could be brought about. The omission was all the more amazing in the case of Dr Radice, who identified the reasons for the failure of the reforms in the 1960s, yet failed to consider why the very same reasons would prevent the reforms she advocated from being effective.[98] Only if such reforms are imposed upon Government by the House will they be effective, a point the reformers seemed unable or unwilling to contemplate. Hence their failure.

The disadvantages of the approach favouring electoral reform are both practical and intellectual. The practical disadvantage is simply stated. The introduction of proportional representation (PR) is a most unlikely prospect at the moment. As Taylor and Johnston have noted, 'there are no technical problems which would prevent proportional representation being created in the British House of Commons. What is lacking is an effective political will to achieve this goal.'[99] PR is opposed by both the Labour and Conservative Parties, the main beneficiaries of the existing system, and it is unlikely that many MPs would be prepared to vote themselves out of their seats, which would be the practical effect in some cases of voting for a Bill to introduce PR for parliamentary elections. The extent to which it is an unlikely prospect has been demonstrated by various votes in the Commons in recent years, including those taken at a time when pressure for electoral reform appeared to reach its peak.[100] It is not an issue whose time has come; indeed, there is less parliamentary support for it now than there was in in 1931. The improbability of its implementation has been conceded by the reformers themselves.[101]

Intellectually, their argument is open to serious questioning. Their case at best is unproven, in part inconsistent, and in part empirically unsound. PR would, as one sympathiser conceded, 'be a leap in the dark'.[102] The argument that it would produce a House representative of the 'more stable and centrist' electorate is unproven. Indeed, the evidence adduced by Professor Finer to show that the electorate is more centrist in opinion than parliamentary parties would appear to consist of data demonstrating that Conservative and Labour voters do not divide on strict partisan lines on certain issues.[103] Does the fact that voters do not divide strictly on party lines in indicating a preference for higher indirect taxes really demonstrate that 'there is a very substantial middle ground in the electorate'? Professor Finer would appear to confuse the distinction between what constitutes the 'ideological centre' and what constitutes 'common ground' among the electorate. The implication of what he writes is that what constitutes 'common ground' among the electorate can be equated with the 'centre ground' of British politics. However, as Ivor Crewe and Bo Sarlvik have pointed out, the 'centre ground' refers to the location of a group of electors along an ideological dimension, whereas the 'common ground' refers to the distribution of electors around that location (whether they be concentrated or dispersed); the two do not always neatly coincide. On certain issues, Crewe and Sarlvik found electors grouping to the right or left of the ideological centre: on what they termed populist-authoritarian issues, for example, their research revealed that 'the electorate clearly does stand on *common* ground: there is almost nothing to distinguish the views of the various electoral groups. But it is a ground far to the right of the ideological mid-point: the electoral centre does not coincide with the ideological centre.'[104] The picture is far from being as clear as Professor Finer would have us believe.

More important, the reformers' critique of the existing system of 'adversary politics' is open to doubt. The instances of policy reversals instanced in *Adversary Politics and Electoral Reform* — a new Government coming in and reversing the policies of its predecessor — would appear to be near-exhaustive, and exceptional. A study by Richard Rose has shown that party government in Britain is best characterised by the 'dynamics of a moving consensus'.[105] A party in Opposition usually opposes only a small proportion of the Bills introduced by the Government. When it is returned to power, it accepts (that is, does not seek to reverse) most of those measures which it opposed when in Opposition. Indeed it will itself often reintroduce measures introduced initially by its opponents, but left stranded because of the calling of the election.

In 1970, for example, the incoming Conservative Government reintroduced fourteen of the twenty-three Labour Bills stranded by the election
(a number far in excess of the small number of Labour Acts that it
reversed — indeed, only three measures introduced in the previous two
sessions were repealed), and in 1974 the new Labour Government
reintroduced fifteen of the twenty-two Conservative Bills stranded at
the February election (again, far in excess of the number of Conservative
measures that it sought to repeal).[106] The first Government Bill of the
1979 Parliament was one inherited from the previous administration.
Thus, the central thesis of the adversary politics critique appears on
shaky ground. Furthermore, the contention that PR would help to
produce policy continuity is unproven. On the one hand, it is argued
that a coalition would probably be formed, capable of ensuring policy
continuity. On the other hand, part of the electoral reform argument is
that PR would result in a loosening of party ties. 'Voters, by expressing
their preferences, can elect a more independent or "rebel" member of
a party if they wish. So no party machine can "discipline" any Member
by depriving him of this seat.'[107] At least one supporter of electoral
reform has appreciated the consequences that more independent voting
behaviour on the part of the MPs could have. In consequence of PR, he
conceded, there would probably be 'shifting coalitions' of Members
'that would alter aspects of this or that law, or even decline to pass
whole new laws, or introduce laws of their own'.[108] In many respects,
no bad thing, but not something that augurs well for stable government
and policy continuity, especially if Members are responsive to volatile
public opinion. Nor can the evidence of countries with PR be called
into account. As the essays in Professor Finer's volume show, no clear
conclusions can be drawn from the experience of PR abroad. The
consequence is that the case for PR, as advanced by the proponents of
the adversary politics thesis, remains unproven, and the onus is on the
reformers, as the advocates of change, to prove their case. They have a
long way to go. Indeed, it could be contended that by advancing the
adversary politics argument they have harmed the case for electoral
reform. As William Waldegrave has commented, 'The more normal, and
to my mind stronger, argument in favour of some form of PR, rests
simply on natural justice.'[109] Though the natural justice, or fairness,
argument is not without its critics,[110] it is a stronger one than that
advanced by Professor Finer and his supporters; by promoting this new
argument the reformers have provided opponents of PR with a more
vulnerable case to which to respond. Finally, we would make the point
that, in order to make effective the Commons' function of scrutiny and
influence, it is not necessary; that can be achieved by less radical means.

The approach favouring the introduction of a Bill of Rights need
concern us less. There are various problems associated with this approach.

There is no existing procedure by which the provisions of a Bill of Rights could be entrenched. There is no agreement on the rights to be embodied in such a measure. (Even the European Convention on Human Rights would not be problem-free, though Britain already is a party to it.) As a committee of the Society of Conservative Lawyers observed, 'The range of rights on which there is fundamental disagreement is frighteningly wide.'[111] There was, the committee argued, insufficient all-party support for an effective Bill of Rights to be implemented; in such circumstances, 'we are wholly unable to see how a Bill of Rights . . . can serve an effective purpose.'[112] The argument over the merits or demerits of such a measure, though, need not detain us. As we have noted already, though this approach constitutes one that falls under the category of external reform, it is not one directed at strengthening the House of Commons in fulfilling its role of scrutiny and influence. Instead, it seeks to limit Government by a judicially enforceable 'higher law' document. Its response to a perceived weak House of Commons is not to strengthen it, but rather to find a more effective alternative to restrict the power, or a possible abuse of power of the 'elective dictatorship' of Government.

Given the limitations of these approaches, how can the House of Commons more effectively fulfil its function of scrutiny and influence? The Norton view posits that the answer lies with MPs themselves. The means by which the House can achieve a greater degree of scrutiny and influence of that part of it which forms the Government exist already, but those means can be employed only if Members themselves are willing to employ them. The two elements of this approach — the powers available to the House, and the willingness of Members to employ them — have been ignored (or in some cases implicitly and not so implicitly rejected) by both internal and external reformers. Yet the House of Commons retains a basic power. If a majority of Members disagree with a proposal or motion advanced by the Government, they can vote against it in the division lobbies. The advent of party government and the consequent degree of cohesion in the division lobbies has led many to assume that this basic power had fallen into disuse. It has not. It is a power which can be, and in recent years *has* been, used by Members.

That this should be so is not that surprising. Members, as we have seen, are returned not just to represent the interests of their party. (Indeed, their party may not constitute a monolithic entity — a Member's local party may not be in accord with the party nationally on a particular issue.) There are many issues on which a party line is not clear. There are many issues on which constituency interests may be important. There are issues on which a party has a clear philosophical approach, but no unity as to how that approach can best be implemented. Though the advent of party government has meant the likelihood, in a parliamentary system, of a high level of party cohesion, it does not mean necessarily complete cohesion. Cohesion, it is true, has been encouraged by a belief that for Government supporters to sustain the Government in office requires them to support the Government in *every* division. Recent research has shown that the assumption motivating this (that is, that a Government defeat would result in the Government's having either to reverse the defeat, or to resign, or to request a dissolution) is based neither on any authoritative source nor on any consistent practice of behaviour – that it is, in short, a 'constitutional myth'.[113] The constitutional reality is, as it has been since the 1840s, that a Government is required by convention to resign or request a dissolution in the event of losing only a declared vote of confidence. If Government backbenchers are in disagreement with their own leaders on a particular issue, they can vote with Opposition Members to defeat the Government without raising necessarily any wider constitutional questions. That they would do so often is unlikely. On most matters, Government backbenchers will vote with their own side. They will normally be in agreement with their colleagues; they will usually want to vote with them. On occasion, though, they will find their leaders taking a step which they regard as unnecessary, unwise, inimical to the party's philosophy, injurious to their constituencies, or possibly threatening to the national interest. On such occasions, they will be tempted to, and can, vote with the Opposition to defeat the Government. By so doing, the House – a majority of the House – is providing the broad parameters within which Government can operate. Thus, a basic power is retained by Members. And on the basis of that power, they can exercise a greater degree of scrutiny and influence. The threat of defeat can force greater Government responsiveness. The combined power of Members can help to implement procedural and more radical reforms, such as the institution of investigative Select Committees. If such committees are to be effective, then it is up to Members themselves to sustain them, and to ensure also a link between committee activities and the floor of the House where their power, through the division lobbies, lies. Once a majority of Members have acquired the habit of flexing their political muscle in the House, the need to do so eventually recedes – the threat of it becomes sufficient to ensure a Government response.

To have argued a decade or so ago that Members retained a basic power through the division lobbies, that they could and should be prepared to use it, and, on the basis of their assertiveness, should force the creation of new machinery for the oversight of Government would have encouraged a dismissive response from reformers, political scientists, and many parliamentarians. However, the strength of this approach was to be demonstrated in the decade of the 1970s. Government back-benchers, first under a Conservative Government and then under a Labour one, proved willing to enter whipped Opposition lobbies to impose defeats on the Treasury bench. Not only did such action have an immediate impact on Government intentions, but it also had wider implications for future parliamentary behaviour. As the decade progressed, the greater was the awareness on the part of Members of what they could achieve. It resulted in Members forcing upon Government the creation of the new Select Committees in 1979. The Leader of the House, as we have noted already, was unable to withstand the pressure from Members on both sides of the House. The events of the 1970s have thus provided the basis on which the House in the 1980s can seek to scrutinise and influence Government more effectively than was previously thought possible. Whether this potential will be realised depends on the Members themselves. It is an effectiveness that cannot be achieved for them, only by them.

How important were the events of the 1970s? In the years from 1945 to 1970, a Government occasionally lost a vote because of poor management by the whips or occasional Opposition ploys[114] (there was a total of eleven defeats in this period), but none as a result of its own supporters

TABLE 9.1

DISSENTING VOTES CAST IN THE HOUSE OF COMMONS, 1945–79

Parliament (number of sessions in parentheses)	Number of divisions witnessing dissenting votes			Number of divisions witnessing dissenting votes expressed as % of all divisions
	Total	Lab.[a]	Con.[a]	
1945–50 (4)	87	79	27	7
1950–1 (2)	6	5	2	2.5
1951–5 (4)	25	17	11	3
1955–9 (4)	19	10	12	2
1959–64 (5)	137	26	120	13.5
1964–6 (2)	2	1	1	0.5
1966–70 (4)	124	109	41	9.5
1970–4 (4)	221	34[b]	204	20
1974 (1)	25	8	21	23
1974–9 (5)	423	309	240	28

[a] As one division may witness dissenting votes cast by Labour *and* Conservative Members, the Labour and Conservative figures do not necessarily add up to the total in the first column.

[b] Excluding the Labour backbench 'ginger group' votes of Februrary–March 1971. See Philip Norton, *Dissension in the House of Commons 1945–74* (Macmillan, 1975), pp. 387–9.

Source: Philip Norton, *Dissension in the House of Commons 1974–1979* (Oxford University Press, 1980), p. 428.

voting with the Opposition; such defeats were not regarded as important and were soon forgotten. The 1960s witnessed a period of restiveness, both within the country generally and in the House itself. Britain was facing serious economic problems; it was unsure of its world role, and concomitantly was divided on whether or not to enter the European Communities. Restiveness within the House was reflected in a slight increase in intra-party dissent in the division lobbies, Government back-benchers voting more often against their own side than had previously been the case; this dissent, though, took place in a Parliament in which the Government had a large majority, and did not extend to Government supporters entering whipped Opposition lobbies to deny the Government a majority. However, there was a significant change in parliamentary behaviour in the Parliament of 1970–4. Conservative backbenchers not only voted against their own front bench on more occasions than in previous Parliaments (see Table 9.1), but they did so more persistently than might be expected in a party of 'tendencies' (that is, the same Members dissented on multiple occasions),[115] and proved willing, for the first time in post-war history, to enter an Opposition lobby and consciously deprive the Government of a majority. During the Parliament, the Government suffered six defeats, three of them on three-line whips, and the most important on the immigration rules in 1972, when fifty-six Conservatives either abstained from voting or entered the No lobby.[116] The variable identified as being responsible for this sudden behavioural change was the prime ministerial leadership of Edward Heath. The radical measures for which he was responsible (which created the potential for conflict in a party which took the name of Conservative),* the manner in which they were introduced and effectively forced through the House, Mr Heath's inability to communicate with his supporters either at the intellectual level of explaining his actions or at the personal level of cultivating friendship, and his failure to make judicious use of his powers of appointment and patronage to keep Members content all coalesced to produce a worried and divided parliamentary party, one in which several Members decided finally to 'put a shot across the Govern-

---

* I am conscious of the argument that many of the pressures motivating some, though not all, of Mr Heath's measures would have faced any Prime Minister and, indeed, were not peculiar to Britain (for example, scarcity of certain energy resources, breakdown of Keynesian economic assumptions, increased regional and national consciousness, pressure of international trade, desire for trans-national economic co-operation in the European Communities), but these pressures in themselves do not account for the *sudden* and distinct change in parliamentary behaviour. Factors peculiar to Britain (Mr Heath's prime ministerial leadership, subsequent minority Government, the undermining of previous assumptions about parliamentary behaviour consequent to these developments, and Britain's lateness *vis-à-vis* other West European nations in applying for EC membership, an application inseparable from a consideration of Mr Heath's premiership) serve to explain the distinctive change, a change which now provides the House of Commons with opportunities not necessarily afforded to comparable national assemblies.

ment's bows'.[117] Though Mr Heath's forcefulness was generally to be successful in the short term, the back-bench response to his approach was to have long-term implications:

> by the strongest assertion of Conservative prime ministerial dominance
> . . . in post-war history, Mr Heath ensured that his result-orientated
> approach was successful in most instances, but created a situation where
> on occasion, through defeat on the floor of the House, it was not, and
> in so doing created the basis for a weakening of Government dominance
> in the division lobbies in future Parliaments.[118]

The Government defeats in the 1970—4 Parliament, and to some extent the significant increase in cross-voting generally, were significant not only in themselves (in that new immigration rules had to be introduced, for example), but also served to dispel or undermine a number of generalisations made previously about Parliament. The whips were shown not to be powerful 'disciplinarians'; through the power of persuasion, the whips helped to limit dissent, but they were unable to respond to the serious dissent that took place with serious disciplinary sanctions — they had none.[119] The belief that any defeat would entail the Government's downfall was dispelled; the question of resigning (or, for that matter, seeking a vote of confidence from the House) was never discussed. Also, the correlation between the incidence of dissent and the Government's overall majority no longer held, and Members by their actions demonstrated less willingness to accept that the Government of the day, through the resources and information at its disposal, 'knew best'.[120] Subsequent experience demonstrated also that dissent was no bar to later promotion.[121]

The defeats served also to provide important precendents. As a dissenter on the immigration rules observed, once one had defeated the Government a first time, it was much easier to do it a second time. (The dissenter in question is now a Government Minister.) The precedent of these defeats was reinforced by those of the short 1974 Parliament. In this Parliament, the minority Labour Government suffered seventeen defeats as a result of Opposition parties combining against it. The Government was returned in October 1974 with a bare overall majority, but through by-election losses and defections this majority gradually disappeared; it became a minority Government nominally in April 1976. As a result of the experience of the past two Parliaments, it was vulnerable to defeats as a result both of Government backbenchers voting with the Opposition, and of Opposition parties (after April 1976) combining against it. Labour MPs and Opposition parties proved willing to exploit this vulnerability. In the Parliament, the Government suffered a total of forty-two defeats in the division lobbies. A minority of these, nineteen, were attributable to Opposition parties combining against it (see Table 9.2). The majority, twenty-three, were attributable to Labour Members entering the Opposition lobby; had they not done so, the Government would have had a majority. It is important to note also that on several occasions the number of Labour Members dissenting was a substantial one; the Government would have gone down to defeat even if it had a sizable working majority.[122]

TABLE 9.2
GOVERNMENT DEFEATS IN THE HOUSE OF COMMONS
DIVISION LOBBIES, 1970–9

Parliament	Number of Government defeats		
	Product of intra-party dissent	Product of Opposition parties combining against a minority Government	Total
1970–4	6	0	6
1974	0	17	17[a]
1974–9	23	19[b]	42[a]
Total	29	36	65

[a] For a list of all Government defeats in the 1974 and 1974–9 Parliaments, see Philip Norton, *Dissension in the House of Commons 1974–1979* (Oxford University Press, 1980), appendix, pp. 491–3.

[b] Includes two defeats attributable to some confusion in the division lobbies.

The defeats themselves took place on important issues. As a result of Opposition parties combining against the minority Government, the rate of income tax was lowered, the Government's policy of employing sanctions against firms breaking its 5 per cent pay limit was abandoned, and ultimately, of course, the Government itself was brought down on a vote of confidence on 28 March 1979. More important for our purposes, dissent by Government backbenchers resulted in a number of legislative changes, in the effective emasculation of the Dock Work Regulation Bill, and in the effective defeat of the original Scotland and Wales Bill and the radical amendment of the subsequent Scotland Bill and Wales Bill. Had it not been for dissent in that Parliament by a number of Labour Members, Britain would now have a new constitutional framework. In addition, various legislative changes were wrought as a result of dissent in Standing Committee, most notably on the 1977 Finance Bill.[123] (In the period from 1974 to 1978, the Government suffered sixty-four defeats in Standing Committee because of Labour MPs' cross-voting.)[124] Again, though, the defeats were important not only in themselves, but also for their implications. They demonstrated that Members could be effective in influencing Government, in imposing their will upon Government if they wished to (not just Government backbenchers, for, though necessary if the Government has an overall majority, they are insufficient to defeat the Government unless they combine with Opposition Members), and that if there was to be a more continuous and structured form of scrutiny than was possible on the floor of the House, it was up to them to do something about it. Towards the end of the Parliament, Members did prove willing to do something about it. The Report of the Procedure Committee, recommending the creation of a comprehensive Select Committee structure to cover Government Departments, was published in August 1978. Initially, it looked as if it would go the way of previous reports – ignored by the Government and not even debated in the House. The Prime Minister and the Cabinet, including the Leader of the House, Mr Foot, were opposed to the Report's recommendations.[125] However, pressure from Opposition Members and Labour backbenchers eventually forced a debate. Mr Foot agreed to one, subject to no vote being held. However, in the debate, the view of Members on both sides of the House was so clear that Mr Foot had again to back down and agreed to arrange for the House to vote on the proposals. As the *Economist* observed of the occasion:

> Is Parliament's control of the executive ever destined to ebb remorselessly away? MPs were inclined this week to answer no, when they forced an unwilling Government to concede them the chance to decide whether major changes should be made in parliamentary procedure . . . some backbenchers have been getting increasingly frustrated and critical of their own ineffectiveness. So, when the Government decided that this report should merely be debated but not voted on they reacted angrily . . . the Government was made to promise that there will be a vote sometime . . . MPs were in no mood to be fobbed off. Support for the proposals and demand for a vote came from all sides of the House.[126]

The May 1979 general election then intervened. The Conservative manifesto expressed 'sympathy' with the Procedure Committee's recommendations, and promised to give the new House an 'early chance of coming to a decision on the proposals'.[127] The promise itself was a compromise one (the Shadow Cabinet had been divided between those, a small minority, who were strongly in favour of the proposals, and a majority who were not), and did not enjoy the wholehearted support of the party leader. Once in office, the new Leader of the House, Norman St John-Stevas, was keen to give effect to the manifesto promise. However, though his support and the speed with which he acted was a necessary condition for its implementation, it was not a sufficient condition. The sufficient conditions were provided by the promise's appearance in the manifesto and, specially important for our purposes, by pressure from backbenchers; the reaction to the Cabinet's proposals on Members' pay demonstrated that Members on both sides of the House were prepared to continue their new assertiveness. A combination of these factors resulted in Mr St John-Stevas's persuading a highly unsympathetic Cabinet to agree that the House debate the Procedure Committee's recommendations,[128] the debate being held on 25 June 1979. Having provided the Leader of the House with the support necessary to bring the proposals before the House, Members then proceeded to approve them; by 248 votes to 12, the House approved the setting up of the proposed Select Committee structure.[129] The membership of the committees (decided upon by the Committee of Selection and not the party whips)[130] was agreed to in November, with the committees subsequently meeting to elect their own chairmen. Other procedural reforms were agreed to by the House in October 1979 (though rejecting a proposal to change the procedure under which applications for emergency debates could be made),[131] and in October 1980; again, the proposals were the product of an alliance of the Leader of the House and private Members (the 1922 Committee under Edward du Cann playing a specially important role) overcoming the reluctance, indeed opposition, of a majority of the Cabinet and the whips. The House of Commons in 1980 had thus come a long way since the House of Commons of pre-1970 days.

The position now is that the House of Commons has a membership which to some extent has learned the lesson of the 1970s; being prepared to dissent if in disagreement with one's leaders became, in the words of one leading Labour dissenter of the 1970s, a 'habit',[132] and one which has not been discarded. Already, the new Parliament has witnessed Conservative Members making clear their preparedness to dissent when occasion demands. The Government has retreated on five occasions in the face of the threat of defeat (this despite an overall majority of forty-three): on the question of Members' pay, an issue which excited bitterness on the back benches (on both sides of the House); on the proposed reduction in the BBC's external services; on proposed charges for eye tests;[133] on the proposal to make sanctions against Iran retrospective;[134] and, apparently, on the immigration rules in 1980. Furthermore, the Government's conduct of the Lancaster House conference on the future of Rhodesia was influenced significantly by the belief that it could not guarantee that a majority of Conservative Members would support the Rhodesian sanctions order when it came up for renewal in autumn. The Government knows that it cannot take its backbenchers for granted;

'unthinking loyalty is no longer a feature of British politics in any party these days'.[135] In addition, the new select committees are in operation. Some have been more adventurous than others, and several have made effective use of their public questioning of witnesses. The success of Members in the creation of the new committees may encourage them to push for further reforms. One leading Conservative backbencher, Kenneth Baker, has noted that 'reflecting on the real nature of their influence, MPs are likely to want a greater say in what is debated', possibly through a Business Committee.[136] As he concluded, 'I don't see MPs transforming the House of Commons into a sort of Congress that undermines or usurps the power of the executive, but I do see them seeking out in Churchill's phrase a less "tame and minor role".'

Members have already started out on the path towards fulfilment of a less tame and minor role. There is still some way to go. Many members have still not learned the lessons of the 1970s. The Select Committees have still to establish themselves as effective investigative bodies with bite. When they were established, the House failed to approve an amendment that would set aside eight parliamentary days each session to debate their reports. Until there is an effective linkage between the committees' activities and the floor of the House, there is the danger that they will follow their predecessors, operating 'in a sort of bipartisan limbo, remote from the main House, unconnected with its procedures and deeply unsure of their role'.[137] As we have observed elsewhere, 'the threat of action on the floor of the House in consequence of a com-mittee's recommendations or findings is the way to ensure an effective Government response.'[138] Though Ministers are pledged to co-operate with the committees, the committees have no power to require a Minister's attendance; again, as we have noted, 'Ministers are likely to be co-operative when they have nothing to hide, and unco-operative when they have.'[139] (Within a few months of operation, some committees – as, for example, the Education Committee in May 1980 – were complain-ing of Ministers' refusals to supply information.) Most Cabinet Ministers – and various leading Shadow Cabinet members, such as Michael Foot – remain unenthusiastic about the committee, and indeed about procedural reform generally. So, there is still some way to go. If the Select Committees are to be effective, if further changes are to take place to improve the effectiveness of the House in fulfilling the function of scrutiny and influence, if the House is to provide the parameters in which that part of it that forms the Government is to operate, then it is up to Members themselves. As one senior Member, Edward du Cann, noted in a debate on the Civil Service in 1979, change generally does not come from Government. 'What is needed is an exercise of political will on the part of the House of Commons.'[140] In recent years, we have seen the limited exercise of such a will. If the House of Commons is to be an effective scrutineer of Government in the 1980s and beyond, then the further exercise of that political will is necessary. The view of this author does not assume necessarily that it *will* be exercised. Rather, it contends that it *should* be exercised, and that the experience of the 1970s has demonstrated that it *can* be exercised. As various Members have conceded, there can be no going back to the cohesion and the 'discipline' of pre-1970 days.[141] How far the lessons learned from the experience of recent years will be carried forward remains to be seen. The experience of the current Parliament to date has not proved discouraging.

Conclusion

Though a number of observers, for very different reasons, have sought to defend the House of Commons on the basis of existing practices and procedures, there has been a fairly widespread realisation in recent decades, and earlier, that the House has not been fulfilling as effectively as it might its function of scrutiny and influence. This century has witnessed in consequence various calls for reform. A number of procedural reforms were implemented in the 1960s, but failed to live up to the hopes of those that advocated them. Given this, those calling for reform divided into different schools of thought. The internal reformers pursued a limited approach, arguing for more procedural reforms within the House. The electoral reformers pursued a more ambitious approach, aiming, through the introduction of proportional representation for elections, to restructure both Government and Parliament, and to provide the basis on which there could be greater stability in economic policy. Seeking primarily to limit Government, those advocating a Bill of Rights with entrenched provisions also pursued an ambitious, constitutionally radical approach. The approach of this author is less ambitious, seeking to work within the existing constitutional and parliamentary framework, emphasising the importance of attitudinal change as a prerequisite for structural change, and drawing on recent parliamentary experience as a guide to possible future behaviour.

Of these approaches, not all are mutually exclusive. Indeed, in its editorial of 5 November 1977, the *Economist* espoused most of them. (It supported a federal system, electoral reform, an elected second chamber, a separation of powers, a constitutional court, and investigative Select Committees, though failing to explain how such changes were to be brought about.)[142] The dividing line between the approaches is not necessarily as distinct as our delineation may imply. A number of traditional internal reformers have on occasion given some implicit recognition that Member's attitudes may be important.[143] Though now taking the argument along new lines, electoral reformers will nevertheless have occasion to call in aid the traditional natural justice argument for PR. Ronald Butt's anti-reform thesis and the Norton thesis share a similar recognition of the power which has always resided with the House, the difference of opinion being over the extent to which it has been employed, and how far it can be taken. Also, the caveat must be entered that the author has interpreted the various approaches as he understands them from the literature available; advocates of each approach may emphasise differently the points made on their behalf in this chapter. The categorisation is also the author's;[144] though to create the category of 'electoral reformers' would appear a fairly straightforward exercise, a number of those included in the 'anti-reform' category may be surprised by such an inclusion. The use of the nomenclature the 'Norton view', which may appear unduly idiosyncratic or immodest, has been employed because it allows the author to express clearly his own approach; with various modifications, it could equally well have been titled the 'Rasmussen view' or the 'Cunningham view'.[145] However aptly or inaptly titled, and however clearly or ambiguously their aims are delineated or pursued, the internal reformers, the electoral reformers (even some Bill of Rights advocates),[146] and those supporting the view or a similar view of this author have one thing in common: to seek for the House of Commons a less 'tame and minor role', to restore to it a more meaningful role of scrutiny and influence in the British political process. The House of Commons can and will have a limited role in the decision-making process, but it need not be so limited as to justify its exclusion from any consideration of how political decisions in Britain are arrived at. The House of Commons should fulfil a worthwhile role in the British political system. In the view of this author and others, it can fulfil such a role. Whether it will or not remains to be seen.

NOTES

1 Samuel H. Beer, *Modern British Politics* (Faber, 1969 ed.), p. 261.
2 Beer, p. 350.
3 Quoted in G. LeMay, *British Government 1914—63* (Methuen, 1964), p. 163.
4 Cited in Hansard Society, *Parliamentary Reform 1933—60*, 2nd rev. ed. (Cassell, 1967), p. 132.
5 Hansard Society, p. 45.
6 Ivor Jennings, *Parliamentary Reform* (Victor Gollancz, 1934), p. 170.
7 See Hansard Society, ch. 3 and *passim*. For one of the most comprehensive calls for procedural reform in this period, see Jennings; his prescient analysis was to be a forerunner of similar tracts in the 1960s.
8 The best single work on Parliament in this period is the much overlooked book by John Eaves, Jr, *Parliament and the Executive 1939—51*.

9   A. Hill and A. Whichelow, *What's Wrong with Parliament?* (Penguin, 1964), p. 9.

10   Quoted in A.H. Hanson, 'The Purpose of Parliament', *Parliamentary Affairs,* 17, 1963–4, p. 284. However, a number of works advocating reform in the 'New Britain' had appeared in the war years.

11   Hansard Society, p. 133.

12   Lord Campion and others, *Parliament: A Survey* (Allen & Unwin, 1952), pp. 25–6.

13   First published in 1964, it was reprinted in 1965 and 1966; a second edition was brought out in 1968, and reprinted in 1969, with a second revised edition being published in 1970.

14   'The Use of Committees by the House of Commons', *Public Law,* 1959.

15   Pall Mall Press, 1959.

16   Secker & Warburg, 1959.

17   Unservile State Papers, No. 1, 1960.

18   Conservative Political Centre, 1963. Published in January, it was reprinted the following month. An Early Day Motion, summarising the pamphlet's proposals, was tabled and soon attracted the signatures of sixty-five Conservative Members; a similar Labour motion attracted the support of twenty Labour Members. See *The Times,* 22 February 1963.

19   PEP, 1965. *The Times*'s article by Michael Ryle is reprinted in H.V. Wiseman (ed.), *Parliament and the Executive* (Routledge & Kegan Paul, 1966), pp. 265–9; see also M. Ryle, 'Committees of the House of Commons', *Political Quarterly,* 36, 1965, pp. 295–308. On attitudes to reform in this period, see generally Kenneth Swinhoe, 'A Study of Opinion about the Reform of House of Commons Procedure 1945–68', unpublished PhD thesis, University of Leeds, 1971.

20   Although pressure for an Ombudsman appears to have largely come from outside the House, certainly in the initial stage. See Frank Stacey, *The British Ombudsman* (Oxford University Press, 1971).

21   See Robin Day, *The Case for Televising Parliament* (Hansard Society, 1963).

22   See Hansard Society, pp. 79–107.

23   Sir William Robson-Brown to author. Sir William was one of the pamphlet's co-authors.

24   Anthony Barker, 'Parliament and Patience', in Bernard Crick, *The Reform of Parliament,* 2nd rev. ed. (Weidenfeld & Nicolson, 1970), p. 201.

25   *Time for Decision,* in F.W.S. Craig (ed.), *British General Election Manifestos 1900–74* (Macmillan, 1975), p. 281.

26   On these committees, see Alfred Morris (ed.), *The Growth of Parliamentary Scrutiny by Committee* (Pergamon Press, 1970).

27   Under the new procedure, a message is sent to the Speaker, who then reads out the names of the Bills to which Assent has been given.

28   Started in March 1975, the amount provided for each party was determined by a formula based on the number of seats won by, and the number of votes cast for, a party at the previous election, with a maximum allowance of £150,000 per party, increased to £165,000 in 1978.

29   On the reforms generally in this period, see Frank Stacey, *British Government 1966–75* (Oxford University Press, 1975), chs 3 and 4.

30   A poll of MPs from the north-west found that they felt the image of the Commons had suffered as a result of the broadcasting; *The Times,* 7 June 1978.

The BBC found that the broadcasts upset and irritated listeners; *Daily Telegraph*, 13 December 1979.

31   Ann Robinson, *Parliament and Public Spending* (Heinemann, 1978), p. 154.

32   Eric Taylor, *The House of Commons at Work*, 9th ed. (Macmillan, 1979), p. 117.

33   Crick, *The Reform of Parliament*, p. 230. Note also his comments in Sussex Tape P1 (1971), 'Reform of Parliament' (Educational Productions, 1975).

34   See *The Times*, 22 October 1976, and Edward du Cann, *Parliament and the Purse Strings* (Conservative Political Centre, 1977).

35   See Tony Benn, 'Technology's Threat to Parliament', *Guardian*, 10 February 1979.

36   'Blowing up a Tyranny', *Economist*, 5 November 1977, p. 11. See the whole article, pp. 11—16.

37   *Big Cyril: The Autobiography of Cyril Smith* (W.H. Allen, 1977), ch. 8.

38   See, for example, Paul Rose, 'I'm Sick of the Whitehall Secret Brigade', *Daily Express*, 7 March 1979, p. 8.

39   Crick, p. 79.

40   *Reforming the House of Commons*, Fabian Tract 448 (Fabian Society, 1977).

41   Cmnd, Paper 6053.

42   *Eleventh Report from the Expenditure Committee*, HC 535, and the *First Report from the Select Committee on Procedure*, HC 588.

43   S.E. Finer in his introduction, S.E. Finer (ed.), *Adversary Politics and Electoral Reform* (Anthony Wigram, 1975), p. 12.

44   See Finer, p. 13, for a diagrammatic representation of this point.

45   Michael Shanks, *Planning and Politics* (PEP, 1977), p. 92. See also S.A. Walkland, 'Parliament and the Economy in Britain', *Parliamentary Affairs*, 32 (1), Winter 1979, pp. 16—18.

46   Some advocates prefer a combination of STV with a regional list system, similar to that which exists in West Germany. For a study of PR, see Enid Lakeman, *How Democracies Vote* (Faber, 1970), and for some of the problems associated with this method, see Geoffrey Alderman, *British Elections* (Batsford, 1978), pp. 34—9.

47   The Conservatives came closest in 1955 with 49.7 per cent of the votes cast. (In the 1979 elections to the European Parliament, the Conservatives did obtain more than 50 per cent of the votes cast, though on a low turnout.)

48   Finer, pp. 30—1.

49   Professor Finer has since argued for further radical reforms, though aimed more at strengthening the role of electors *vis-à-vis* parties than strengthening Parliament. S.E. Finer, *The Changing British Party System 1945—1979* (American Enterprise Institute, 1980).

50   For example, 'Whither the Commons?', ch. 12 in S.A. Walkland and M. Ryle (eds), *The Commons in the Seventies* (Fontana, 1977); 'The Politics of Parliamentary Reform', *Parliamentary Affairs*, 29 (2), 1976, pp. 190—200; and 'Parliament and the economy in Britain'.

51   In addition, support was forthcoming from a commission set up by the Hansard Society to study the subject; *The Report of the Hansard Society Commission on Electoral Reform* (Hansard Society, 1976).

52   The pamphlets were published by the Fabian Society, the Liberal Party, and the Conservative Political Centre, respectively. Details are to be found in Michael Zander, *A Bill of Rights?* (Barry Rose, 1975), pp. 5–10.

53   Cited in Zander, pp. 7–9.

54   For a brief chronology of the period up to and including 1977, see Emlyn Hooson, *The Case for a Bill of Rights* (n.d.), pp. 15–23.

55   See the bibliography in Simon J. Wilson, 'Should Britain Have a Bill of Rights?', third-year undergraduate dissertation, Hull University Politics Department, 1980.

56   Leslie Scarman, *English Law — New Dimensions* (Stevens, 1974).

57   Lord Hailsham, *Elective Dictatorship* (BBC, 1976). He made such a call previously in four articles in *The Times*, 2, 16, 19 and 20 May, 1975, and repeated it in the Richard O'Sullivan Memorial Lecture (1977) and in his book, *The Dilemma of Democracy* (Collins, 1978), especially chs 20 and 21.

58   It is by no means the only argument. See, for example, Scarman, and Zander, pp. 18–25.

59   Hailsham, *Elective Dictatorship* (my emphasis).

60   Hailsham, *Elective Dictatorship*.

61   As recommended by Peter Wallington and Jeremy McBride, *Civil Liberties and a Bill of Rights* (1976), and supported, for example, by Hooson.

62   See Zander, p. 50.

63   *The Times*, 19 May 1975.

64   Also, in April 1979, a Conservative MP, Sir Frederic Bennett, introduced a Bill of Rights under the ten-minute rule. Given that the Parliament was about to end, though, little attention was paid to it, and no one rose to oppose it. *House of Commons Debates*, 965, c. 1318–21. Sir Frederic did not emphasise the partisan aspect of his case.

65   *The Times*, 19 April 1980.

66   Ian Gow, MP, January 1980, quoted in Wilson, 'Should Britain Have a Bill of Rights?', p. 29.

67   In 1979, Lord Wade's Bill of Rights actually passed through all its stages in the House of Lords, though with no chance of further success.

68   *Conservative Manifesto 1979*, p. 21. In May 1980, the Leader of the House revealed that meetings were being held between representatives of the Government, the Liberal Party, and the Labour Party, on the issue of devolution; no mention was made of a Bill of Rights. Parliamentary written answer, *House of Commons Debates*, 985, c. 35.

69   Published by Constable. A second edition came out in 1969.

70   Methuen, 1968.

71   Crick, *The Reform of Parliament*, preface to the second edition.

72   The Private Bills introduced in the nineteenth century covered parochial matters considered beyond the scope of limited Government at that time.

73   Fairlie, *The Life of Politics*, p. 253.

74   Philip Norton, 'The House of Commons in the 1970s: Three Views on Reform', *Hull Papers in Politics No. 3* (Hull University Politics Department, 1978), p. 11.

75   *First Report from the Select Committee on Procedure, 1977–8*, Vol. 2: Minutes of Evidence (HC 588–2), p. 64.

76   *First Report*, pp. 68 and 69.

77   'Are we Worse Governed?', *New Society*, 19 May 1977.

78   J.J. Richardson and A.G. Jordan, *Governing Under Pressure* (Martin Robertson, 1979), p. 121.
79   *First Report*, Minutes of Evidence, p. 30.
80   'Mutiny on the Benches', *Times Literary Supplement*, 12 March 1976.
81   In 1977 a survey showed a large majority of respondents believing that Parliament represented their interests not very or not at all well — cited in M. Beloff and G. Peele, *The Government of the United Kingdom* (Weidenfeld & Nicolson, 1980), p. 6 — while another survey the same year showed that respondents rated Parliament as second only to the law courts in 'doing a good job' (ahead of unions, the Civil Service, the newspapers, the parties, and industry), and second only to the trade unions in 'having a lot of influence'. *Sunday Times*, 18 September 1977. (In 1966, an ORC poll, also for the *Sunday Times*, found that 53 per cent of respondents were 'satisfied with Parliament and the way it works'.)
82   Ralph Miliband, *The State in Capitalist Society* (Quartet Books, 1973), pp. 49—50 and 148—9.
83   At least as interpreted by this author. See Steven Lukes, *Power: A Radical View* (Macmillan, 1974).
84   Bob Jessop, 'Capitalism and Democracy: The Best Possible Shell?', in G. Littlejohn (ed.), *Power and the State* (Croom Helm, 1978), pp. 10—51, especially pp. 44—5.
85   In the post-Keynsian period, according to this analysis, it is necessary to secure the active and continuous involvement of labour (as well as capital) in economic intervention: hence the growth of corporatism. Parliamentarianism is necessary to provide a forum for popular—democratic struggles beyond the ambit of economic intervention and to secure the legitmacy and popular accountability of state intervention. 'But corporatism is associated with the centralisation and concentration of state power and with the consolidation of the domination of monopoly capitalism. Parliamentary government, on the other hand, is associated with local representation and favours small and medium capital as well as regionalised or localised minority interests. Thus monopoly capital has stronger interests in promoting corporatism, small and medium capital have stronger interests in promoting parliamentarianism.' The result is a 'contradictory unity'. Jessop, 'Capitalism and Democracy', pp. 44—5.
86   See the comments of Jessop, above. Given the growth of corporatism, the 'popular accountability' of state intervention may be considered a not unimportant function.
87   That is, it is rare for a Member to oppose a measure or vote against the Government on a supply vote because of an unsatisfactory response from the Government to a question or representation on a constituency problem. However, it is not unknown, though the last Member to do so with much effect was probably the late Dame Irene Ward.
88   See Ivor Crewe, 'Electoral Reform and the Local MP', in Finer, *Adversary Politics and Electoral Reform*, pp. 320—1.
89   *ibid.*
90   S.A. Walkland, 'The Politics of Parliamentary Reform', p. 192.
91   H. Helco and A. Wildavsky, *The Private Government of Public Money* (Macmillan, 1974), p. 253. See also the comments of John Mackintosh, 'Reform of the House of Commons: The Case for Specialization', in G. Loewenberg (ed.), *Modern Parliaments: Change or Decline?* (Aldine/Atherton, 1971), p. 40. Mackintosh

contended, though, that support for the committees had grown by the end of the Parliament; see pp. 57 and 59.

92   Barker, 'Parliament and Patience', p. 202.

93   Richard Crossman, *The Diaries of a Cabinet Minister*, Vol. III (Hamish Hamilton/Jonathan Cape, 1977), p. 355.

94   Walkland, 'The Politics of Parliamentary Reform', pp. 192—3. Henry Fairlie makes a similar point.

95   See the Crossman *Diaries, passim,* and the extracts as reproduced in Ferdinand Mount, 'The Knights Purse their Lips', *Spectator,* 3 March 1979.

96   Crossman, *Diaries,* 6 September 1967, p. 466.

97   Philip Norton, *Dissension in the House of Commons 1974—1979* (Oxford University Press, 1980), p. 479.

98   The pamphlet was marred generally by poor argument, and was castigated by Bernard Crick in an editorial in *Political Quarterly,* 48 (3), July 1977, p. 258.

99   P.J. Taylor and J. Johnston, *Geography of Elections* (Penguin, 1979), p. 433.

100   In the 1974—9 Parliament, for example, PR for the proposed Scottish Assembly was rejected on a free vote by a majority of 183, and PR for the 1979 elections to the European Parliament was rejected by a majority of 97 despite a Government recommendation to support it.

101   As, for example, by Walkland, 'Whither the Commons?', pp. 255—6, and to some extent by Finer, *Adversay Politics and Electoral Reform,* p. 31.

102   Alderman, p. 39. A similar point is made by Taylor and Johnston, p. 433: 'We are literally working in the realms of speculation.'

103   Finer, *Adversary Politics and Electoral Reform,* pp. 15—16.

104   Ivor Crewe and Bo Sarlvik, 'Popular Attitudes and Electoral Strategy', in Z. Layton-Henry (ed.), *Conservative Party Politics* (Macmillan, 1980), pp. 244—75, especially p. 258 (emphasis in original).

105   Richard Rose, *Do Parties Make a Difference?* (Macmillan, 1980), conclusions.

106   Rose, table V.7.

107   'Fair Voting is Safer', *ER Leaflet No. 40* (Electoral Reform Society, n.d.), p.1.

108   Joe Rogaly, *Parliament for the People* (Temple Smith, 1976), p. 5.

109   William Waldegrave, 'The Case Against', *Spectator,* 25 October 1975.

110   As Ferdinand Mount has written, 'the whole assumption that PR is fairer depends on an implied definition of fairness which is by no means self-evident.' See his article, 'Roy Stops the Clock', *Spectator,* 1 December 1979, p. 4.

111   *Another Bill of Rights?,* a report by the Bill of Rights Committee of the Society of Conservative Lawyers (Conservative Political Centre, 1976), p. 11.

112   *Another Bill of Rights?,* p. 12.

113   See Philip Norton, 'Government Defeats in the House of Commons: Myth and Reality', *Public Law,* Winter 1978, pp. 360—78.

114   That is, Opposition MPs pretending to leave the House to go home, hiding in nearby Houses, and then returning when a division was called. See, for example, Lord Wigg, *George Wigg* (Michael Joseph, 1972), pp. 165—7; *The Times,* 8 July 1965; and Colin Thornton-Kemsley, *Through Winds and Tide* (Standard Press, 1974), p. 234.

115   The classification of 'tendencies' is provided by Richard Rose, 'Parties, Factions and Tendencies in Britain', *Political Studies,* 12, 1964, pp. 33—46. For the

extent to which the Conservative parliamentary party came close to experiencing 'factional' dissent in this Parliament, see Philip Norton, *Conservative Dissidents* (Temple Smith, 1978), pp. 244—54.

116   Philip Norton, 'Intra-party Dissent in the House of Commons: A Case Study. The Immigration Rules 1972', *Parliamentary Affairs*, 29 (4), Autumn 1976, pp. 404—20. For details of the six defeats, see Philip Norton, *Dissension in the House of Commons 1945—74* (Macmillan, 1975), pp. 440—1, 505—7, 515—17, 523—5, 560, and 582—4.

117   See Norton, *Conservative Dissidents*, pp. 239—41, and 'Intra-Party Dissent in the House of Commons', pp. 414—15.

118   Norton, *Conservative Dissidents*, p. 274.

119   See Norton, *Conservative Dissidents*, ch. 6, and also Philip Norton, 'The Organisation of Parliamentary Parties', in S.A. Walkland (ed.), *The House of Commons in the Twentieth Century* (Oxford University Press, 1979), and above, Chapter 3.

120   Norton, *Dissension in the House of Commons 1974—1979*, pp. 460—2; these points are developed further in Philip Norton, 'The Changing Face of the House of Commons in the 1970s', *Legislative Studies Quarterly*, 5 (3), August 1980.

121   Norton, *Dissension in the House of Commons 1974—1979*, pp. 464—5.

122   For instance, if a Government has an overall majority of fifty, the cross-votes of twenty-six or more of its supporters would result in a Government defeat. In one defeat in the 1974—9 Parliament, the number of Labour Members cross-voting was seventy-nine: a Government overall majority of 158 would have been necessary to avoid a defeat.

123   The so-called Rooker/Wise amendments. See above, Chapter 8.

124   John Schwarz, 'The Commons Bites Back', *Financial Times*, 2 June 1978. See also, by the same author, 'Exploring a New Role in Policy Making: The British House of Commons in the 1970s', *American Political Science Review*, 74 (1), March 1970, pp. 23—37.

125   Geoffrey Smith, 'Reform of Parliament: Not Whether but When', *The Times*, 30 November 1978. The divisions within the Cabinet have been confirmed to the author by a parliamentary source.

126   'Parliament Prepares to Seize Power', *The Economist*, 24 February 1979, pp. 23—4.

127   *Conservative Manifesto* 1979, p. 21.

128   The Leader of the House succeeded 'against much pressure from his Cabinet colleagues'. *Spectator*, 13 October 1979, p. 15.

129   *House of Commons Debates*, 969, c. 247—50.

130   An attempt was made by the Labour whips to persuade Labour MPs on the Committee to support the names put forward by the whips, but the attempt eventually floundered. Partly as a result of this, the Committee made a decision not to appoint to Select Committees MPs who were chairmen of the pertinent party committees.

131   *House of Commons Debates*, 972, c. 1268—1391.

132   George Cunningham, MP, to author.

133   'The World Tonight', BBC Radio 4, 15 May 1980.

134   *House of Commons Debates*, 985, c. 30—48, 254—63. *The Times*, 20 May 1980.

135   Geoffrey Smith, 'The Younger Men that Mrs Thatcher Must Convince of Her Strategy', *The Times*, 21 March 1980. 'Taken all in all', as Hugh Stephenson noted, 'on the experience of her first year Mrs Thatcher had no reason to suppose that she could count on a docile Parliament for the rest of her first term in office.' *Mrs Thatcher's First Year* (Jill Norman, 1980), p. 104.

136   Kenneth Baker, 'The New Pattern of Parliament in the 1980s', *The Guardian*, 10 December 1979, p. 9.

137   Walkland, 'Whither the Commons?', p. 246. Only one of the first thirty reports emanating from the new committees was debated on the floor of the House.

138   Norton, *Dissension in the House of Commons 1974—1979*, p. 481.

139   Norton, *Dissension in the House of Commons 1974—1979*, p. 481.

140   *House of Commons Debates*, 960, c. 1342.

141   The view was variously expressed by MPs in the BBC Radio 4 programme, Talking Politics', broadcast 28 October 1978.

142   *Economist*, 5 November 1977. Its calls for such a variety of reforms were not unique. Two years previously, Sam Brittan had made a similar call. See S. Brittan, 'A 'Manifesto' for 1975', in J. Hicks (ed.), *Crisis '75*, Occasional Paper Special No. 43 (Institute of Economic Affairs, 1975).

143   Bernard Crick touched upon it, for example, in *The Reform of Parliament*, including in his section on 'Disquiet among MPs', but the section is tucked away in three pages at the end of a chapter, and records merely MPs' attitudes on pay and the like, without drawing wider conclusions.

144   For a somewhat different categorisation (though geared more to party than parliamentary reform), see Finer, *The Changing British Party System 1945—1979*, ch. 6.

145   George Cunningham, MP, has expressed views similar to the author's. See, for example, his peroration to a speech delivered from the Opposition Front Bench in October 1979: 'When they elect us, the electors give us only one thing — the right to vote in the House of Commons. That is all an hon. Member has but it is all he needs.' *House of Commons Debates*, 972, c. 1362. Mr Cunningham has variously put his views into practice, and was responsible for engineering various Government defeats in the 1974—9 Parliament, most notably on the issue of devolution. Professor Jorgen Rasmussen has also advanced a similar view. Jorgen Rasmussen, 'Was Guy Fawkes Right?' in Isaac Kramnick (ed.), *Is Britain Dying?* (Cornell University Press, 1979), especially p. 116. Also, see below, Chapter 10.

146   Some advocates of a Bill of Rights believe that such a limitation on Government would help to strengthen the House in fulfilling its role of defending the individual, minorities, and the rule of law.

10
The House of Commons: the future?

Well, it's dead . . . power has now bypassed the House of Commons.

Humphry Berkeley, MP (1963)[1]

There's life in the old dog yet.

George Cunningham, MP (1979)[2]

One of the remarkable and most important features of Parliament in Britain has been its adaptability to changing conditions. However, in adapting to the changes of the nineteenth and twentieth centuries it has been left with no clear agreed role in the British political process. That it has shed some of the functions previously ascribed to it, and that the balance in its relationship with that part of it which forms the Government has shifted significantly in favour of the latter, would appear to be generally accepted by most (albeit not all) observers. In this respect, it is not unique. Other national assemblies in industrialised or developing democracies have witnessed a similar imbalance, though research would appear to suggest that it is marked in British-style parliamentary systems as opposed to Continental parliamentary systems and presidential systems;[3] there are exceptions,[4] though the generalisation remains a useful one. In Britain, the response to these changes has resulted in ambiguity and confusion over the purpose of the very Mother of Parliaments.[5] It has ceased to form a regular part of the decision-making process. We have identified it as occupying an unusual place in the British political process, having an important relationship with, yet not being a major part of, the decision-making process. In Figure 1.3 (p. 7), we have emphasised its position as a scrutinising and legitimising body. John Wahlke has emphasised its role as one of the 'supports' of the political system.[6] As a result of the changes of the 1970s, John Schwarz has suggested that it might be considered to form again part of the decision-making 'black box'.[7] We have attempted to bring some coherence to the different formal and real functions posited for the House (Chapter 4), yet those we have identified are far from problem-free. Even in so far as they enjoy some measure of support, there is no agreement as to the extent to which they are, or could be, fulfilled. The concept of representation has been variously defined and argued about. The liberal theory has had to contend with the Whig, Tory, radical and socialist theories, and with the reality of organised, mass-membership parties and group representation. The tension this has created has been commented upon by Stuart Walkland.[8] The function of supporting and sustaining the Government and the Opposition has been challenged by the adversary politics thesis (see Chapter 9); some would wish the Commons to fulfil a more forceful function than that of scrutiny and influence of Government (the adversary politics school of thought would apparently wish it to play a more positive role in reviewing economic policy; John Schwarz believes it already fulfils a more positive function); some would wish to hive off the remnants of the elective power that is held by elements now within the House; indeed, some — supporters of referendums — would wish to hive off much or part of its role of legitimisation. Not surprisingly, such uncertainty and disagreement as to the purpose of Parliament has resulted in different approaches to the question of whether or not Parliament should be reformed. These approaches we have outlined in Chapter 9. Seeking a more positive role for the House of Commons in the formulation and scrutiny of economic policy, and wishing it to be strengthened as a 'support' of the political system (through being a more 'representative' assembly), the adversary politics school advocates reform through the introduction of a new electoral system. Ronald Butt, ascribing a negative checking function to the House, believes that it is not in need of any radical surgery. Wanting strong Government with a strong Opposition, and regarding the main purpose of the House as an informing or educating one, various reformers have contented themselves with pressing for limited procedural reform. This author has stressed the function of scrutiny and influence, and has argued that for it to be achieved, an attitudinal change on the part of Members is a prerequisite to structural change. Other writers have weighed in with supporting or alternative approaches. The picture facing the student is, in short, a complex one.

The purpose of this work has been to try to give some coherence to the complexity of facts and figures facing the student when he or she sets out to study the House of Commons. The picture, as we have seen, is not simple. History has seen to that. We have sought to detail the important developments of the nineteenth and twentieth centuries, and to identify the effect on the relationship of the House to that part of it which forms the Government. In the changed environment of British politics after 1867, the purpose of the House of Commons has not been a clearly defined one. As we have pointed out, there is no formal or binding document delineating authoritatively the functions of the House.

What we have tried to do is to identify those functions on which there is some, if by no means total, agreement. Some observers would stress the importance of certain functions over others. For our part, we have stressed what we consider the most important function of the Commons in relation to Government, that of scrutiny and influence. In exploring the extent to which the House fulfils this function (Chapters 5 to 8), we have identified a number of limitations or deficiencies. Though it is a function which the House collectively and individually seeks to fulfil, it does so only to a limited extent. As Government has grown, and has developed new techniques to respond to the increasingly complex demands and expectations of an advanced industrialised society, Parliament has failed to keep pace with these developments. Realisation of this fact has helped and helps to fuel the pressure for parliamentary reform. This pressure, and the various forms it has taken, we have outlined already. Though seeking to identify the various approaches that currently exist, we have argued the case especially for one approach — that which emphasises the need for MPs themselves to realise and to utilise the power which still resides with them. It is important to stress, though, that no one approach is the 'right' approach. The advocates of each approach believe that their prescription provides the best means of achieving the role that they posit for the House of Commons. No one approach has a monopoly of knowledge or wisdom. Each must be subject to the debate that seeks to determine 'Whither the Commons?'

Whither the Commons?

The debate on the future role of the House of Commons does not take place in isolation. Perceptions of what the Commons should do are influenced by what it is or has been. This point can be gleaned from the foregoing pages. As we have seen, perceptions clearly differ. Some polls have revealed that many members of the public believe the Commons to play a near-central role in British politics. A survey in 1977 revealed that respondents ranked Parliament as second only to the trade unions in 'having a lot of influence'.[9] This perception, we would argue, is based on a confusion of the formal with the real powers of the House. Because the legislative outputs of Parliament are binding, it is often assumed that Parliament must be an important decision-making body. Conversely, many academics — observing the factors that have strengthened Government in the nineteenth and twentiety centuries — have emphasised the weakness or even the irrelevancy of the House of Commons in the making of political decisions in Britain. In their book *Governing Under Pressure*, published in 1979, Richardson and Jordan speak of a 'post-Parliamentary Democracy'. Stuart Walkland and others have stressed the inability of the House of Commons to play any positive role in the determination or influence of economic policy; indeed, the adversary politics thesis suggests that its contribution is a negative one. We would argue that this emphasis is at times a little overdone. The House of Commons certainly cannot be written off as irrelevant. However limited it may be, it has exerted and does exert some influence in the decision-making process.[10] To be fair to some critics, they do concede this point. Richardson and Jordan, as one reviewer of their book noted, 'hedge their bets' in discussing Parliament;[11] they concede that the House 'can on occasions be important as a veto power on legislation and can play an important role in getting a problem recognised as needing political action'.[12] (Indeed, their section on Parliament is both interesting and sensible.) Our argument, though, is that many contemporary reformers base their approaches on perceptions derived from parliamentary experience of the 1950s and the 1960s, a period of notable quiescence in the House of Commons. Though the arguments of the external reformers, especially those pressing for a new electoral system, came to the fore and gained ground in the 1970s, their analyses had their roots in past experience. And having become wedded to a particular approach, many advocates of reform have tended to ignore or discount the changes in parliamentary behaviour that have taken place over the past decade. As a result, they appear unaware of what could be achieved by the Commons *in the near future* in strengthening its function as a scrutineer and influencer, as what we have referred to as a watchdog, of Government. Admittedly, even when the changes of recent years are taken into account, the Commons still does not act as an adequate watchdog of Government. Our argument, though, is that is could.

Recent years have witnessed a change in the attitude of many, if not all, Members of Parliament. A number have become aware of their ability to help provide the parameters within which Government can govern, and to do so within the context of party government. This attitudinal change, as we have argued, is a necessary prerequisite for effective procedural or structural changes. 'The issue', as Jorgen Rasmussen has succinctly noted, 'is not structure but behaviour. Are MPs now willing, as they were in the past, to cross-vote? If so, the Commons can check the Cabinet effectively; if not, no package of legal reforms will increase executive responsibility.'[13] With the growth of this awareness, this willingness, on the part of Members has come the ability to influence and sustain new structures designed to provide a more thorough scrutiny of Government and its component parts. This was reflected in the manner in which the new Select Committee structure recommended by the Procedure Committee in 1978 was established, and to some extent in the way in which the committees have operated. It is a beginning. As we have suggested, there is still some way to go. The new committees have the potential to scrutinise Departments, to question their officials and informed witnesses from outside (a task they fulfil already with some success), to provide information and, if necessary, advice to the House. Nevertheless, there is always the danger that they will go the way of their predecessors. If this is to be avoided, it is for Members collectively to be prepared to sustain them and, if necessary, press for their strengthening. One of the most radical proposals designed to strengthen the committees has come from Geoffrey Smith of *The Times*.

Noting that Parliament is most deficient in its scrutiny of public expenditure, he has suggested that the Consolidated Fund Bill be split up after receiving its Second Reading, with each Department's Estimates being sent to the appropriate Select Committee. Each committee would have the right to change the distribution of funds between different functions on a departmental vote, and to reduce the Estimates for the Department. The Treasury Committee would have responsibility for the Estimates as a whole.[14] Traditionally, the power of the House lay in its control of the national purse strings, and to some extent this proposal would help to turn the wheel full circle. The chances of its implementation, though, are not good, and even critics of the existing structure, such as Brian Sedgemore, have criticised it as constituting a 'direct attack on Cabinet government'.[15] It is nevertheless valuable in directing attention to the need for the Commons to establish a more effective oversight of departmental Estimates; the traditional procedure is generally recognised as being woefully inadequate, a fact recognised by the decision in 1980 to appoint a Procedure Committee to study Supply procedure. The new committees have already the opportunity to start moving in the right direction. They have the power to examine the Estimates, and they do now receive copies of the relevant Estimates in draft form prior to publication. If they are to continue moving in the direction of more effective oversight, the willingness and the momentum must be provided by the committees' own members. It is the one area where ministerial resistance is likely to be strongest. Cabinet Ministers are not keen on the Select Committees as such; others, especially those from the spending Departments, are unlikely to be very sympathetic to greater committee incursions into departmental needs and costings. (And any that are may find themselves unable to carry their officials with them.) If the committees are to develop and acquire new functions, especially effective oversight of expenditure, then pressure must come from Members on both sides of the House. Support from some Ministers or Opposition front benchers would obviously help, but in itself would not be a sufficient condition for success. The comments of Edward du Cann in 1979 remain apt: 'What is needed is an exercise of political will on the part of the House of Commons as a whole.'[16]

Parliamentary experience of recent years has demonstrated that collectively Members can exercise the political will necessary to provide the parameters within which the Government can govern, albeit of necessity in a limited and generally negative way. The 'habit', as George Cunningham termed it, of greater voting freedom acquired in the 1970s is not likely to be discarded. As Members have conceded, there can be no going back to the quiescence of the 1950s and early 1960s;[17] 'The old days of party discipline', according to one MP, are 'dead and buried,'[18] a point that would appear to be borne out by the experience of the current Parliament. If the Government goes beyond what is acceptable to a majority of the House, and certainly if it pursues a policy which is clearly unacceptable, it knows that it cannot guarantee its acceptance in the division lobbies. However, what is now important is the extent to which the experience of recent years can be built upon by the House. That experience, as we have argued, provides the basis on which it can move forward to make more effective its scrutiny and influence of Government. It has made a start. It now needs to go further. In particular, it needs, as we have just mentioned, to achieve an effective scrutiny of the Estimates (probably through the new Select Committees), and to scrutinise more effectively not only the activities of Ministers but, more important, what is done in the name of Ministers, in other words, the activities of civil servants; the second of these may result if the first is achieved. (In certain circumstances, as we have commented already, a more assertive House may actually serve to strengthen a Minister in relation to his officials, paradoxical though it may seem.)[19] The House of Commons can never hope to overcome all the obstacles placed in its path in seeking to achieve effective scrutiny and influence through more open and responsive Government (no legislature or national assembly, not even the United States Congress, has or can hope to overcome *all* such problems), but it can move in the direction of removing some of them. As we have just said, it has made a start. Whether or not it will build on what it has already begun remains to be seen. Our argument is that it can do so, and that it should. It is an opportunity not to be missed.

NOTES

1   Speaking in a BBC TV symposium, quoted in Ronald Butt, *The Power of Parliament* (Constable, 1967), p. 10.
2   George Cunningham, MP, to author.
3   See especially the comments of Malcolm Shaw in his conclusion to J.D. Lees and M. Shaw (eds), *Committees in Legislatures* (Martin Robertson, 1979), pp. 398–404, 417; see also the comments of Ergun Ozbudun, *Party Cohesion in Western Democracies: A Causal Analysis* (Sage, 1970), pp. 355–63.
4   When compared with legislatures worldwide, including those in Communist countries, the picture is less clear-cut. See especially Michael Mezey's typology of

legislatures; M. Mezey, *Comparative Legislatures* (Duke University Press, 1979), especially ch. 2 and table 2.1.

5   The term 'Mother of Parliaments' should be taken as a reference to the number of parliaments set up elsewhere on the lines of the British Parliament (or rather the House of Commons) under British influence, and not to its age; the Icelandic Parliament has a claim to be the 'Grandfather of Parliaments'.

6   See John C. Wahlke, 'Policy Demands and System Support: The Role of the Represented', in Gerhard Loewenberg (ed.), *Modern Parliaments* (Aldine/Atherton, 1971), pp. 141–71.

7   John Schwarz, 'Exploring a New Role in Policy-Making: The British House of Commons in the 1970s', *American Political Science Review*, 74 (1), March 1980, pp. 23–37.

8   See, for example, the introductory chapter to David Coombes and S.A. Walkland (eds), *Parliaments and Economic Affairs* (European Centre for Political Studies/PSI, 1980).

9   *Sunday Times*, 18 September 1977.

10   For a balanced evaluation of its role in a comparative perspective, see Mezey, chs 2 and 5.

11   Review by A.M. Potter, *Public Administration*, 58, Spring 1980, pp 120–1.

12   J.J. Richardson and A.G. Jordan, *Governing under Pressure* (Martin Robertson, 1979), p. 128.

13   Jorgen Rasmussen, 'Was Guy Fawkes Right?', in Isaac Kramnick (ed.), *Is Britain Dying?* (Cornell University Press, 1979), p. 116.

14   Geoffrey Smith, 'How Parliament can Grab Back the Purse Strings', *The Times*, 9 May 1980, and, by the same author, *Westminster Reform: Learning from Congress*, Thames Essay No. 20 (Trade Policy Research Centre, 1979).

15   Brian Sedgemore, *The Secret Constitution* (Hodder & Stoughton, 1980), p. 172.

16   *House of Commons Debates*, 960, c. 1342.

17   'Talking Politics', BBC Radio 4, broadcast 28 October 1978.

18   Eric Heffer, MP, in 'Talking Politics'.

19   See above, Chapter 7, and the comments in Philip Norton, *Dissension in the House of Commons 1974–1979* (Oxford University Press, 1980), p. 462.

Select bibliography

The number of general works on the House of Commons, as we mentioned in the preface, is not great. Among the most recent works are S.A. Walkland (ed.), *The House of Commons in the Twentieth Century* (Oxford University Press, 1979), and S.A. Walkland and Michael Ryle (eds), *The Commons in the Seventies* (Fontant, 1977), now revised as *The Commons Today.* The OUP volume is an original work of use to the academic; the Fontana text is designed for student use. Other works include Peter Richards, *The Backbenchers* (Faber & Faber, 1972); Fred Willey, *The Honourable Member* (Sheldon Press, 1974); Michael Rush, *Parliament and the Public* (Longman, 1978); and Eric Taylor, *The House of Commons at Work,* 9th ed. (Macmillan, 1979). Sir Ivor Jenning's *Parliament,* 2nd ed. (Cambridge University Press, 1957) continues to be regarded as a classic, destined for ritual consultation and occasional citation. There are few works which provide a detailed analysis of Parliament's history from its origins to the present day; for the student, Ronald Butt's *The Power of Parliament,* revised ed. (Constable, 1969) is the best work to consult. Similarly, there are few good works placing Parliament in a comparative perspective. Of those that do exist, Michael Mezey's *Comparative Legislatures* (Duke University Press, 1979) is the most recent.

On party organisation in the House of Commons (the subject of Chapter 3), the main work is Philip Norton, 'The Organisation of Parliamentary Parties', in Walkland, *The House of Commons in the Twentieth Century,* ch. 1. There is no one work that deals thoroughly with the functions of the House of Commons (see Chapter 4), but A.H. Birch, *Representative and Responsible Government* (Allen & Unwin, 1964) is the standard text for a consideration of the function of representation. On the legislative process (see Chapter 5) the best introduction remains S.A. Walkland, *The Legislative Process in Great Britain* (Allen & Unwin, 1968); Malcolm Barnett, *The Politics of Legislation* (Weidenfeld & Nicolson, 1969) constitutes still a useful case study — as does Uwe Kitzinger's *Diplomacy and Persuasion* (Thames & Hudson, 1973), extending beyond the Commons — while J.A.G. Griffith's *Parliamentary Scrutiny of Government Bills* (Allen & Unwin, 1973) has added a useful empirical, if rather critical (and now dated), study to the literature. The most thorough and interesting study of Private Members' legislation is Peter Richards, *Parliament and Conscience* (Allen & Unwin, 1970); more recent data is to be found in his chapter on the subject in Walkland, *The House of Commons in the Twentieth Century.* On scrutiny of executive acts (see Chapter 6), the standard work on parliamentary questions is D.N. Chester and N. Bowring, *Questions in Parliament* (Oxford University Press, 1962), with more recent material to be found in J. Rose, 'Questions in the House', in D. Leonard and V. Herman (eds), *The Backbencher and Parliament* (Macmillan, 1972); Sir Norman Chester, 'Questions in the House', in Walkland and Ryle, *The Commons in the Seventies;* and R.L. Borthwick, 'Questions and Debates', in Walkland, *The House of Commons in the Twentieth Century.* There is as yet no useful analysis of private correspondence from Members to Ministers (as opposed to constituency correspondence). On debates, see Borthwick, 'Questions & Debates'. On the Ombudsman see the two works by Frank Stacey, *The British Ombudsman* (Oxford University Press, 1971) and *Ombudsmen Compared* (Oxford University Press, 1978). On select committees see A. Morris (ed.), *The Growth of Parliamentary Scrutiny by Committee* (Pergamon Press, 1970); Nevil Johnson, 'Select Committees and Administration', in Walkland, *The House of Commons in the Twentieth Century,* and *The First Report from the Select Committee on Procedure, 1977—78* (HC 588), a minefield of useful material on this and other subjects. On ministerial and Civil Service relationships (discussed in Chapter 7) see Bruce Headey, 'Cabinet Ministers and Senior Civil Servants', in V. Herman and J. Alt (eds), *Cabinet Studies: A Reader* (Macmillan, 1975), and, by the same author, *British Cabinet Ministers* (Allen & Unwin, 1974), as well as G. Marshall and G. Moodie, *Some Problems of the Constitution,* 4th rev. ed. (Hutchinson, 1967), and *The Civil Service: Eleventh Report from the Expenditure Committee, 1977* (HC 535). On Parliament and the EC, see David Coombes, 'Parliament and the European Communities', in Walkland and Ryle, *The Commons in the Seventies,* and, more generally, the Hansard Society, *The British People: Their Voice in Europe* (Saxon House, 1977). There are few useful sectoral analyses (see Chapter 8); Peter Richards, *Parliament and Foreign Affairs* (Allen & Unwin, 1967), and Ann Robinson, *Parliament and Public Spending* (Heinemann, 1978), are the two most worthy of note.

On parliamentary reform (see Chapter 9), the best background works, detailing the reforms that have taken place, are the Hansard Society, *Parliamentary Reform 1933—60,* 2nd rev. ed. (Cassell, 1967), and Frank Stacey, *British Government: Years of Reform 1966—75* (Oxford University Press, 1975). The main works in the debate on reform are, of course, Bernard Crick, *The Reform of Parliament,* 2nd rev. ed. (Weidenfeld & Nicolson, 1970); Ronald Butt, *The Power of Parliament* (Constable, 1967); Henry Fairlie, *The Life of Politics* (Methuen, 1968); Lord Hailsham, *Elective Dictatorship* (BBC, 1976); and S.E. Finer (ed.), *Adversary Politics and Electoral Reform* (Anthony Wigram, 1975). One might usefully read as well Timothy Raison's *The Power of Parliament*

252   THE COMMONS IN PERSPECTIVE

(Basil Blackwell, 1979). As the comments in Chapter 9 reveal, these works constitute but the tip of an iceberg.

As is also pointed out in Chapter 9, the House of Commons has witnessed important behavioural changes in recent years. The main works to consult here are the author's: *Dissension in the House of Commons 1974—79* (Oxford University Press, 1980), *Conservative Dissidents* (Temple Smith, 1978) — which constitutes also a case study of a particular Parliament — and *Dissension in the House of Commons 1945—74* (Macmillan, 1975). Recent articles touching upon changes in the Commons include Jorgen Rasmussen, 'Was Guy Fawkes Right?', in Isaac Kramnick (ed.), *Is Britain Dying?* (Cornell University Press, 1979); Philip Norton, 'The Changing Face of the British House of Commons in the 1970s', *Legislative Studies Quarterly*, 5 (3), August 1980; John Schwarz, 'Exploring a New Role in Policy-Making: The British House of Commons in the 1970s', *The American Political Science Review*, 74 (1), March 1980; and, more generally, Leon Epstein, 'What Happened to the British Party Model?', *American Political Science Review*, 74 (1), March 1980. To keep abreast of parliamentary developments, one should consult the journals listed below.

Reference works and journals

The main reference work on parliamentary procedure is *Erskine May's Treatise on the Law, Privileges, Proceedings and Usage of Parliament* (known as *Erskine May*), the latest edition being the nineteenth, edited by Sir David Lidderdale (Butterworth, 1976); the latest edition of *The Standing Orders of the House of Commons: Public Business* was published in 1979 (HMSO). A useful reference work on Parliament generally is *Dod's Parliamentary Companion*, now in a new larger format, published annually; various interesting data are to be found also in David Butler and Anne Sloman, *British Political Facts 1900—79* (Macmillan, 1980). *The Political Companion*, published regularly by Parliamentary Research Services (18 Lincoln Green, Chichester), provides valuable material, including details of Members' voting frequency and the number of parliamentary questions they table each session.

The two main journals that publish articles on the House of Commons are *Parliamentary Affairs*, the journal of the Hansard Society, and the *Parliamentarian*, the journal of the Commonwealth Parliamentary Association; the readership of the former tends to comprise academics and students, that of the latter parliamentarians. Other journals which sometimes carry articles dealing with the Commons include *Public Law, Legislative Studies Quarterly, Government and Opposition, Political Studies*, and, on occasion, *The American Political Science Review*. Of weekly publications, the *Economist* provides a useful coverage (its

'Schools Brief' on Parliament, 'Parliament redivivus?', 23 February 1980, is useful especially for sixth-formers), though somewhat better in its reporting than in its editorialising on the subject; among the daily newspapers, *The Times* provides the most thorough coverage.

For the serious student wishing to keep abreast of daily proceedings in the House of Commons, the *House of Commons: Official Report (Hansard)* is published in daily and weekly parts, as well as in the more impressive bound volumes, and a summary of proceedings given in the BBC Radio 4 programme 'Today in Parliament' each evening while the House is in session; the BBC also broadcasts on Radio 4 on Saturday mornings during parliamentary sessions the more analytical 'The Week in Westminster'.

Information

For those wishing to obtain more information on specific points about the House of Commons, the House now has its own public information service. Questions about the history and work of the Commons (including current business) can be addressed to the Public Information Office at the House of Commons, London SW1A OAA, or by telephone on 01–219–4272.

Index of names

Index of subjects